Let's have a conversation

TEENS 101
A parent's survival guide

BUILDING TRUST WITH TEENS

"Parenting has never been easy and families face more challenges than ever as we navigate the 21st century.

"The cyber age has provided enormous opportunities but also poses many challenges. We have countless communication tools, but this hasn't necessarily made it easier to communicate with our kids. Technology is changing how we interact and forcing institutions to be more transparent, inclusive, dynamic and personalised. Trust has shifted back to individuals, with profound implications for society.

"At the same time, trust and influence have grown among family, friends, classmates, colleagues and even strangers. No longer is the 'top down' influence of elites, authorities and institutions a given. That's why Parent Guides are so important. Our credible and easy-to-digest resources empower parents and carers to create trust and communicate with their children about what matters to them.

"This compendium of five Parent Guides – *Drugs 101*, *Social Media 101*, *Sex 101*, *Respect 101* and *Mental Health 101* – tells it like it is. *Teens 101* is an evidence-based resource that offers parents and carers all they need to know about what their kids are doing and how to keep them safe.

"We want to encourage open and honest family conversations on topics such as drugs, sex, mental health, social media, respect, gambling and gaming. The aim is to inform, not alarm.

"Our comprehensively researched guides draw on the latest available data and expert advice to facilitate these important discussions and build confidence in families of all shapes and sizes.

"No-one has all the answers. But arming yourself with the best information and communicating openly with your kids is a great start. Together, we can maximise their chances of becoming healthy and happy adults."

From the Editor // Eileen Berry

WHAT WE DO

A GUIDE TO PARENT GUIDES

We must equip young people with the skills and strategies needed to deal with taboo topics and build resilience

MENTAL HEALTH 101 *Let's have a conversation*

This important guide looks at how families can avoid and/or deal with issues such as suicide, anxiety, depression, ADHD, self-harm, eating disorders and other mental illnesses.

CONTENT: Honest and open conversation is a must for parents and carers dealing with teen mental health. *Mental Health 101* covers important issues including suicide, anxiety, depression, ADHD, self-harm, eating disorders and other mental illnesses. It contains statistics, expert advice and case studies involving families and health professionals.

Parents, carers and teachers can use the information, drawn from reputable sources, to start important conversations with teenagers about mental health. Young people have never had so many communication tools yet communicating with them is as tricky as ever. *Mental Health 101* hopes to help break down barriers and encourage meaningful dialogue between generations.

KEYWORDS:
Education; parenting; parent guide; parent resource; mental health; mental illness; mental disorder; anxiety; depression; teenagers; children.

RESPECT 101 *Let's have a conversation*

Respect 101 identifies what respectful behaviour is, how to turn disrespectful into respectful, create life-long relationships and embed respect within the culture of adolescence.

CONTENT: *Respect 101* helps families to define respect and encourage it in their children. Written by education and psychology experts with input from students, educators and other teen specialists, it is designed as a starting point to build respect and develop resilience in children.

It looks at how adults can provide positive role models while guiding young people through today's cyber minefields and empowering them to be strong and respectful.

Experts look at family life, values and how family breakdown and domestic violence can affect children. There are sections on sexism and equality, racism, social media and LGBTIQ+, as well as pointers to more assistance.

KEYWORDS:
Education; parenting; parent guide; parent resource; respect; resilience; relationships; racism; sexism; homophobia; teenagers; children.

SOCIAL MEDIA 101 *Let's have a conversation*

Social Media 101 helps parents understand what their kids are doing online, when it might be a problem and how to make the most of the positive aspects of cyberspace.

CONTENT: Young people have never had so many communication tools yet communicating with them is as tricky as ever.

For parents, teachers and carers, the cyber age provides enormous opportunities but also brings many challenges. *Social Media 101* provides them with information about what kids are doing online, when it might be a problem and how to make the most of the positive aspects of cyber space.

Speaking to a range of experts, we cover apps, websites, gaming, gambling, cyber-bullying, cyber laws, privacy laws and 'device advice'.

Armed with this information, adults will find discussing these issues with children and teenagers easier and more fruitful.

KEYWORDS: *Education; parenting; parent guide; parent resource; social media; online; internet; cyber safety; cyber bullying; teenagers; children.*

DRUGS 101 *Let's have a conversation*

Drugs 101 is a resource for parents, carers and teachers of children aged 8-17. It features what drugs are, their effects, interviews with users and tips from experienced experts.

CONTENT: *Parent Guides* are a resource that creates trust, credibility and confidence in families to deal with issues affecting young people, in this case using and abusing drugs.

We want to encourage open and honest conversations between parents, carers, teachers and young people, to educate and minimise harm.

Drugs 101 aims to empower adults with information and strategies to help guide those important discussions. *Drugs 101* explains what drugs are, who takes them and how to educate kids about them.

It covers everything from marijuana to ecstasy and heroin, profiles former users, speaks to experts who help those with drug problems and provides links to useful resources and services.

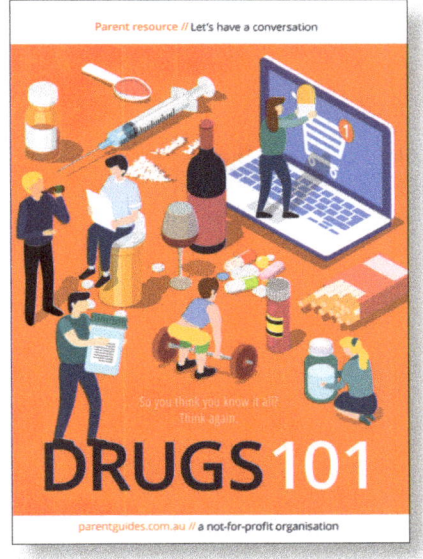

KEYWORDS: *Education; parenting; parent guide; parent resource; drugs; drug problem; addiction; teenagers; children.*

SEX 101 *Let's have a conversation*

Let's talk about Sex. *Sex 101* tells parents and carers what their teens are doing – or not doing – and offers advice on how to keep them safe as they navigate relationships.

CONTENT: *Sex 101* looks at sexual activity, growing up, sex education, relationships, safer sex, sexting, the law, STIs, and LGBTIQ+ issues.

The no-nonsense guide informs adults about what their kids are doing and thinking, and arms them with information that can facilitate positive conversations about sex and sexuality.

It also emphasises the importance of accepting and embracing diversity, so all teens feel comfortable with their individual sexual identity. Useful contacts for more detailed resources are also provided.

KEYWORDS: *Education; parenting; parent guide; parent resource; sex; relationship; sexuality; LGBTIQ+; gender; diversity; teenagers; children.*

© Parenting Guides Ltd

CONTENTS

MENTAL HEALTH 101

Prevalence // **8**
On the bright side // **10**
Don't ignore the problem // **11**
Depression // **12**
PROFILE //
I didn't think I could recover // **14**
PROFILE // A friend in need // **15**
PROFILE // How to be brave // **16**
ADHD // **17**
Resilience // **18**
Is my child OK? // **20**
Am I OK? // **21**
Eating disorders // **22**
PROFILE //
Coping with anorexia // **24**
Anxiety // **25**
PROFILE //
Why I chose to hurt myself // **26**
Self-harm // **27**
Suicide // **28**
PROFILE //
My first suicide attempt was at 14 // **30**
Bullying // **31**
PROFILE //
The behavioural interventionist // **32**
Psychosis // **33**
Profile // True to yourself // **34**
More at risk // **35**
Personality disorders // **36**
Remote areas // **37**
International students // **38**
CAT Team // **38**
Assistance // **39**

RESPECT 101

R.E.S.P.E.C.T.
What it means to us // **42**
Focus on respect // **44**
FIRST PERSON //
The Casual cruelties of Childhood // **47**
GROWING & LEARNING //
Respect yourself // **48**
RESPECTING OTHERS //
Do unto others // **50**
FAMILIES // All in the family // **52**
FAMILY VIOLENCE //
Violence of all kinds is wrong // **54**
SEXISM & EQUALITY //
Two sexes on one level // **56**
RACISM & XENOPHOBIA //
Australia fair? // **58**
LGBTIQ+ // Vive la difference // **60**
INDIGENOUS CULTURE //
First Australians // **62**
DISABILITY //
Positively enabling // **63**
SOCIAL MEDIA // **64**
SCHOOLS //
Learned behaviour // **66**
COMMUNITY //
One in, all in // **68**
ELDERLY // Elder abuse:
A growing problem // **70**
ASSISTANCE // **71-73**

PARENTING GUIDES LTD IS A REGISTERED CHARITY
To purchase resources or for school bundles contact;
Eileen Berry // 0407 542 655
or visit // parentguides.com.au

SOCIAL MEDIA 101

Teen use // **76**
Web Weavers // **78**
Life's A Gamble // **80**
PROFILE // Gambling online // **81**
What you need to
know about gaming // **82**
PROFILE // Intelligent gaming // **83**
eSafety tips // **84**
Cyber-bullying // **86**
State by state // **88**
Territories law // **90**
PROFILE // Digital nutrition // **91**
PROFILE // The policeman // **92**
PROFILE // The cyber expert // **93**
Apps & sites // **94-97**
Stay in control // **98**
PROFILE // The lawyer // **100**
PROFILE // The privacy expert // **101**
PROFILE // The Author // **102**
Family technology user agreement // **103**
ASSISTANCE // **104**

DRUGS 101

Youth & drugs // **108**
Alcohol // **110**
PROFILE // The physician // **112**
Lead by example // **113**
Cannabis // **114**
PROFILE // The teenager // **116**
PROFILE // The parent // **117**
Parent Q&A // **118**
Inhalants // **119**
Amphetamines // **120**
PROFILE // The paramedic // **122**
Heroin // **123**
PROFILE // The addict // **124**
Ecstacy // **125**
PROFILE // The psychologist // **126**
Cocaine // **127**
NBOMe freakout // **128**
Hallucinogens // **129**
PROFILE // The psychiatrist // **130**
Steroids // **131**
PROFILE // The professor // **132**
Analgesics & tranquillisers // **133**
PROFILE // The police // **134**
Ingredients in Illicit Drugs // **135**
PROFILE // The psychologist // **136**
History // **137**
ASSISTANCE // **138**

SEX 101

Sexual activity // **142**
Parent Q&A // **144**
PROFILE // Positive bystander // **145**
Young people have their say on sexting // **146**
PROFILE // The new standard // **147**
Safer sex // **148**
Growing up // **150**
PROFILE // Understanding enthusiastic consent // **151**
Sex education // **152-154**
PROFILE // Talking sex // **155**
Teen Q&A // **156**
LGBTIQ+ // **157**
Live your way // **158**
STIs // **160**
HIV/AIDS // **162**
Sex & the law // **164-165**
Know the law // **166**
PROFILE //
Sex & relationships // **167**
PROFILE // Open communication & connectedness // **168**
Parent Q&A // **169**
PROFILE // The expert // **170**
PROFILE // The addict // **171**
ASSISTANCE // **172**

// PARENT GUIDES

Yvonne Hackett // CEO
yvonne@catalystanz.com.au

Eileen Berry // Editor
0407 542 655
eileen@parentguides.com.au

David Corduff // Ambassador

Sarah Marinos & Cheryl Critchley // Writers

Anita Layzell // Art Director

Sue Richardson // Designer

Max Hunter, Beverley Johanson, Andrew Ryan, Fiona O'Connor, Sally Bornholt // Production Editors

Julian Healey, Mary Riekert & Smith Brothers Media // Social Media Editors

Kimberly Barry // Marketing Director
0439 900 350
kimberly@parentguides.com.au

Our Advisory Committee //
Dr Peter Briggs (GP);
Kirsten Cleland (social worker, headspace);
Shane Jacobson (partner, PKF Melbourne);
Helen Kapalos (former chair commissioner, Victorian Multicultural Commission);
Stephanie Kelly (parent);
Julie Podbury (president — Victorian Branch, Australian Principals Federation);
Julian Riekert (partner, Lander & Rogers);
Ian Robertson (former deputy principal Firbank Grammar School); and
Dr Tony Mordini, Assistant Principal, Mt Ridley P-12 College.

Every attempt has been made to contact holders of copyright for material used in this book.
Parent Guides welcomes inquiries from anyone who thinks they may have a copyright claim.

Parenting Guides Ltd disclaim all liability resulting from any views or any information written or posted. We recommend you seek appropriate independent professional advice before entering into any commitment based on these views. You should not rely on these views.

Links from our social media to other sites are not endorsed by parentguides.com.au. We are not accountable for content on linked sites or your access to those sites via the links.

MENTAL HEALTH 101

The A to Z of understanding our health and well-being

PREVALENCE

Never have parents been so worried about their children's mental health.

Young people face unprecedented pressure to do well at school, shine on social media and find meaningful employment in an ever-changing job market. On top of that, many will need to pay for their tertiary education.

The mental health of some young people has suffered as a result, with worrying rates of some conditions and suicide. Young LGBTIQ+ and Aboriginal Australians face even higher rates of many illnesses and suicide than their peers. But families are more likely to access a growing number of health services and schools are much more likely to offer support.

Support services and programs are backed by a solid body of research, such as the Australian government's 2015 paper, *The Mental Health of Children and Adolescents; Report on the second Australian Child and Adolescent Survey of Mental Health and Wellbeing.*

Based on a survey of more than 6300 families with children aged four to 17, it followed a similar 1998 study. Overall, the prevalence of mental illness was stable and more families were accessing help. But there were several troubling trends in areas such as self-harm and suicide.

OVERALL PREVALENCE
The overall prevalence of mental health disorders did not change much between 1998 and 2013-14, but there were changes in disorders covered by both surveys. The prevalence of major depressive disorder increased from 2.1 per cent to 3.2 per cent, attention deficit hyperactivity disorder (ADHD) decreased from 9.8 per cent to 7.8 per cent and conduct disorder fell slightly from 2.7 per cent to 2.1 per cent.

In 1998, only 31.2 per cent of 16 to 17-year-olds with mental health disorders had accessed a service in the previous six months. This rose to 68.3 per cent in 2013-14, which covered the previous year.

// TIPS FOR PARENTS

IF SOMETHING IS WRONG...
- Many adolescents have emotional ups and downs.
- Some suffer from depression or anxiety.
- If changes in mood, behaviour, school performance and social isolation last at least two weeks, consider seeing a GP.
- Seek help early. Effective treatments include counselling.

NORMAL ADOLESCENT MOOD FLUCTUATIONS

NORMAL ADULT MOOD FLUCTUATIONS

Graphic used with permission copyright Michael Gordon, Monash Health, 2018.

// PREVALENCE OF MENTAL HEALTH DISORDERS

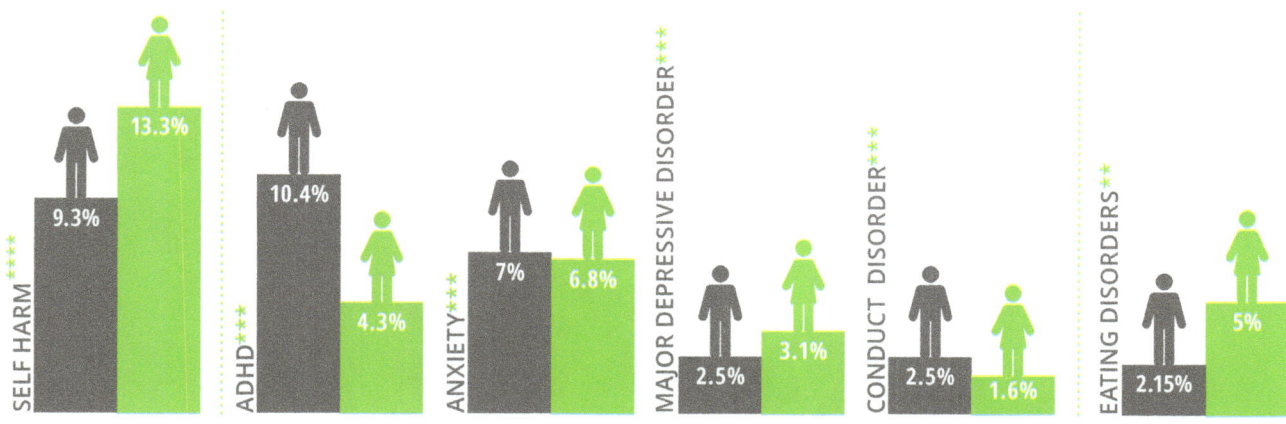

- SELF HARM****: 9.3% / 13.3%
- ADHD***: 10.4% / 4.3%
- ANXIETY***: 7% / 6.8%
- MAJOR DEPRESSIVE DISORDER***: 2.5% / 3.1%
- CONDUCT DISORDER***: 2.5% / 1.6%
- EATING DISORDERS**: 2.15% / 5%

**** Self-harm in the past 12 months in 12-17-year-olds, *The Mental Health of Children and Adolescents; Report on the second Australian Child and Adolescent Survey of Mental Health and Wellbeing (2015).*
*** Prevalence of mental disorders in 4-17 year-olds in the past 12 months.
The Mental Health of Children and Adolescents; Report on the second Australian Child and Adolescent Survey of Mental Health and Wellbeing (2015).
** Estimated prevalence of total eating disorders in Australia in 5-19 year-olds.
Nip it in the bud: Intervening early for young people with eating disorders. Melbourne: Orygen, The National Centre of Excellence in Youth Mental Health, 2016.

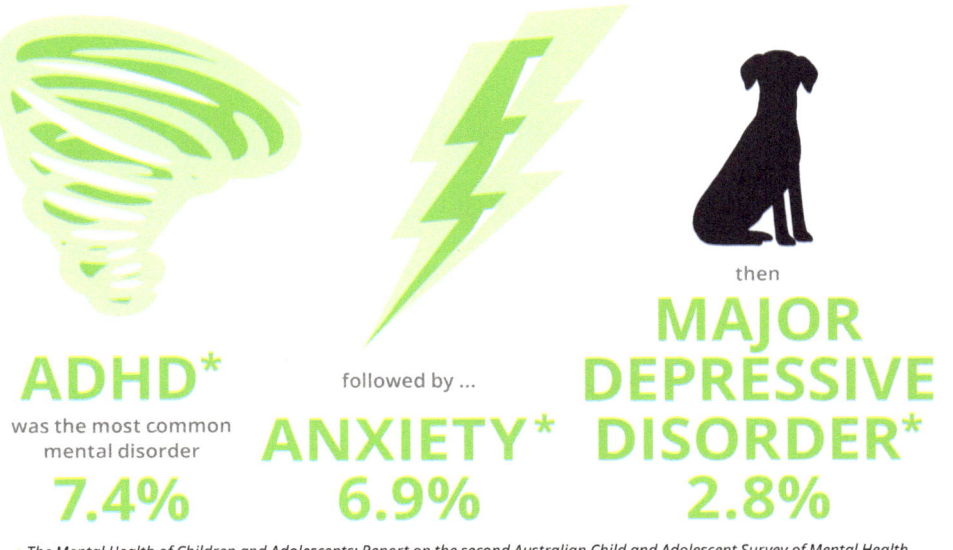

16.3%

11.5%

MALES WERE MORE LIKELY THAN FEMALES*
to have experienced mental health disorders

ADHD* was the most common mental disorder
7.4%

followed by ...
ANXIETY*
6.9%

then
MAJOR DEPRESSIVE DISORDER*
2.8%

ASKING FOR HELP

1998
31.2%
16 to 17-year-olds with mental disorders had accessed a service in the previous six months

2013-14
68.3%
16 to 17-year-olds with mental disorders had accessed a service over the previous 12 months

* The Mental Health of Children and Adolescents; Report on the second Australian Child and Adolescent Survey of Mental Health and Wellbeing (2015).

// MISSION AUSTRALIA YOUTH SURVEY

Mental health is a huge issue for young people and a growing concern for them.

The Mission Australia Youth Survey highlights the concerns of young people aged 15 to 19 each year. In 2016, almost 22,000 respondents identified alcohol/drugs and equity/discrimination as the most important issues in Australia today, with mental health entering the top three for the first time in the survey's 15-year history, after concerns about it doubled in the previous five years.

Mission Australia also produced a *Youth Mental Health Report / Youth Survey 2012-2016* with the Black Dog Institute. It found:
- One in four young people were at risk of serious mental illness;
- Mental illness risk increases as adolescents age, becoming most prevalent in the older teen years; and
- The risk is greater in indigenous groups and young women.

The prevalence of probable serious mental illness among young people had continued to increase, even since the last report in 2015.

THE YOUTH MENTAL HEALTH REPORT / YOUTH SURVEY 2012-2016 **FOUND THAT IN 2016:**
- Just under one in four young people met the criteria for a probable serious mental illness, up from 18.7 per cent in 2012 to 22.8 per cent in 2016;
- Older teenagers were much more likely to have a probable serious mental illness. The proportion rose from 20.8 per cent at 15 to 27.4 per cent at 18 to 19 years;
- More than three in 10 (31.6 per cent) Aboriginal and Torres Strait Islander respondents had a probable serious mental illness, compared with 22.2 per cent of non-Aboriginal or Torres Strait Islander respondents;
- The top three issues of personal concern for those with a probable serious mental illness were coping with stress, school or study problems and depression;
- While the proportions of males and females with a serious mental illness rose from 2012-2016, the increase was higher among females (22.5-28.6 per cent from 2012-2016), than males (12.7-14.1 per cent); and
- Those with a probable serious mental illness said the top three sources for help with important issues in their lives are friends, parents and the internet. Those without an illness list friends, parents and relatives/family friends.

ON THE BRIGHT SIDE
6 IN 7 DO NOT
HAVE A MENTAL HEALTH DISORDER

While mental health is a serious issue, it is important to remember that most people don't have a mental illness.

In 2014-15, 4 million Australians (17.5 per cent) reported having a mental or behavioural condition. This meant 82.5 per cent, or about 19.5 million Australians, did not.

PROMOTING MENTAL HEALTH IN YOUNG PEOPLE

Adolescents are finding their place in the world and need a safe, caring space so they can:
- come to terms with their identity and adjust to their changing looks and new found sexuality;
- explore their own values;
- learn how to negotiate and set themselves limits; and
- plan a future they are happy with.

POSITIVE MENTAL HEALTH // PARENT TIPS

- Spend time together. Find activities that you and your adolescent enjoy and make a regular time for them. Make time to eat together and talk about current issues.
- Remember to let them know you love them. Take an interest in what is happening in their lives.
- Adolescents still need limits. Explain why you need to set limits. Let them know that you set limits because you care about them.
- Adolescence is a time of experimentation, change and increasing independence. As young people become older and more independent, families change.
- Be open to your adolescent's ideas. Adolescents can be very idealistic. If you listen and try not to be judgmental, they are more likely to share their concerns with you.
- Many adolescents will experiment with sex and drugs. Try to talk about these topics with them. There are often stories in newspapers or on TV about sex and drugs that you can use as a talking point.
- Try to just listen without reacting. There are times when you may be concerned about behaviour or problems. Try to be supportive and assist them to find solutions.

// WHY TEENAGERS NEED SLEEP

If you think your teenager or adolescent is trying to make life difficult when they go to bed late, they're not. Blame it on natural changes in their body clock. But getting enough quality sleep is important for mental health, says Professor Sarah Blunden, a sleep researcher and psychologist at the Australian Centre for Education in Sleep.

Sleep patterns change during adolescence because a teenager's body clock or Circadian rhythm shifts, making them feel sleepier later. At night, the pituitary gland in the brain releases a hormone called melatonin, which is a sleep hormone. During adolescence, melatonin is released later, so teenagers don't feel sleepy until later.

"Around 80 per cent of young people show a significant delay in sleep onset and if parents don't know about this delay, it can cause friction. Parents think adolescents don't want to go to bed for the sake of it, but it's a physiological issue and it's not their fault," says Professor Blunden.

If a teenager can't sleep, they will probably use a smartphone or tablet to amuse themselves. But exposure to light further delays the release of melatonin. Most teens get seven to eight hours sleep a night when they need about nine hours.

"Without sleep people are more irritable, aggressive and withdrawn. There's greater incidence of depression, anxiety and stress because teenagers haven't got the energy and capacity to cope with frustrations – and those years are filled with frustrations as they manage school, exams and learning how to be independent," says Professor Blunden.

"Learning, memory and attention are affected too. Sleep is a foundation of health. Without it, nothing else goes right."

BETTER SLEEP TIPS

- Catching up on sleep by lying in at weekends doesn't help – it continues the cycle of sleeping late and struggling to get up the next morning. Restrict weekend sleep-ins to an hour either side of weekday wake time.
- Changes to a teenager's sleep patterns are not their fault, so relax expectations that they need to sleep by a certain time – the stress will make sleep more difficult.
- Help your child with sleep hygiene. Keep their room dark, cut screen time at least half an hour before bedtime and try and get them to swap their screen for something relaxing, such as listening to calming music in the dark or using guided meditation.

Profile // Professor Patrick McGorry

DON'T IGNORE THE PROBLEM

Early diagnosis and treatment for mental illness is vital.

"Experience during adolescence predicts very strongly how young people will be doing at age 30. If you had a certain number of mental health problems during the transition from youth to adulthood, you will have fewer friends, you are more likely to not have completed your education, you will be earning less money – if indeed you have got a job – you might be on disability support, you might be homeless. And, you might be dead – from suicide." Professor Patrick McGorry, European Society for Child and Adolescent Psychiatry 2017 Keynote Speech.

In the next 20 years, the World Economic Forum expects 35 per cent of the loss of gross domestic product to be due to mental illness. Despite this alarming statistic, Professor McGorry believes there's a 'massive double standard' between recognition and treatment of mental illness versus illnesses such as heart disease or cancer.

"If you're diagnosed with heart disease, you will be taken seriously. You'll get access to expert care. But if that person presents to the same GP or health service with a significant mental health problem, there will be problems in accessing expert care and the quality of care will vary," he says.

Professor McGorry is particularly concerned about how this double standard affects young people with mental illness, such as anxiety, depression, eating disorders and psychosis. He believes early intervention is essential so young people can recover or manage mental illness. While some experts warn of 'over-treatment' if intervention happens too early, Professor McGorry says under-treatment is the issue.

"Scaremongers have promoted the idea of every minor problem in young people being labelled as a mental health problem. That's far from reality. It is still a minority of young people with these problems who get treatment."

Early intervention includes community education – young people, parents, family and friends knowing what signs to look for and helping a young person seek help. Professor McGorry says help may include user-friendly venues such as headspace and flexible outreach approaches that take support to young people in places where they feel comfortable.

First-line treatment is often cognitive behavioural therapy, followed by medication when needed. Research is providing new insights to potential effective treatments – recent studies have shown SSRIs or antidepressants can be potent in treating anxiety. Professor McGorry is about to undertake trials of cannabidiol – a component of cannabis – on young people with anxiety. Cannabidiol works on neurotransmitters in the brain and

Photo: Supplied

"Scaremongers have promoted the idea of every minor problem in young people being labelled as a mental health problem."

may help young people for whom traditional therapies don't work. Anti-inflammation treatments are also being investigated because inflammation seems to play a role in anxiety and depression.

Professor McGorry says parents have a key role to play in early intervention.

"Don't sweep it under the carpet. If the issue has been hanging round for more than a couple of weeks, talk to the young person and try to understand what they are going through. Talk to their friends," he advises.

"They may not want to talk but don't ignore the problem. If your gut feeling is to be worried, if a person has changed, is distressed, has become withdrawn, is struggling at school – don't put it off because you may regret it for the rest of your life. After a suicide, it's very sad to see parents say they had no idea what was going on because usually they had a feeling but didn't realise it was serious enough to kill their child."

If a young person won't seek help, talk to professional services yourself or consider other adults in your network with whom a young person will be able to talk.

"Sometimes it needs a few bites of the cherry before a young person gets over the line and seeks help. Just because it's been knocked back once doesn't mean it is a permanent decision," says Professor McGorry.

"And parents are critical and should be involved in the provision of care by any services, because nobody cares about a kid more than the parents."

// Professor Patrick McGorry AO is a psychiatrist, a former Australian of the Year and the executive director of Orygen, The National Centre of Excellence in Youth Mental Health. He is also Professor of Youth Mental Health at the University of Melbourne.

DEPRESSION

A study has found that depression is more common than previously believed.

Parents and carers may not realise the extent of depression in young people. A major Australian study* found that the prevalence of major depressive disorder was much higher than parents and carers believed.

One in 13 adolescents aged 11 to 17 (7.7 per cent) met the diagnostic criteria for major depressive disorder over the past 12 months. While 7.7 per cent self-reported that they had the condition, only 4.7 per cent of parents and carers thought their young person had it.

Major depressive disorder was more common in females, affecting 19.6 per cent of girls and 7.2 per cent of males aged 16 to 17. One in five adolescents (19.9 per cent) had very high or high levels of psychological distress. The incidence was almost twice as high for girls – 25.9 per cent compared with 14.8 per cent for boys.

IMPACT

Major depressive disorder has a bigger impact on schooling than other mental illnesses. Those who have it miss an average of 20 school days a year due to the symptoms. One in three young people with major depressive disorder (34.3 per cent) say their schooling is affected severely; another one in three (34.1 per cent) say it is moderately affected*. Two in five (42.8 per cent) report that their disorder has a severe impact on their general functioning, while 35.8 per cent reported a moderate impact.

BARRIERS TO SEEKING OR RECEIVING HELP

The most common reasons that 13 to 17-year-olds with major depressive disorder gave for not seeking or receiving help related to stigma or poor mental-health literacy. Two in three (62.9 per cent) worried what others might think or didn't want to talk to a stranger. Almost two in three (61.7 per cent) thought the problem would get better by itself and 57.1 per cent wanted to work the problem out without help from family or friends[1].

SELF-HARM

Young people with major depressive disorder are much more likely to self-harm than those who don't have it. One in two young females (54.9 per cent) and one in four young males (25.8 per cent) with major depressive disorder have harmed themselves in the past year[1].

STAYING POSITIVE

Two in three adolescents (62.9 per cent) say they are receiving informal help or support for emotional and behavioural problems, mostly from parents and friends. This is much higher (93.9 per cent) for adolescents who self-report with major depressive disorder.

Two thirds (66.4 per cent) of all young people use other strategies to help manage or avoid emotional or behavioural problems. Most did positive things, such as more exercise or sport (37.9 per cent), more activities they enjoyed (45.1 per cent), seeking support from friends (24.4 per cent) and improving their diet (23.2 per cent).

Almost one in 12 (7.9 per cent) reported smoking cigarettes, or using alcohol or drugs to help. The proportion was much higher (31.5 per cent) for those who reported having major depressive disorder[1].

---

[1] Symptoms of these conditions can range from mild to severe. They are treatable and the sooner treatment is sought the better.
Find out more // **healthyfamilies.beyondblue.org.au**

// PREVALENCE OF MAJOR DEPRESSIVE DISORDER AND SELF-HARM*

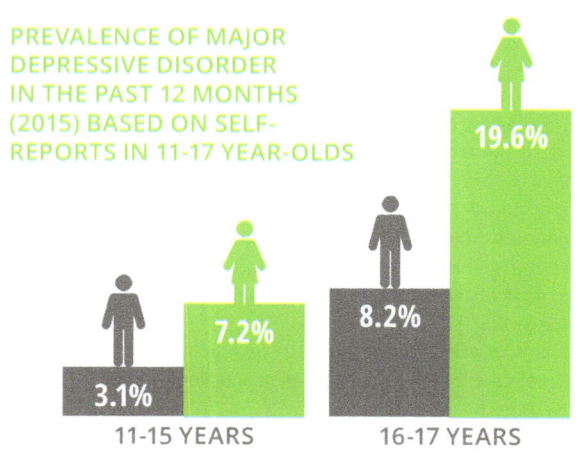

PREVALENCE OF MAJOR DEPRESSIVE DISORDER IN THE PAST 12 MONTHS (2015) BASED ON SELF-REPORTS IN 11-17 YEAR-OLDS

- 11-15 YEARS: 3.1% / 7.2%
- 16-17 YEARS: 8.2% / 19.6%

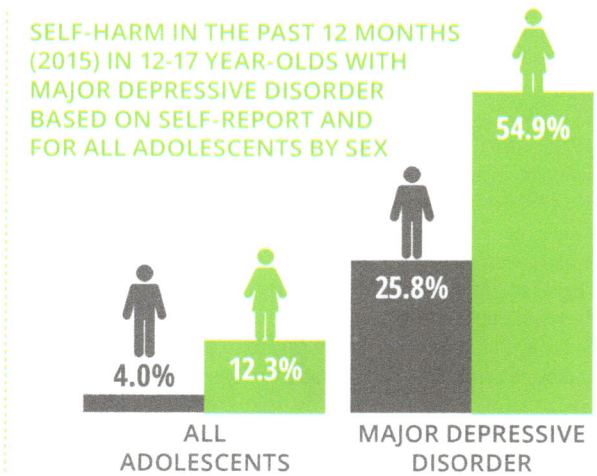

SELF-HARM IN THE PAST 12 MONTHS (2015) IN 12-17 YEAR-OLDS WITH MAJOR DEPRESSIVE DISORDER BASED ON SELF-REPORT AND FOR ALL ADOLESCENTS BY SEX

- ALL ADOLESCENTS: 4.0% / 12.3%
- MAJOR DEPRESSIVE DISORDER: 25.8% / 54.9%

*The Mental Health of Children and Adolescents; Report on the second Australian Child and Adolescent Survey of Mental Health and Wellbeing (2015).

// TYPES OF DEPRESSION

MAJOR DEPRESSION
Sometimes called major depressive disorder, clinical depression, unipolar depression or simply depression, major depression involves low mood and/or loss of interest and pleasure in usual activities, as well as other symptoms most days for at least two weeks.

MELANCHOLIA
A severe form of depression with many of the physical symptoms, melancholia sees a person start to move more slowly and be more likely to have a depressed mood characterised by complete loss of pleasure in everything, or almost everything.

PSYCHOTIC DEPRESSION
Psychotic depression occurs when someone with a depressive disorder loses touch with reality. It can involve hallucinations or delusions, or paranoia about being watched or followed.

ANTENATAL & POSTNATAL DEPRESSION
Women are at an increased risk of depression during pregnancy (known as the antenatal or prenatal period) and in the year following childbirth (known as the postnatal period).

BIPOLAR DISORDER
Bipolar disorder used to be known as manic depression because the person experiences periods of depression and periods of mania, with periods of normal mood in between.

CYCLOTHYMIC DISORDER
Often described as a milder form of bipolar disorder, this disorder involves chronic fluctuating moods over at least two years, periods of hypomania (a mild to moderate level of mania) and periods of depressive symptoms, with periods of up to two months of normality between.

DYSTHYMIC DISORDER
The symptoms are less severe than major depression but last longer.

SEASONAL AFFECTIVE DISORDER (SAD)
This mood disorder has a seasonal pattern characterised by mood disturbances (either periods of depression or mania) that begin and end in a season such as winter.

beyondblue

TALKING ABOUT DEPRESSION // PARENT TIPS

- Choose a time when the young person is relaxed and unlikely to be distracted.
- Be natural and don't overthink it. Start by sharing your concern.
- Be prepared for rejection. If they don't want to talk, try again later.
- Check your emotions and be realistic, while telling them you care and want to help.
- Discuss what you have noticed and why you are concerned.
- Ask questions about how they feel.
- Let them guide the conversation.
- Tell them it is important to discuss their feelings.
- Try to understand their reaction and help them to feel at ease. Let them know that crying is OK.
- Seek a balance between helping and encouraging their independence.
- Provide information about depression and the types of help available.
- Respect their privacy but explain the benefits of telling trusted people. Let them know that professional help is confidential and easy to access.

Other helpful tips can be found at //
healthyfamilies.beyondblue.org.au

// RISK FACTORS

- Emotional difficulties between a child and parent/parents e.g. more arguments, conflict, lack of communication.
- Physical and sexual abuse or neglect.
- Sudden death of a loved one, family member or pet.
- A loved one experiencing serious physical illness.
- Sudden separation of parents.
- A family history of depression – genetic and biological factors, such as chemical imbalances, can increase the risk.
- Social isolation and poor social/friendship networks.
- Being bullied.
- Changing schools or starting high school.
- Not doing as well at school – not getting the same kind of marks or having behaviour issues.
- Self-critical thinking and seeing oneself as a failure, a loser, unloveable, worthless etc.
- A tendency to ruminate and dwell on issues, sometimes turning them into bigger problems than they really are.
- Risk-taking behaviours.
- Having trouble sleeping and feeling irritable and grumpy.
- Lacking motivation, e.g. everything seems too hard.
- Losing interest in usual activities.
- Appetite changes, e.g. not eating regularly or overeating and weight changes.

Profile // Depression

I DIDN'T THINK I COULD RECOVER

Hannah has spoken about her experiences with schizophrenia as part of a campaign for SANE Australia.

// "I was around 12 years old when I began to experience depression and anxiety, which continued throughout my teenage years. I struggled to concentrate on my school work and I stopped enjoying sport and other activities that I usually liked. I found it extremely difficult to get out of bed. Everything took so much energy.

"I constantly felt a fear that I can't describe. I had extremely low self-worth and confidence in my abilities. High school was a difficult time. Depression and anxiety weren't as widely understood when I was at school so people thought I wasn't trying, that I didn't care or that I was 'attention seeking'.

"But I couldn't control the symptoms I was experiencing and I didn't have the tools required to effectively manage them. I didn't know how to seek help from people around me and I didn't feel safe to ask. I talked to friends but they didn't know how to help me, and this caused them a lot of emotional distress, which wasn't my intention. I desperately needed understanding and support.

"The depression and anxiety eventually got to a point where the symptoms were so severe that the adults around me couldn't ignore them. I was admitted to adolescent psychiatric wards a few times. I started experiencing psychosis towards the end of high school, although I didn't really understand what was happening at the time.

"The stress and pressure of the transition from school to university, as well as a culmination of other traumatic experiences, triggered the psychosis and ultimately resulted in a schizophrenia diagnosis when I was 18. I experienced auditory and visual hallucinations, delusions, paranoia and confused thinking. This made day-to-day life extremely challenging.

"When I was diagnosed, I didn't have much of an understanding of schizophrenia at all. The only thoughts that came to mind were the 'horror movie' stereotypes that many people think about when they think of schizophrenia. I didn't think that it was possible to recover – I believed that my life was over. One of the most common myths is that people with schizophrenia are inevitably dangerous and violent. This is not the case. Another common myth is that schizophrenia causes people to have multiple personalities. This is also false.

"One of the main things that struck me when I was diagnosed were the low expectations that many people had of me – particularly mental-health professionals. I was told that I would most likely have schizophrenia for the rest of my life. Not once was I given any sense of hope, or told that it's possible to recover and live a fulfilled life.

"For me, recovery will most likely not be a complete cure but I have worked hard to build an arsenal of supports, coping skills and strategies. I have been prescribed medications, but, unfortunately, they cause me some serious side-effects. I see my psychologist regularly. Volunteering and becoming involved in mental-health advocacy has played a huge role in my recovery. It has given me a sense of purpose and confidence. I know how essential it is for people who experience psychosis or schizophrenia to be empowered to develop self-efficacy and to have a meaningful input into their treatment, because finally being given that opportunity was instrumental in my recovery.

"I'm not a parent, but I can understand how powerless people can feel and how terrifying it can be when someone you love is suffering from a mental illness.

"No matter how out of reach or hopeless recovery may seem, I believe that it is always possible with holistic support and love. Continue to see young people as themselves, not as a diagnosis. Always show them that they are worthy of respect and love, and remain hopeful that they can recover – whatever recovery looks like for them."

Photo: Supplied

// SANE AUSTRALIA

SANE Australia is a national mental-health charity working to support 4 million Australians affected by complex mental illness including schizophrenia, bipolar, borderline personality disorder, eating disorders, OCD, PTSD and severe depression and anxiety.

Find out more // **www.sane.org**

// Hannah, 24, is studying a bachelor of human services and is a mental-health advocate. She is also a volunteer at headspace.

Profile // Depression

A FRIEND IN NEED

When a friend turned to Russell Farmer because they were experiencing depression and suicidal thoughts, Russell didn't know the best way to help.

// "We live in a society where it's not OK to not be OK. There's stigma around talking about how you feel, particularly if you're a guy. You have a problem and your first reaction is to deal with it on the inside, to try to fix it yourself rather than asking for help.

"We don't like to accept that things aren't perfect. In social and friendship groups, we want to be laid-back and fun – not a burden. We want to be the person that is looked up to, not the guy who is sad and bumming everyone out. We talk about the footy more than how bad our Saturday night was because we were stuck in bed feeling anxious or depressed.

"I want to challenge the idea that we all have a perfect life. It's normal to struggle sometimes. Things come up that are out of our control – we don't get the ATAR we want, we get sick or our parents split up – but those things can be dealt with. Research suggests three in five young men who acknowledge they are struggling don't seek help.

"I realised this during year 11 when a friend was struggling. I was quite clueless until they started sharing things with me and I had no idea how to deal with it. I was quite shaken. They had anxiety and depression and felt suicidal and they were trusting in me and another friend to help them get back on their feet.

"They didn't want to speak to their parents initially and I needed help to help my friend. I chatted to a school counsellor, then directed my friend towards a psychologist and got their parents involved. It was about keeping our friendship while involving the right people. They're getting help, and I've learnt through that experience.

"I think it's a natural thing initially not to want to tell your parents. It can be uncomfortable and sometimes you don't know how they will react. For a while my friend's excuse was that they didn't want to worry their parents and that they already had a lot on their plate. They were very supportive but I think it can be hard for parents to get an insight into how their kids are going – it may be that their friends more quickly see a problem.

"Friends have a responsibility to ask their friend if they are all right and to be serious about it. Don't ask in passing. Give friends an opportunity to say if they aren't doing well, but be a normal friend to them. Don't try and be their psychiatrist or the only person to make them feel better – get support yourself. Acknowledge they're having a rough time, be sensitive, but don't change your friendship. Keep the normal parts of their life secure and strong so they can hold on to those while other parts of their life are not going so well.

"Parents need to make it clear that they are on the same side as their teenager. Get professional help so you know how to best help your child and make sure they know you love them."

EDITOR'S NOTE // R U OK? DAY is Thursday 13 September 2018.

> "I want to challenge the idea that we all have a perfect life."

Photo: iStock

// Russell Farmer, 18, is a former vice-captain at Trinity Grammar School in Melbourne. Russell had spoken at school assemblies urging young people to ask for help if they or a friend are struggling with their feelings.

Profile // Professor Sue Spence

HOW TO BE BRAVE

Professor Sue Spence is a clinical psychologist who focuses on the prevention and treatment of anxiety and depression in young people.

"We know about 7 per cent of young people experience anxiety disorder to a level that it interferes in their daily life and justifies treatment – it is one of the most common problems in mental health. Many teenagers don't just grow out of it and a lot of adults with anxiety will tell you that the problem started when they were young and they suffer for years," says clinical psychologist Professor Sue Spence.

"Some degree of anxiety is a good thing. Evolution-wise it's a good idea to be afraid of wild animals and high places from which you could fall, for example. So there is commonsense as to why we've evolved a degree of fear. Some worry is also useful because it helps us pay attention to a situation, to prepare and to remember to do things.

"But anxiety and worry transition into a problem when they stop people doing things that are important in their life, like going out with friends, not going on school camp, spending a lot of time at home and not wanting to go to school. When it starts to disrupt their lifestyle, it becomes a problem, and the sooner you do something about it the better."

To lessen the incidence and impact of anxiety for young people, Professor Spence developed an in-clinic program, where children and families attended a clinic. Young people did 10 therapy sessions and parents completed six sessions. The program achieved positive results and Professor Spence and her colleagues, Dr Caroline Donovan and Dr Sonja March, converted it into an online format, BRAVE Online, to help a wider group of young people and parents.

The sessions look at the different kinds of anxieties that teenagers experience, the symptoms, and typical feelings and bodily reactions. Sessions also look at the relationship between thoughts and feelings; how we can learn to change our thinking and swap negative thoughts to more positive and effective thinking, and so reduce anxiety. Teenagers also learn coping skills and relaxation methods to help them reduce their anxiety.

The program uses an exposure hierarchy that breaks fears into small parts and helps young people begin facing their fear step-by-step.

"Each week a teenager gradually does something that is a little scarier. So if they have a fear of talking in front of others in the classroom, they might start practising talking in front of a mirror. Once they are comfortable doing that, they then find a parent or someone they trust to practise with them and gradually they work up to a point where they feel confident enough to talk in front of the class," explains Professor Spence.

Photo: Supplied

"Parents can try and make sure they don't inadvertently reward fearful behaviour by allowing young people to avoid a situation."

BRAVE also has dedicated sessions to help parents recognise and support a child with anxiety. Sessions begin by explaining different types of anxiety and how to distinguish between normal worries versus problematic worries. The sessions also illustrate parenting styles that can help a young person with anxiety. Parents are shown how to help their child with the exposure hierarchy – by ensuring steps between tasks are not too big and encouraging them to practise their tasks.

"Parents can try and make sure they don't inadvertently reward fearful behaviour by allowing young people to avoid a situation. When a teenager doesn't want to go to school, parents need to be firm and say, 'you really have to go to school', rather than saying 'you poor darling, I can see you're worried, take today off and stay home with me'," says Professor Spence.

"Don't give too much attention when young people express fears and worries but always be supportive, loving and warm."

// Professor Sue Spence helped develop BRAVE Online, a free online treatment program for anxiety that offers support to young people and to parents. To find out more, visit // brave4you.psy.uq.edu.au

ADHD

Attention deficit hyperactivity disorder is more common than you may think.

Attention deficit hyperactivity disorder (ADHD) is the most common mental-health disorder in children and adolescents. A major Australian study* found 7.4 per cent of those aged 4-17 had ADHD, followed by anxiety disorders (6.9 per cent), major depressive disorder (2.8 per cent) and conduct disorder (2.1 per cent).

This means about 298,000 Australian children and adolescents have ADHD. Most cases – 65.7 per cent – are mild, and more boys than girls – 10.4 compared to 4.3 per cent – have had the condition in the past 12 months (2015).

Girls are less likely to have ADHD as adolescents (2.7 per cent compared with 5.4 per cent at ages 4-11), but there is little difference for boys (10.9 per cent at 4-11 years old and 9.8 per cent at 12-17). In the past 12 months (2015), students with ADHD took an average five days off school due to its symptoms.

WHAT IS ADHD? *
ADHD is a persistent pattern of inattention and/or hyperactivity-impulsivity more frequent and severe than in other individuals at a similar developmental stage. Children and adolescents may find it difficult to pay attention and see tasks or activities through to the end or make careless mistakes with schoolwork or other tasks.

Children and adolescents with hyperactivity problems may talk excessively, have trouble staying still when it is appropriate or expected, and act like they are always "on the go".

// CONDUCT DISORDER

WHAT IS CONDUCT DISORDER?
Conduct disorder is repetitive and persistent behaviour that violates the basic rights of others, major societal norms or rules in their aggression towards people or animals, destruction of property, deceitfulness or theft and serious violation of rules. Behaviours often include bullying, frequent fights, deliberately destroying others' property, breaking into properties or cars, staying out late without permission, running away from home or frequent school truancy.

WHO HAS IT?
About 2 per cent of Australian children and adolescents – or 84,000 – have conduct disorder. More boys (2.5 per cent) than girls (1.6 per cent) have it. Like ADHD, conduct disorder is more prevalent in children and adolescents living in families with lower levels of income, education and employment and with poorer family functioning.

More young people outside capital city areas have conduct disorder than those in the city (3.2 per cent compared with 1.4 per cent). Compared to other disorders, a higher proportion of those with conduct disorder had a severe impact in the family domain (29.5 per cent). Only 4.3 per cent of those with conduct disorder have no impact on their family.

// PARENT TIPS

- Work with health professionals to develop a behaviour management plan that teaches skills to boost co-operative behaviour and reduce challenging behaviour.
- Give clear, easy-to-follow instructions while maintaining eye contact.
- Ask them to repeat instructions to ensure they understand them.
- Avoid over-tiredness by encouraging a healthy diet, good rest/sleep patterns and manageable screen time.
- Have regular routines using lists and timetables.
- Teach strategies so they can self-monitor their behaviour and deal with conflict.
- Speak to teachers about classroom strategies such as a visual checklist of tasks.

Find out more at Raising Children Network //
www.raisingchildren.net.au

// ADHD RISK FACTORS *

- Original families where at least one child lives with both natural, adoptive or foster parents without step-children have the lowest ADHD rates (5.7 per cent). The rate for those in lone parent or carer families is 11.1 per cent and blended families 13.4 per cent.
- ADHD is most prevalent in children in the lowest-income families (less than $52,000 a year) – 11.7 per cent. It falls to 6.6 per cent in middle-income and 5.2 per cent in high-income families.
- Of those whose parents left school in year 10 or below, 11.7 per cent have ADHD, compared with 5.4 per cent whose parents had a bachelor degree or higher. Rates are also higher in families with both parents unemployed.

// AUTISM SPECTRUM DISORDERS

Autism spectrum disorders (ASD) refers to a group of developmental disorders — Autistic, Asperger's, Childhood Disintegrative Disorder, Rett's and Pervasive Developmental Disorder — that often affect a person's ability to interact socially and communicate with others.

The signs and symptoms of an autism disorder will typically manifest before the age of three and can include repeating activities, showing an extreme resistance to changes in routine and various speech problems.

---

* The Mental Health of Children and Adolescents; Report on the second Australian Child and Adolescent Survey of Mental Health and Wellbeing (2015).

RESILIENCE

Children need to experience life's ups and downs to become resilient young people.

Helping adolescents and young people build resilience is one of the most valuable gifts a parent can give their child. Why is resilience important, and how do parents and carers help their child develop this essential characteristic?

"We are living in a time when children are less resilient, so by the time they get to adolescence they are floundering in a world that has changed more rapidly than ever. It's tricky out there. We've always had a generation gap, but now it's a chasm," says Maggie Dent, a parenting and resilience author and educator.

"We have a generation of wonderful young people whose parents have done so much for them that they've disabled those young people from doing things for themselves."

Dent says a generation of millennial adolescents are growing up and entering adulthood without resilience – a quality or characteristic she defines as being able 'to manage your day-to-day life and to recover from setbacks and adversity'.

WHAT IS RESILIENCE?

The *Promoting Resilience in the Millennial Adolescent* report, prepared by Dent with the Department for Communities' Office for Youth in WA, says resilience refers to "the ability of a person to successfully manage their life, and to successfully adapt to change and stressful events in healthy and constructive ways. It is about survivability and 'bounce-back-ability' to life experiences – both the advantageous ones and the challenging, traumatic ones".

Dent says the failure to build resilience begins in younger children.

"We've changed games like pass the parcel so every child gets a prize. Everyone gets trophies and ribbons even when they don't win. We've softened children's natural ability to experience things like disappointment and setbacks," says Dent.

"Yet we've changed the education system to become such a testing regime, so children are experiencing more opportunities to fail without having the capacity to manage failure. And, with great love, parents are doing too much for their children and are further reducing their capacity to do things for themselves."

WHY RESILIENCE MATTERS

Researchers say a lack of resilience in adolescents and young people is leading to issues, including depression, anxiety disorders, stress, low self-esteem, drug abuse, family dysfunction, disconnection and struggles at school. Resilience is protective against these kinds of problems and helps young people deal with adversity.

"Adolescence is a time of transformational change on all levels. They move from being a child to being an adult. They are searching for identity and at the same time young people are marinated in a sexualised culture," Dent says.

"They see the world through a distorted windscreen and develop self-loathing and self-disgust. At the same time, an adolescent needs to learn to separate from their parents."

Dent says resilience helps young people safely navigate a rapidly changing modern world and helps them be competent to make the right choices and decisions in their life.

// THE RESILIENCE PROJECT

After spending time volunteering in an Indian village, former teacher Hugh van Cuylenburg was inspired to create The Resilience Project, which educates Australian parents, children and organisations about the importance of gratitude, empathy (compassion) and mindfulness. "In this desert community, there was no running water, no electricity and no beds; everyone slept on the floor," van Cuylenburg says. "Despite the fact these people had very little to call their own, I was continually blown away by how happy they were."

The Resilience Project delivers presentations to a range of organisations including elite sporting clubs and primary and secondary schools. In addition to the presentations schools receive they have the opportunity to complete a curriculum specifically designed to encourage self-awareness through focusing on what you have as opposed to what you don't have, understanding the benefits of helping others and being healthy and active. Here are some simple tools to build resilience:

KEEPING A GRATITUDE JOURNAL

In the journal, answer these two questions every night.
- What are three things that went well for you today?
- What are you looking forward to most tomorrow?

This simple exercise will help build positive emotion and reduce levels of anxiety.

MEDITATE

Meditation has many well-known benefits. Most notably, it teaches you to appreciate the moment you are in.

BE KIND

Try to perform one random act of kindness a week. It can be something small, such as giving someone a compliment. When we do something kind, our brain releases a hormone called oxytocin, which makes us feel happier.

SLEEP

Never underestimate the power of sleep. Adolescents require 8-10 hours of sleep a night for optimal cognitive development. A child at primary school requires 10-12 hours.

EXERCISE

Research tells us that regular exercise is linked closely to our resilience and well-being. Twenty minutes a day is enough. Even if it's just a brisk walk, make sure you are putting time aside to be active.

For more information, visit // **theresilienceproject.com.au**

HELPING CHILDREN BUILD RESILIENCE

Parents and trusted, significant adults – whom Dent calls 'lighthouses' – play a pivotal role in helping young people develop resilience. 'Lighthouses' are adults who have a caring, genuine and meaningful involvement with a young person and who are willing to support them in their bumpy journey towards adulthood.

LIGHTHOUSES

'Lighthouses' support adolescents as they develop and build resilience in a number of ways. They:
- Have knowledge and understanding of adolescence;
- Have the courage to care;
- Are trustworthy and respectful;
- Give hope and encouragement;
- Build connectedness through genuine acceptance;
- Encourage mastery and teach life skills;
- Help adolescents manage 'big ugly emotional states';
- Practise caring, empowering communication;
- Give guidance when asked; and
- Strengthen the spirit – including laughter and lightness.

Dent says parents need to focus more on being a 'lighthouse' and less on being the 'perfect parent'.

"Parents want to hide their own embarrassment around their own disappointments and failures. They don't want to be seen to be a 'bad' parent. They want their children to think they have never mucked up so they don't model what to do when you get stressed or angry or fail," she says.

Be a mean but loving parent. Don't overindulge children in the pursuit of keeping them happy, adds Dent. Life isn't always going to be happy and children need to learn that and practise how to navigate disappointment, failures and things not going according to plan.

"Give them opportunities to fail well and reassure them that failure doesn't make them bad people. Reassure them that things can be bumpy but nothing they do will ever make you, as a parent, not want to be there for them. You can tell them you love them and they will probably roll their eyes! But your child needs to know you love them fiercely and unconditionally," says Dent.

Day-to-day, give young people responsibilities around your home so they learn life skills that are not only useful but that build their confidence and sense of capability.

"Give them opportunities to develop grit and persistence and an 'I can do that' attitude. And remember it's a coaching process. Don't yell and shout because that will alienate a young person. Remember that they can already feel lost and confused because of all the changes happening around them," says Dent.

"Look at what gaps they have in their coping capacities and help them fill those gaps. And have 'what if' conversations with your teenagers. Ask them what they would do if gatecrashers turned up at a party. Put them in some real-life situations and see what their explanations are."

Help young people foster healthy friendship groups and welcome and co-parent those children.

"We want their parents to co-parent our children because often children listen to the parents of their friends. Encourage friendships that can help children transition from home because when they leave home, often they consult a good friend before mum or dad," says Dent.

Photo: iStock

// PARENT TIPS

Start building life skills by encouraging your teenager to do tasks such as:
- Wiping down the kitchen bench after preparing food;
- Sweeping and mopping the floor;
- Learning basic food preparation skills;
- Knowing how to use a washing machine;
- Not leaving clothes, shoes and wet towels around the house;
- Eating meals at regular times;
- Saying hello to people when they first see them;
- Learning to be assertive without being aggressive;
- Listening when someone is speaking to them;
- Being punctual for meetings – or 10 minutes early;
- Saying sorry when they make a mistake;
- Learning how to save money, and repaying money if they borrow it; and
- Learning how to laugh at themselves when they muck up.

// *Saving Our Adolescents*, by Maggie Dent
www.maggiedent.com

IS MY CHILD OK?

Is your child going through normal adolescent ups and downs? Angelina Chisari shares some of the lessons she's learnt and signs to look out for.

More than half the callers to Kids Helpline are 13 to 18 years old and about one in five callers are worried about mental health – their own, or a person close to them.

"Most of the time they are seeking support and strategies to manage an already diagnosed or established mental health condition, but we also get contacts from children who aren't diagnosed and who are concerned about initial symptoms or some quite serious symptoms," says Angelina Chisari.

Most mental-health concerns involve depression, anxiety, self-harm and suicide.

"At night, they can be left with their thoughts and have difficulties sleeping, and they call us because they can't see their usual psychologist or counsellor then. They also call for crisis support if they have urges around suicide and self-harm – we build a safety net for young people," says Ms Chisari.

She says it can be hard for parents to work out whether their teenager's behaviour is normal, or whether it's something to be concerned about. And she adds that it's normal for parents to feel anxious and concerned about how to approach mental health concerns with their child.

"We know teenagers tend to be a little more emotional than at other times in life. They are going through a lot of changes developmentally, socially, academically, physically and emotionally.

"The teenage brain is still developing, and this can leave young people feeling really tired, emotional and exhausted. Emotions like anger, sadness, stress and anxiety can be normal, but if those emotions are excessive, consistent and prolonged over weeks to months, that needs to be explored further," Ms Chisari says.

> "We know teenagers tend to be a little more emotional than at other times in life."

// WHAT IS NORMAL AND WHAT ARE THE SIGNS THAT A CHILD MAY BE STRUGGLING EMOTIONALLY?

"Is your child retreating from family, friends or everyday activities? Or have you noticed other changes in their behaviour? Is your child avoiding school? Have they become more irritable or aggressive? Are they using drugs or alcohol? Usually teenagers don't want to spend as much time with their parents and their focus shifts to their friends. If you see a change in how much time your child is spending with their friends, that can be a sign that something is going on," says Ms Chisari.

If your child shows persistent signs of hopelessness or pessimism, don't minimise those feelings by trying to normalise them. "When you minimise their feelings, your child is less likely to talk to you again about those issues," says Ms Chisari. "If the issue worsens and those feelings escalate from depression to self-harm. They're not going to come back to you for help."

Is your child showing increased sensitivity and heightened reactions to challenges, failure or rejection? Are they more self-critical than usual? Do they talk about feeling guilty or worthless? Your first reaction as a parent is important. "Be supportive and don't try to convey that everything is in their head, that it's normal teenage hormones and it will all get better," says Ms Chisari. "Ask your child what is going on, how they are feeling, acknowledge and validate their feelings and involve them in options for support. Ask them if they want to speak to a counsellor or a doctor or to call an anonymous service like Kids Helpline so what they're experiencing can be looked at further."

Experts usually agree that if a condition is affecting a child's ability to function day to day, or their ability to enjoy life, they may need professional help.

It's normal for parents to feel worried about how to talk to their kids about mental health. "As parents, we don't always know what to do or say. It's OK to feel this way and help is available," says Ms Chisari. Parentline is a confidential telephone counselling service for parents and carers offering information, referrals and assistance on a range of parenting issues.

Parentline // **1300 30 1300**

The Kids Helpline website has a dedicated section for parents that includes advice on how to start a conversation with a young person about their mental health. It also gives information on different forms of mental illness, signs, symptoms and support and treatment options.

Kids Helpline // **www.kidshelpline.com.au** or **1800 55 1800**

// *Angelina Chisari is a senior practice supervisor at Kids Helpline, a national phoneline that provides counselling and support to children and young adults aged between 5 and 25.*

AM I OK?

Parenting young people can be tough at times, but it can be even trickier if you're not feeling supported yourself.

Like young people, adults too can struggle with the challenges of life. The *Jean Hailes Women's Health Survey 2017* found about 40 per cent of women had been professionally diagnosed with depression or anxiety. Those aged 18-35 were most anxious.

Nearly half of the women surveyed said that on several days of the week they worry excessively about different things, become easily annoyed or distracted and have trouble sleeping.

Clinical psychologist Dr Janet Hall says it is a great advantage for young people if their parents are mentally well.

"Parents are their primary models and their communication, habits, routines and relationship can set a fine model for a teen," she says.

Dr Hall says if they are struggling, parents may need someone to listen to them and offer advice.

"Close relationships offer support and feedback for parents who are not thinking straight or feeling OK," she says. "The challenge may be for an unwell parent to share with the appropriate person."

Warning signs that a parent may need professional help include being unable to cope with normal life routines, no motivation, talking too fast or not at all, anxiety attacks, being unable to make decisions or solve everyday problems, lack of self-care and hygiene, explosive anger and inability to stop crying.

Dr Hall says parents often believe it's better to avoid talking to children about their mental illness to protect them from stress and confusion.

"Yet research shows that when parents talk openly about their struggles, in language their child can understand, it actually helps the child to cope better," she says.

"It can help them to make sense of the changes that they observe in you when you're unwell and to know that they're not at fault or somehow responsible for them.

"It is inappropriate, however, to 'overshare' by giving too much information about their mental illness and perhaps set up an expectation that the teen has to give the parent counselling and advice."

Keeping yourself mentally well
- Have a healthy routine – exercise, eat foods with good nutrition, have a good night's sleep.
- Communicate with people who are constructive – talk to positive friends and family regularly.
- Belong to a group of positive people who share a common interest such as sport, reading or contributing to community activities.
- Be realistic about your stress levels – learn to say no so you don't get burnt out.
- Be responsible about your choices for pleasure – avoid escaping into drugs, alcohol, social media and television. Get professional help early if you know you are abusing yourself or if others who care for you recommend that you need help.

For more information, visit // www.drjanethall.com.au

Photo: iStock

// SEEKING HELP
- Talk to other parents, your partner or other family and friends.
- There may be parenting groups in your area that meet and talk about adolescents.
- If talking to friends and family does not help or reassure you, talk to your child's teacher or a trusted health professional.
- Don't give up if you can't find the right person. It may take time.

Most states and territories have parent help lines, and raisingchildren.net.au has a good list. The following are some national numbers.

Department of Mental Health // www.health.gov.au/internet/main/publishing.nsf/content/mental-ba-fact-pat

Family Relationship Advice Line // 1800 050 321, 8am-8pm Monday to Friday, 10am-4pm Saturday

Lifeline // 131 114

MensLine Australia // 1300 789 978

Sane Australia Mental Health Helpline // 1800 187 263, 9am-5pm Monday to Friday

1800 RESPECT (National Sexual Assault, Domestic and Family Violence Counselling Service) // 1800 737 732

COPMI (Children of Parents With a Mental Illness) // www.copmi.net.au

EATING DISORDERS

Early intervention is crucial for young people who develop eating disorders.

Eating disorders are complex and can remain well-hidden unless the person living with it suffers from serious physical illness. Many people live with them for years and may never seek treatment.

A 2016 report by Orygen, The National Centre of Excellence in Youth Mental Health, paints a detailed picture of eating disorders, which are not one diagnosable illness but a set of neuropsychiatric illnesses with biological, psychological and socio-cultural risk factors.

They include anorexia nervosa, bulimia nervosa, binge-eating disorder and several other specified or unspecified feeding and eating disorders.

Those who have them may move from one to another and then back again. Some will experience an eating disorder with another condition such as anxiety, depression, drug and alcohol disorders and obesity.

Treatment requires a complex response to all related physical and mental ill-health, while recovery needs medical, psychological and nutritional treatments that, particularly for young people, also require a significant commitment from the entire family.

Orygen's *Nip it in the bud: Intervening early for young people with eating disorders*** estimates that 9 per cent of Australians have an eating disorder. This includes a significant proportion affected by binge-eating disorder.

Binge-eating disorder is the most prevalent eating disorder and rates appear to be rising.

Conversely, dieting is a big issue for many. Another study (Tucci, 2007), found 90 per cent of 12 to 17-year-old girls and 68 per cent of 12 to 17-year-old boys had been on a diet of some form.

Nip it in the bud found that many people with eating disorders were either not diagnosed or only accessed treatment after an extended period of illness. "At present, a young person with the onset of an eating disorder may potentially not seek treatment for four to 10 years," it found.

"While evidence-based treatment provided within two to three years of diagnosis has been shown to be successful, the costs of delayed, or no treatment, are devastating for young people experiencing the illness, their family and the community."

WARNING SIGNS AND TRIGGERS

Many young people, particularly girls, are dissatisfied with their bodies. Preoccupation with weight and shape is one of the most potent and replicated risk factors for bulimia and anorexia nervosa.

Intense dissatisfaction with body size and shape can lead to disordered eating behaviours, such as fasting, use of laxatives, self-induced vomiting and binge eating. This does not always result in an eating disorder but is a serious health problem and the most common indicator of risk for the development of an eating disorder.

An estimated one in five females have disordered eating, which could be a conservative figure given its secretive nature.

Numerous psychological, biological, socio-cultural and environmental factors may trigger a vulnerable young person into a cycle of disordered eating. It may appear to be quite minor, such as an off-hand comment by a parent about gaining weight.

// PREVALENCE OF EATING DISORDERS**

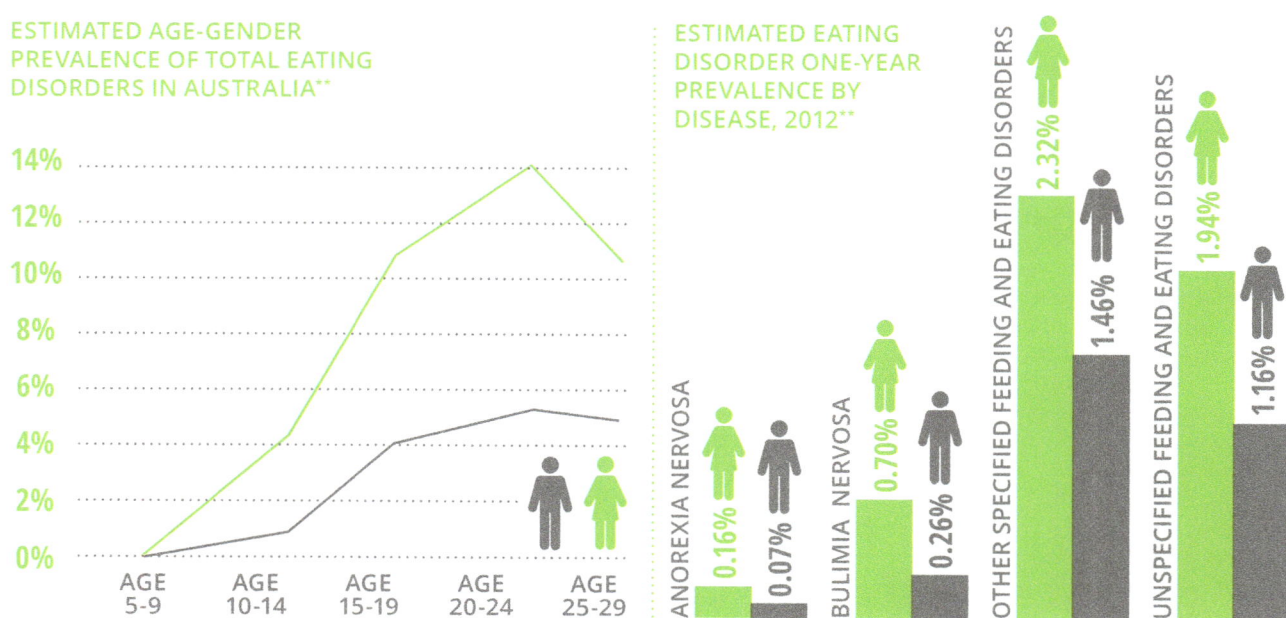

** *Nip it in the bud: Intervening early for young people with eating disorders. Melbourne: Orygen, The National Centre of Excellence in Youth Mental Health, 2016.*

// EATING DISORDER TYPES**

ANOREXIA NERVOSA
Involves a persistent restriction of energy intake leading to significantly low body weight. A person with it has either an intense fear of gaining weight or becoming fat, or persistent behaviour that interferes with weight gain, even though they are already significantly underweight.

It also includes disturbances in the way one's body weight or shape is experienced, undue influence of body shape and weight on self-evaluation, or a persistent lack of recognition of the seriousness of current low body weight.

BINGE-EATING DISORDER
Recurring episodes of eating significantly more food in a short period of time than most people would under similar circumstances, with associated feelings of lack of control, distress, guilt, embarrassment and disgust. This occurs, on average, at least once a week over three months.

BULIMIA NERVOSA
Involves recurrent episodes of binge eating, followed by recurrent inappropriate behaviour to prevent weight gain, such as self-induced vomiting, misuse of laxatives, diuretics or other medications, fasting or excessive exercise. These behaviours both occur, on average, at least once a week for three months.

OTHER SPECIFIED FEEDING AND EATING DISORDER (OSFED)
Refers to situations where a person has clinically significant feeding and eating disorder symptoms but does not meet the full criteria for another diagnostic category. e.g. atypical anorexia nervosa (weight is within normal range).

UNSPECIFIED FEEDING AND EATING DISORDERS (UFED)
Clinically significant feeding or eating disorders that do not meet the criteria for another eating or feeding disorder.

** Nip it in the bud: Intervening early for young people with eating disorders. Melbourne: Orygen, The National Centre of Excellence in Youth Mental Health, 2016.

// SEEKING HELP

Early intervention is critical. Those who have had an eating disorder for less than two years are likely to respond faster to treatment and have fewer physical health consequences.

However, most people with an eating disorder don't seek help. *Nip it in the bud* found only 17–31 per cent of those with a diagnosable eating disorder seek specific treatment. If they do, it is often after an extended period of illness, up to 10 years later.

Under 18s are more likely to experience good outcomes from intervention. Family therapy within three years of onset is the most effective approach for young people with anorexia nervosa.

Australia's eating disorder rates are increasing, most notably for bulimia nervosa and binge-eating disorder. The anorexia nervosa rate has been generally stable in recent years.

Read // *Life-Size* by Jenefer Shute
Watch // *The Karen Carpenter Story*

// RISK FACTORS**

- Women and girls are 2.5 times more likely to have an eating disorder than men and boys. Nine out of 10 of those with anorexia are female.
- More young men are reporting body dissatisfaction and eating problems, including weight control and weight gain behaviours. Up to 50 per cent of boys have reported wanting to change their body size and about one in four children with anorexia nervosa are boys.
- No single cause has been identified for eating disorders, which may develop in vulnerable individuals through a combination of biological, psychological, socio-cultural and environmental factors.
- There is no eating disorder gene, but a number of genes within biological systems that relate to food intake, appetite, metabolism, mood and reward-pleasure responses may be involved.
- Psychological factors may include perfectionism, obsessive compulsiveness, impulsivity, body dissatisfaction, neuroticism and core low self-esteem.
- There is also evidence that socio-cultural influences play a part in the development of eating disorders, particularly in Western cultures, which promote a thin body ideal through media, family, friends and sporting cultures.
- Few studies have looked at risk factors for binge eating, but those available identified family neglect, low self-esteem and low perceived social support as contributing factors.

For more information, visit // www.oyh.org.au
For more help, visit// www.thebutterflyfoundation.org.au

// PARENT TIPS

- Set a good example with your dietary habits; children learn from parents.
- Avoid dieting and don't encourage your child to. Discuss the dangers of dieting.
- Be aware of the impact of negative body talk around your children, about your own body or other people's.
- Exercise regularly, and keep the focus on health and fun.
- Be critical of media messages and images that promote thinness or masculine ideals.

www.betterhealth.vic.gov.au

// NIP IT IN THE BUD

**Orygen Youth Health (OYH) is a world-leading youth mental health program based in Melbourne, Australia. OYH has two main components: a specialised youth mental-health clinical service and an integrated training and communications program.
For more information visit // www.orygen.org.au**

Profile // Anxiety & eating disorder

COPING WITH ANOREXIA

People often don't realise that an eating disorder is a psychological issue. As she moved to year 7, Ashleigh's anxiety manifested as an eating disorder.

"I was 12 when the problem began. I did a lot of competitive gymnastics and dancing and put a certain amount of pressure on myself. I associated being worthy with being smaller. I also have an obsessive, perfectionistic personality – when I commit to something, I do anything to get there. I felt that I needed to be perfect to be accepted/loved and that led to an implosion. A range of factors led me to develop anorexia – it's a very complex illness.

"I was incredibly anxious all the time. Despite being very successful in all areas of my life, I felt that I was never good enough, and I felt that way every day, all the time. Anorexia was a manifestation of my anxiety and a subconscious coping mechanism – so I didn't have to worry about everything, I would worry about my food and my size. It's a spiral and it gets completely out of control. I desperately wanted to get out but I didn't know how to escape. I felt constant self-loathing and would say the nastiest things to myself. I just wanted to disappear.

"I didn't talk to anyone about what was happening because this was my activity. And I knew that if I told anyone they would interfere and stop me doing what I was doing. People were concerned but for a long time I said I was fine. The illness berates you for not adhering to the rules and it was hard to speak out because the illness is also secretive and deceitful.

"I did see a school counsellor at the start of year 8. I said I think I have a problem with food, I'm hungry all the time but I won't allow myself to eat, and she was completely dismissive. She said I was probably not hungry but thirsty and to have some water. When I told her about the anxiety she told me I should skip rope when I felt stressed. This completely fed into my disordered behaviours and self-loathing. It essentially gave my anorexia a 'free pass' as it told me that if I was truly sick, the school counsellor would have picked up on it.

"My parents were worried and tried to have a conversation and I'd say I'm fine. My illness didn't want to be disturbed so I withdrew from family and friends. From anorexia's point of view, they were an obstacle trying to derail me from what I was doing. They would get in the way of the plan.

"Mum tried to take me to appointments with doctors and dietitians, and one night my parents sat on my bed and cried and begged me to eat. But I physically couldn't eat. You can't help it. It is similar to how people with drug addictions do horrendous things to get their hit; you are so desperate and driven by the illness that you do anything it says. But while parents can't make a child eat, the behaviour does need to be addressed with professional support – it can't be ignored.

"The next day dad said he was taking me to an orthodontist appointment and took me to an emergency department instead and I was diagnosed with anorexia. I was initially sent to an outpatient's clinic and then I was admitted for a couple of weeks but I deteriorated rapidly after I was discharged because they didn't address the psychological component and I was re-admitted. People often don't realise an eating disorder is a psychological issue.

"I began seeing a private psychologist and so began my slow journey to recovery. She taught me how to separate the illness from myself – she called it the snake. When I could separate myself, I had a foundation to help me push back against negative and self-destructive thoughts.

"As parents, don't focus on the food. Don't tell your child just to eat. We know we need to do that but we can't. Parents can be aggressive because they are worried. Self-care for parents is important, too. Get support. Eating Disorders Victoria has support groups for family and friends. Create a space so children know they aren't going to be told off or judged. Create a safe space for conversation.

"Parents tend to want to 'fix' it but that can make the illness retreat more. Instead, listen to what a young person is saying. Remind them they are loved and support them to believe in themselves because when people have belief in you, that rubs off."

> "The illness berates you for not adhering to the rules and it was hard to speak out because the illness is also secretive and deceitful."

For more information, visit Eating Disorders Victoria //
www.eatingdisorders.org.au or 1300 550 236
Body image movie *"Embrace"* //
www.youtube.com/watch?v=__2AayArYfs

// Ashleigh, 27, lived with anorexia for 10 years. Today she is about to become a lawyer.

ANXIETY

While anxiety is normal, it can develop into a disorder.

Most of us feel anxious at times. But for some people the anxiety is serious enough to negatively affect their enjoyment of life. Almost 7 per cent of Australian children and adolescents – or 278,000 – have an anxiety disorder. Most are considered mild.

Anxiety disorders generally include social phobia, separation anxiety, generalised anxiety and obsessive-compulsive disorder. A major Australian study* found that these affected 6.9 per cent of those aged four to 17. There was little difference in prevalence between girls and boys.

Young people in the most-disadvantaged socioeconomic group (10.4 per cent) were twice as likely to have an anxiety disorder than those in the least-disadvantaged group (5.3 per cent).

Young people with an anxiety issue need support to cope with the challenges they face, such as doing well in year 12, taking on leadership roles at a younger age and pressure to feel accepted on social media. Parents must be alert for signs that they are not coping and seek professional help if needed.

// RISK FACTORS

- A family history of anxiety;
- Having a perfectionistic personality;
- Lack of confidence or self-esteem;
- Family and relationship problems;
- Having a controlling or over-protective parent, or parents who are often critical or negative in their parenting style;
- Death or loss of a loved one;
- A traumatic or negative life experience;
- Verbal, sexual, physical or emotional abuse or trauma;
- Serious physical illness; and
- Girls, or women, are more likely to develop anxiety disorders.

// ANXIETY DISORDERS

SOCIAL PHOBIA // Intense anxiety caused by social situations leading up to and during the event, such as going out with friends or giving a speech.
SEPARATION ANXIETY // An overwhelming fear of being parted from parents, carers or those to whom someone has a strong attachment.
GENERALISED ANXIETY // Excessive anxiety and worry about common issues, such as family or friends, health, work, money or forgetting important appointments.
OBSESSIVE COMPULSIVE DISORDER // An obsessive compulsion to do something, such as checking doors and windows to see if they are locked, or ensuring everything is orderly in cupboards and drawers.

// TIPS FOR PARENTS

- Anxiety is normal. Excessive anxiety is not.
- Young people with genuine anxiety disorders are not naughty or defiant.
- Look for persistent physical symptoms such as headaches, stomach aches, vomiting, tiredness as well as missing school and avoiding social activities.
- If the anxiety relates to a mental-health disorder such as generalised anxiety, obsessive compulsive disorder, phobias, social anxiety and panic attacks, seek professional help.
- Teaching and modelling resilience can help young people cope with anxiety.
- Admit when you are anxious; no one is perfect.

// PREVALENCE OF ANXIETY DISORDERS AMONG 4-17-YEAR-OLDS*
(In the past 12 months [2015] by sex and age group)

	Social phobia %	Separation anxiety %	Generalised anxiety %	Obsessive compulsive %	Any anxiety disorder %
Males 4-11 years	1.8	4.9	1.8%	1.3	7.6
Males 12-17 years	3.3	3.8	2.3	0.9	6.3
Females 4-11 years	1.3	4.8	1.5	0.3	6.1
Females 12-17 years	3.4	3.1	3.4	0.7	7.7

* The Mental Health of Children and Adolescents; Report on the second Australian Child and Adolescent Survey of Mental Health and Wellbeing (2015).
'Any anxiety disorder' is not the sum of individual anxiety disorders as some children and adolescents had more than one type of disorder

Profile // Anxiety & self-harming

WHY I CHOSE TO HURT MYSELF

For Sarah, anxiety, heightened emotions and the pressure to be perfect contributed to self-harming. She describes it as an outlet for her emotional distress.

"Self-harming got pretty bad when I was 15. For me, it was the pressure of adolescence and everything that goes with that. I was OK at school but I wanted to be the best and I started getting anxious about schoolwork. I put pressure on myself. I wanted everything in my life to be 'perfect'.

"I was anxious and really stressed. I lost my appetite because anxiety made me feel sick. But then it felt good not to eat – I had control over food if nothing else in my life. In a weird way, I felt it was something I was good at. I felt I couldn't do anything well enough.

"Halfway through year 10, I stopped doing school work. I'd sit in class but thought I'd fail so I decided to fail myself – again, I had some control that way. Because I was a high achiever previously, the school was happy for me to go to class and the teachers and welfare staff who knew me well were my main support. They were part of the reason why I went to school. But I felt I didn't know what I was doing or who I was and I didn't want to face anything or anyone. I felt I was losing everything. I thought I was pretty worthless.

"I began self-harming to control the pain I felt inside, as it gave me something else to focus on. It was also a way to communicate to people that things weren't going well, because I wasn't able to openly talk to anyone about it. Self-harming was an outlet for my emotional anxiety and distress. I needed to get it out somehow. Every time I self-harmed, it helped calm me down. There were so many emotions – anxiety, self-hatred and feeling like I was alone and I didn't know how to soothe myself. It was a routine. I'd get everything set up, harm myself and then bandage myself and I'd feel calmer.

"I did minor stuff most days but a couple of times a month I needed medical intervention. I'd hide it from my family and was really angry if they found out. My parents would get angry and upset when they saw it, and that made things more difficult because I was already anxious. During an argument is not the moment to talk about self-harm. It's a scary thing for parents and so they feel they need to ask about it now. Taking a step back and thinking about how to have the conversation is more helpful. Young people need to see it is safe to talk, and it doesn't feel safe when a parent is really emotional.

"There's a misconception that self-harm is linked with thoughts of suicide, or leads to suicide. It's often not the case. Parents miss that. For people doing it, it can be their way of coping with the pain, distress and difficulty in their life. It can also be an attempt to take control in situations that seem uncontrollable. It's almost like a form of resilience – it's that person trying to cope with difficulty the best way they know how, and it might be all they know to get them through that moment.

"Counselling and being able to talk about what I was going through has helped. Being able to get really upset and show that to someone meant I didn't need to self-harm.

"I think it's helpful if parents focus on what is behind the self-harm rather than the self-harm itself. It's a symptom. Nobody does it for no reason. There's always a need that isn't being met. Ask what is going on for your child and how you can help."

> "My parents would get angry and upset when they saw it, and that made things more difficult because I was already anxious."

// Sarah, now 23, is studying at university. She has worked with headspace to provide a lived-experience perspective in developing courses for young people, parents, carers and health professionals to help them better understand what's behind self-harm.

SELF-HARM

Typically associated with difficulty managing emotions, without assessment and help self-harm can become a risky mechanism for coping with distress.

Self-harm affects almost 200,000 young Australians. It involves deliberately hurting or injuring yourself without trying to end your life and is often done secretively.

A major national 2015 study* found about one in 10 Australian adolescents (10.9 per cent) reported having self-harmed at some point, which is about 186,000 young people aged 12 to 17.

Three in four (137,000) had done so in the previous 12 months. Another 7.5 per cent answered "prefer not to say" about self-harm, so the rates could be higher.

Self-harm was more common among girls than boys, with 16.8 per cent of girls aged 16 to 17 doing it in the previous 12 months and 22.8 per cent at some point. This compared with 6.2 and 9.1 per cent for boys.

Of those aged 12 to 15, 9.8 per cent of girls had self-harmed over the past year and 11.1 per cent at some point, compared with 3 per cent and 5.7 per cent for boys.

More than half of females who had self-harmed had done so four times or more, and one in 10 young people who had self-harmed in the past year received medical treatment.

Excluding young people with a major depressive disorder, self-harm rates were higher in those from stepfamilies than original families – 14.7 per cent versus 7.8 per cent had self-harmed at some point and 6.4 per cent versus 2.5 per cent in the past year.

WHAT YOUNG PEOPLE TELL US ABOUT SELF-HARM

- One in 10 adolescents aged 12- to 17-year-olds (10.9 per cent) have ever self-harmed, or 186,000 people. Three in four had done so in the past year.
- Self-harm is roughly twice as common in girls than boys.
- It is more common in older than younger adolescents.
- Girls aged 16 to 17 years had the highest rate (16.8 per cent in the past year).
- Young people with major depressive disorder are much more likely to self-harm – 25.8 per cent of boys and 54.9 per cent of girls with it have self-harmed in the past year.
- Of those who self-harm, 0.8 per cent are admitted to hospital.

// SELF-HARM IN THE PAST 12 MONTHS (2015)*
(in 12-17 year-olds by sex and age group)

- 12-15 YEARS: 3.1% / 9.8%
- 16-17 YEARS: 6.2% / 16.8%

// TIPS FOR PARENTS

- Don't force or push your child into stopping self-injuring. If they could they would. Self-injury is their way of coping with stress, so before asking them to stop, we need to equip them with other, more adaptive coping skills.
- Talk openly and honestly about self-injury. Avoid fostering an environment of secrecy, shame, isolation and guilt.
- Remain calm and avoid emotional extremes: for example, anger or effusive sympathy, as this may further reinforce the behaviour.
- Be emotionally supportive, actively engage with and listen to your child.
- Watch for signs that your child is experiencing intense emotions and help distract them by employing their alternatives or simply comfort them.
- Encourage and explore alternative coping strategies with your child: for example, taking up a new hobby, sport, sit down and watch TV with them.

// Dr Madeline Wishart
www.madelinewishart.com
facebook.com/thebodyasavoice

Photo: pixabay.com

// RISK FACTORS*

- Mental-health issues including depression, anxiety and personality disorders increase the risk of self-harm.
- Low self-esteem, anger and feeling isolated are also risk factors.
- Grief or a traumatic life event.
- Childhood emotional, physical or sexual abuse.

*The Mental Health of Children and Adolescents; Report on the second Australian Child and Adolescent Survey of Mental Health and Wellbeing (2015).

SUICIDE

While uncommon in young people, suicide is still a big concern.

In 2015, more Australian young people aged between 15 and 24 died by suicide than any other cause, including transport accidents and accidental poisonings. A major national 2016 Orygen report** found that suicide accounted for almost a third of deaths in this age group.

Twice as many young women aged 15 to 19 died by suicide in 2015 than in 2005. Despite this increase, young men still suicide at much higher rates. In 2015, 72 per cent of suicide deaths among those aged 15 to 24 were male (ABS[6], 2016).

While rare, the number of children under 14 taking their lives has also risen.

Mental ill-health is one of the strongest risk factors and is a factor in about 90 per cent of youth suicides. This includes schizophrenia and borderline personality disorders, eating disorders and a history of self-harm. Substance misuse appears to further increase the risk.

Suicide among Aboriginal and Torres Strait Islanders aged 5 to 17 are five times that of non-Aboriginal and Torres Strait Islander young people (ABS[6], 2016). Suicide, and anxiety and depression have all increased among Aboriginal and Torres Strait Islander young people in recent years.

Other factors that elevate risk include being LGBTIQ+, recent contact with the justice system, living in rural and remote areas, contact with statutory care and exposure to suicide or related behaviour such as self-harm.

SUICIDE CLUSTERS

Suicide clusters are more likely to involve young Australians than adults. A cluster means several people in one geographical area or linked to an institution, such as a school, taking their lives. An Australian analysis of 12 clusters involving 190 suicides between 2010-2012 found five involved young people, accounting for 5.6 per cent of youth suicides. The adult figure was 2.3 per cent[†].

In 2011-2012, 12 young people who were at school, or had just left, took their lives in the Berwick and Pakenham areas outside Melbourne.

SUICIDAL BEHAVIOURS*

Suicidal behaviours include suicidal ideation (serious thoughts about taking one's own life), suicide plans and suicide attempts.

- About one in 13 (7.5 per cent) 12 to 17-year-olds had seriously considered attempting suicide in the previous 12 months. This is about 128,000.
- One in 20 (5.2 per cent) had made a plan.
- One in 40 (2.4 per cent), or around 41,000 12 to 17-year-olds, reported having attempted suicide in the previous 12 months.
- Suicidal behaviours were more common in females than males and in 16 to 17-year-olds compared with younger adolescents.
- About one in seven (15.4 per cent) females aged 16 to 17 years had seriously considered attempting suicide and one in 20 (4.7 per cent) had attempted suicide in the previous 12 months.
- The rates of all suicidal behaviours were markedly higher in young people with major depressive disorder.

// SUICIDAL BEHAVIOURS IN THE PAST 12 MONTHS (2015) AMONG 12-17 YEAR-OLDS* *(by sex and age group)*

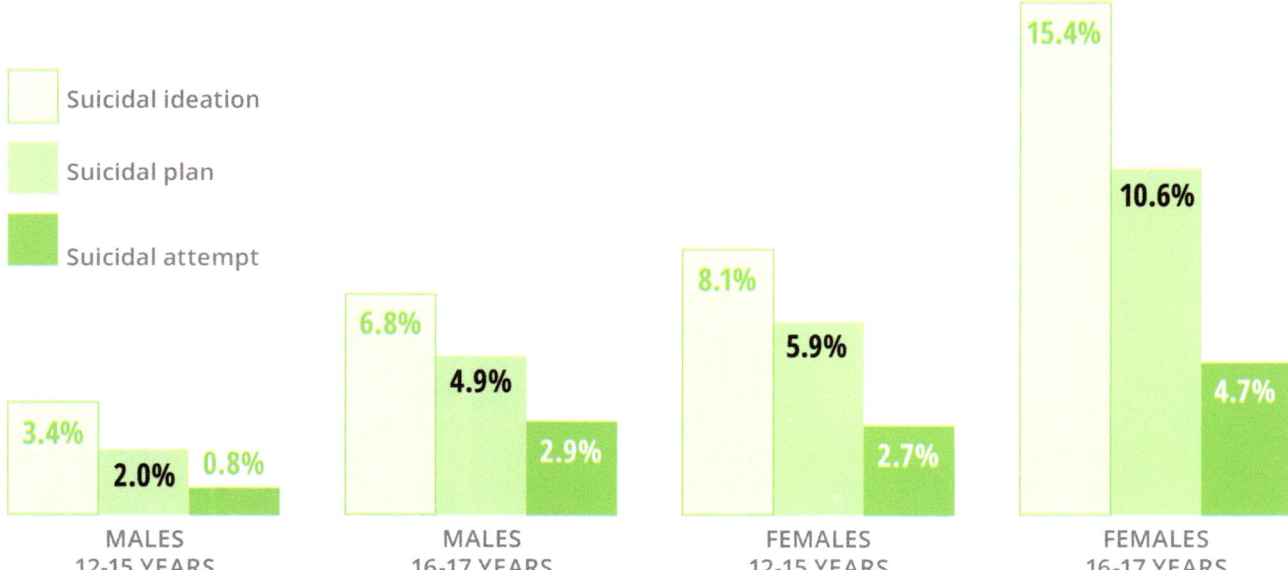

* *The Mental Health of Children and Adolescents; Report on the second Australian Child and Adolescent Survey of Mental Health and Wellbeing (2015).*
** Robinson, J, Bailey, E, Browne, V, Cox, G & Hooper, C. *Raising the bar for youth suicide prevention, Orygen, the National Centre of Excellence in Youth Mental Health, 2016*

// PARENT TIPS

- Remind young people that any feelings of distress are valid and warrant support.
- Acknowledge the factors that may increase a person's risk of suicide.
- Remind young people that support is available for any type of issue.
- Encourage them not to give up if their first experience of seeking help fails.
- Point out the supports available e.g. friends, family, a trusted adult (teacher, school counsellor or family doctor) or mental health service.
- Support them to seek help, if necessary.
- Encourage continued participation in enjoyable activities (such as sports or hobbies).
- Explain that suicide is complex and that many people who suicide experience mental-health difficulties, such as depression.
- Emphasise that suicide is never heroic or romantic – it is a tragedy with devastating consequences.
- Avoid judgmental language that may glamorise or sensationalise suicide, or reinforce negative stereotypes it is a 'selfish' or 'immoral' act.
- Remind them that suicide is final and those who do it do not get to witness other's reactions or experience a sense of resolution.

For more information visit //
www.headspace.org.au
www.healthyfamilies.beyondblue.org.au
esafety.gov.au
www.esafety.gov.au/YoungandeSafe

// RISK FACTORS

- Depression;
- A history of other mental health issues, such as anxiety and bipolar;
- Drug and alcohol problems;
- Relationship problems and conflict with parents or with a boyfriend or girlfriend;
- Ongoing bullying, including online or cyber-bullying;
- The death of someone close to the young person;
- Experiencing illness or disability;
- A past suicide attempt;
- Family history of suicide;
- Being male – males have a statistically higher risk of suicide than females; and
- Talking or writing about death or suicide and/or being a burden to others.

beyondblue says that the more challenges a young person has in their life, the greater risk of suicide.

beyondblue // headspace

// MEDIA RESPONSIBILITY

Media has responsibilities when it comes to reporting on mental-health issues. They include:

- Take the opportunity to educate the public about suicide;
- Avoid language that sensationalises or normalises; suicide, or presents it as a solution to problems;
- Avoid prominent placement and undue repetition of stories about suicide;
- Avoid explicit description of the method used in a completed or attempted suicide;
- Avoid providing detailed information about the site of a completed or attempted suicide;
- Word headlines carefully;
- Exercise caution in using photographs or video footage;
- Take particular care in reporting celebrity suicides;
- Show due consideration for people bereaved by suicide;
- Provide information about where to seek help; and
- Recognise that media professionals themselves may be affected by stories about suicide.

www.who.int/mental_health/prevention/suicide/resource_media.pdf

// 13 REASONS WHY

In the controversial Netflix series *13 Reasons Why*, a young woman suicides after outlining 13 reasons. She appears to seek revenge from the grave against those who "drove her to it".

Concerns have been raised about the show glamorising suicide and implying that revenge is a legitimate motivation for taking your life.

In the USA, at least two families have claimed their 15-year-old daughters, who already had issues, were inspired to suicide by the show.

Netflix told KTVU news: "We have heard from many views that *13 Reasons Why* has opened up a dialogue among parents, teens, schools and mental-health advocates around the difficult topics depicted in the show."

Australian schools and mental-health organisations have contacted parents to offer advice on how to handle the issue. In a fact sheet, headspace outlines the concerns raised and how to deal with them.

Dr Steven Leicester from eheadspace said clinicians working for the service had been dealing with a steady stream of concerned parents and young people since the show first aired.

eheadspace is urging school communities, parents, and mental-health services to be aware of the dangers and risks associated for children and young people who have been exposed to this content. The national suicide media initiative, Mindframe, also has significant concerns and warnings related to this content.

For the full fact sheet, visit // www.headspace.org.au/news/dangerous-content-in-13-reasons-why/
www.jedfoundation.org/13-reasons-why-talking-points/

Profile // Suicide

MY FIRST SUICIDE ATTEMPT WAS AT 14

Keiah endured years of bullying through primary school and high school. She became depressed and attempted to take her own life.

"I was bullied my whole life but it got particularly bad when I was 10 and revealed I'd been sexually abused. I told a friend and it spread around the school and I was called a 'slut'. I was also overweight and picked on for that, too.

"I was bashed regularly at high school. Mum and dad told the school it wasn't acceptable but it continued. I was bashed walking to class, during lunch, and when I retaliated, I was suspended. It was heartbreaking and it's hard to put into words how I felt.

"I went to another high school in year 8 and was bashed three times in the first two months. I dreaded the morning alarm. The bullying caused arguments with my parents because I was so angry. I'd argue with them intentionally because I was hurting inside and I needed a release. I went down the wrong path with drugs – they took the pain away for a while. I started cutting myself and when my parents took me to hospital they were told I was attention seeking.

"My first suicide attempt was at 14, and there were a few other attempts. Even though I knew my parents loved me, and I knew they were there for me, I felt worthless. I felt I was a burden and it would be easier for them if they didn't have to look after me and fight with me to go to school. I didn't want to wake up any more. It hurt to breathe, it hurt to talk.

"People asked me if I was OK and if I said 'no', they'd want every detail and to try and fix me. But it's hard when you're depressed to have people tell you that you just need to be happy, it's not a big deal, you're young and things will be better in the future because I wasn't planning to live any longer. As a parent, you look into the future for your kids but if your child doesn't think there's going to be a tomorrow, there's no point talking about years down the track and telling them they have so much to live for.

"If they talk to you about how they are feeling, listen and hear what they are saying. Don't assume you know what they want and need because you're their parent. Don't push the point if they don't want to talk, and ask them if they would like to chat with someone else. Some kids might want to see a counsellor because they're scared of what their parents might think.

"Create a safe zone for your teenager. My mum would tell me I could talk about anything with her and that she wouldn't get angry. She might say she wasn't very happy about something but then she'd say, 'let's work this out'. She never punished me when I found courage to tell her something and I always felt better afterwards. I think parents can benefit from doing the Youth Mental Health First Aid program – it teaches parents how to have conversations with their children.

"From year 9 until the end of year 12 I went to Caldera School – a non-mainstream school for about 30 kids. It saved my life. I hated school with a passion until I went there. The teachers took time to get to know me and I felt safe to talk about how I felt.

"My life isn't perfect and I have days when I don't want to get out of bed. But I have support. I'm in counselling, I have my true friends and family and I've learnt to love who I am."

> "Don't assume you know what they want and need because you're their parent. Don't push the point if they don't want to talk, and ask them if they would like to chat with someone else."

Photo: Supplied

// Keiah, 22, is studying community services, volunteers with headspace and is an instructor for the Youth Mental Health First Aid program.

BULLYING

Young people's self-esteem can be shattered by bullies.

Bullying can have a big impact on the mental health of young people. A major Australian mental health study[*] looked at face-to-face teasing, threatening, spreading rumours, physically hurting another person and cyber-bullying using mobile phones and/or the internet.

It found that one in three 11 to 17-year-olds (34.3 per cent) had been bullied in the past 12 months (2015). More than one in 10 (11.3 per cent) felt a lot or extremely upset when bullied. One in four were bullied every few months or less often, and 10 per cent every few weeks or more often.

The study also found that young people who had mental illnesses were more likely to be bullied than those who did not. Three in five who self-reported with major depressive disorder (62.8 per cent) had been bullied in the past year. They were three times more likely than all adolescents to be picked on every few weeks or more often (28.3 versus 10 per cent).

Four in 10 felt a lot or extremely upset when bullied. Those with major depressive disorder were also twice as likely as all adolescents to bully others (22.5 per cent).

SOCIAL MEDIA*

A 2017 UK report[2] found social media had positive and negative effects on the mental health of young people. Seven in 10 had been cyber-bullied. While much online interaction was positive, bullies could continue their abuse after school. "Instant messaging apps such as Snapchat and WhatsApp can also become a problem as they act as rapid vehicles for circulating bullying messages and spreading images," the report said.

More than one in three young people (37 per cent) were bullied "on a high-frequency basis". They were twice as likely to be bullied on Facebook than any other social network. "These statistics are extremely worrying for the overall health and well-being of our young people," the report found.

"Victims of bullying are more likely to experience low academic performance, depression, anxiety, self-harm, feelings of loneliness and changes in sleeping and eating patterns – all of which could alter the course of a young person's life as they undertake important exams at school or university, and develop personally and socially."

#STATUSOFMIND[2]

- Ninety-one per cent of 16 to 24-year-olds use the internet for social networking.
- Social media has been described as more addictive than cigarettes and alcohol.
- Rates of anxiety and depression in young people have risen 70 per cent in the past 25 years.
- Social media use is linked with increased rates of anxiety, depression and poor sleep.
- Cyber-bullying is a growing problem, with seven in 10 young people saying they have experienced it.
- Social media can improve young people's access to other people's experiences of health and expert health information.

Photo: iStock

// BE ALERT TO BULLYING

Parental and peer behaviours can influence the risk of depression in children who have been bullied at school, even after intervention, a Queensland expert says.

University of Queensland psychologist and researcher Dr Karyn Healy urges schools to focus on stopping bullying behaviours and parents and teachers to look for symptoms of depression in children who experience bullying.

Dr Healy says symptoms can range from persistent sadness and increased irritability to changes in sleep or appetite and loss of interest in previously enjoyable activities. "Parents also need to be aware that some of their parenting behaviours may increase the risk of depression in these children," she says.

These include conflict with their child, giving too many directions, not allowing the child to develop independence and aggressively attacking others in defence of the child.

Dr Healy says parents can play an important role in helping protect their child from the risk of depression by maintaining a warm, supportive relationship and coaching them in social and emotional skills with their peers.

Her paper, *Antecedents of Treatment Resistant Depression in Children Bullied by Peers*, looked at factors influencing ongoing depression in children aged 6 to 12 who were bullied at school. "Our research ... with families of children who had been bullied has found that supportive practices by parents and peers following victimisation can help reduce risks of later depression," Dr Healy says.

---

[*] *The Mental Health of Children and Adolescents; Report on the second Australian Child and Adolescent Survey of Mental Health and Wellbeing (2015).*
[2] *UK Royal Society for Public Health report, #StatusOfMind. Social media and young people's mental health and wellbeing*

Profile // Frank Zoumboulis

THE BEHAVIOURAL INTERVENTIONIST

Clinical psychotherapist Frank Zoumboulis says 'helicopter' or 'tow-truck' parenting affects the emotional development and well-being of young people.

"Helicopter parents take an overactive and excessive interest in their child's life. All parents want the best for their child but they can become over-involved, smothering, overbearing, interfering and over-controlling. I also call them tow-truck parents because they wait for an accident to happen and then steam in and clear up the mess.

"They have clear opinions about who is the right teacher for their child, what sport they should play, they want their child to be in the popular group and they offer disproportionate assistance, rather than allowing their teenager space. These parents don't enjoy uncertainty, so they over-prepare and supervise intensely and interfere with their child's opportunity to do something for themselves and to deal with the natural consequences of their actions.

"In the 1940s and 1950s the approach to parenting was not to smother or spoil a child. John Bowlby was a contemporary British psychiatrist and child-development specialist who saw attachment as complementary to exploration. He said a child needed to feel secure enough and good enough about themselves to explore, but helicopter parents shut down exploration. They dampen a child's confidence and interfere with their ability to develop resilience and to find their own feet. Kids end up ill-equipped to deal with basic day-to-day stuff, they can't manage emotional responses and they are super-dependent on the parent. In my practice, I'll see a 16-year-old with their parent and the parent completes the child's sentences and answers their questions for them.

"Some parents don't risk a child participating in something because they feel their child may fail, but children need to experience failure to thrive."

Photo: Eliana Schoulal

"Helicopter parenting isn't to be confused with parents who are present – young people need a present parent. That's a parent who can manage their own anxiety so when their child challenges their authority or questions them, that parent doesn't go into a meltdown. A present parent is one who listens to their child because when your child talks, it encourages them to develop independent thoughts and they begin to have some critical thinking skills. Give your child some time with a problem so they can try and solve it themselves while making it clear you are available and allow them to come to you when they need help.

"Some parents don't risk a child participating in something because they feel their child may fail, but children need to experience failure to thrive. They need to sit with the burden of upset. Helicopter parenting alleviates that burden of suffering, but this interferes with a child's ability to develop their own experience of struggle and success, or struggle and trauma and then recovery.

"When your child feels hurt or defeated, sit with them and let them feel it and then your child will move on. Parents think that when a child is hurt and they fail at something that it is the beginning of a downhill slide and that their child will keep going downhill – they don't. A child sits with it for a while and then moves on to the next thing. Parents are more likely to be the ones who catastrophise, but that's about their anxiety of being a good enough mother or father.

"Ask yourself 'how much am I hovering?'. Ask someone who knows you and who is prepared to tell you the truth. Often parents don't realise they're stifling their child's potential for greater development. So be more of an observer rather than a doer and remember that your child needs to master the ordinary to be extraordinary."

// Frank Zoumboulis is a clinical psychotherapist in private practice in South Yarra who works with adults and teenagers.

PSYCHOSIS

Being psychotic is much more serious than simply being delusional.

Some people who have a mental illness develop a psychosis, which sees them lose the capacity to tell what's real from what isn't. They may believe or sense things that aren't real, and become confused or slow in their thinking. Psychosis often occurs as a part of other mental illnesses. It is treatable.

SANE Australia provides useful advice about psychosis and common misconceptions, such as that all people who develop a psychosis are dangerous. Psychotic symptoms vary from person to person and even between one episode and another.

PSYCHOSIS FACTS

The causes are complex: genetics, early childhood development, adverse life experiences, drug use and other factors increase your chances of experiencing psychosis.

In any given 12-month period, just under one in every 200 adult Australians will experience a psychotic illness.

PSYCHOTIC EPISODES

In most cases, a psychosis is an episode of acute symptoms such as delusions and hallucinations. But it often begins with general, hard-to-pin-down changes in a person's thinking and behaviour, such as trouble with attention and concentration, irritability, depression, anxiety, suspiciousness, insomnia, social withdrawal and trouble at work or school.

These issues don't necessarily mean someone is developing psychosis, just that something might not be right. The following changes are much stronger indicators of psychosis:
- Preoccupation with a subject;
- Speech or writing that is very fast, muddled, irrational or hard to understand;
- Talking much less;
- Loss of concentration, memory and/or attention;
- Increased sensitivity to light, noise and/or other sensory inputs;
- Withdrawing from relationships or hobbies;
- Increased anger, aggression or suspiciousness;
- Decreased or disturbed sleep;
- Behaving in a way that's reckless, strange or out of character;
- Laughing or crying inappropriately, or being unable to laugh or cry;
- Inattention to personal hygiene;
- Depression and anxiety; or
- Being unable to feel or express happiness.

If untreated, these symptoms can develop into a full psychotic episode. If a parent or carer suspects that their young person may be in danger of developing a psychosis, they should see a doctor immediately.

// CAT TEAM

A Crisis Assessment and Treatment (CAT) Team supports people experiencing a mental health crisis. The team is made up of health professionals with different areas of expertise, including psychiatric nurses, social workers, psychiatrists and psychologists.

// PSYCHOSIS SYMPTOMS

DELUSIONS
False, irrational beliefs that can't be changed by evidence and aren't shared by other people from the same cultural background.

HALLUCINATIONS
Seeing, hearing, feeling, tasting or smelling something that isn't there. The most common are voices that are often very negative.

DISORDERED THINKING
Thoughts and speech that become jumbled or slowed. They might make up words or use them in strange ways, use mixed-up sentences or change topic frequently. They may also have memory problems.

DISORDERED BEHAVIOUR
They might become agitated, act in a child-like way, mutter, swear or act inappropriately, or neglect their personal hygiene and housework. In severe cases, they may become unresponsive to the world around them.

Sane

DIAGNOSIS AND TREATMENT

If needed, your GP can make an assessment and refer you to a psychiatrist for full diagnosis and treatment. Psychosis is usually diagnosed as part of another mental illness, such as schizophrenia, schizoaffective disorder or bipolar affective disorder.

Over time, your diagnosis might change or stay the same. Treatments include antipsychotic medication, specialist psychological therapies and community support programs to help with social connection, physical health, accommodation and work or school.

Find out more // **www.sane.org.au**

HELPING SOMEONE WITH PSYCHOSIS
- Try to be calm and supportive; experiencing psychosis can be frightening and confusing.
- If you are worried about a friend/family member, see your GP or local mental-health service, and encourage the young person to get professional treatment ASAP.
- Practical help, such as paying bills or getting them to appointments, can assist a person to stay safe and feel secure.
- If someone is suggesting they will harm themselves, call your mental-health service or hospital for urgent specialist attention.
- Remember the person may be responding to things that are real to them but do not make sense to you.
- There are support groups for family and friends of people with psychosis.

Find out more // **www.headspace.org.au**

Profile // LGBTIQ+

TRUE TO YOURSELF

Adrian, 22, knew in primary school that he was gay. When he came out at high school he endured bullying and struggled with self-acceptance.

"I wasn't drawn to the more masculine activities such as sport and wrestling and those stereotypical male things. I naturally gravitated towards females – I felt more comfortable. Although I felt different from other boys, that feeling was authentic and natural to me. I didn't question it because I knew it was part of who I was. There was no label for the feelings I experienced. At that point, I didn't know what it meant to identify as gay. I had to allow myself to grow and acknowledge that I was different.

"Around this time, sex education played a part. It helped me realise that there isn't just a boy and a girl relationship. It is more diverse than that and it's about what the heart wants. I'd secretly find books in the school library about being gay or about sexuality in general.

"When I was 12 I knew very much that I was gay and I came out to mum. She said, 'you are telling me something I already know as a mother'. She was and still is very supportive. I wasn't initially comfortable coming out at high school but in year 8 a bully approached me in class and abruptly asked me if I was gay. For me, saying yes or no can hurt you as a person because if you say 'no' you are a liar to yourself. If you say 'yes' you are going to have more weight on your shoulders. I said yes and the bullying began.

"I was nagged and bullied for being who I was. This happened throughout high school but each year it got easier – it's about perception. If someone called me a 'poofter' in year 8, I would be upset and think my world was over. I was that teenager who walked around with his head down, long hair covering his face because I didn't want people to look at me at that point. It affected my self-worth.

"I was too focused on trying to gain people's acceptance and I couldn't accept myself. It was emotionally draining and depressing. I also felt a sense of anger because I found it unfair that I was given this life and I didn't understand why I was made this way. I went to school every day but I felt empty – I wasn't really there.

"By year 12, I'd developed a thick skin. I wasn't willing to let one word like that hurt me and stop me studying and graduating high school. I was very close to my nan – she helped raise me – and I'd promised her I would graduate.

"My biological dad knows I am gay but he's not fully accepting. He grew up in a very Catholic family and doesn't really accept me as a gay man. If a parent is not accepting, just be humane. You don't have to accept me as a gay man, but the least you can do is accept and respect me as a human being and we don't have to bring up sexuality. It's part of my life but I'm able to be who I am without making my father uncomfortable.

"I got help from a counsellor and I always had support from my family. Mum never gave up on me when I was deeply depressed. Parents and family can be very important counsellors and mentors – not just people who happen to live in the same house as their children."

> "I also felt a sense of anger because I found it unfair that I was given this life."

// Today Adrian is a community volunteer and has qualifications in hairdressing and beauty therapy.

MORE AT RISK

LGBTIQ+ young people and mental health.

While some young people who don't identify as heterosexual have positive experiences growing up, many face an increased risk of mental-health issues. A disproportionate number have worse health outcomes than non-LGBTIQ+ peers in a range of areas, especially mental health and suicidality. Some find it extremely difficult to come out.

It is important for parents to unconditionally support their children regardless of their sexuality or gender identity. Using inclusive language and encouraging open communication can help. Families who need it can access support services.

INCREASED RISKS

Rates of suicide and self-harm are up to six times higher among LGBTIQ+ young people than the general population (Dyson et al., 2003) with an association between homophobic abuse and suicide and self-harm reported in an Australian national study of LGBTIQ+ young people.

A recent report exploring self-harm, suicidal feelings and help-seeking among LGBT youth in the UK found that of the young people in the study, more than 70 per cent experienced discrimination, bullying, rejection, physical and verbal violence, threats and/or other forms of marginalisation related to their sexual orientation and gender identity. Those who felt affected by this abuse were 2.18 times more likely to plan or attempt suicide than those unaffected; and almost 83 per cent had not told everyone they needed to about their sexuality and gender, and almost 75 per cent indicated that not being able to talk about their feelings or emotions influenced their self-harm and suicidal feelings either very much or completely.

Robinson, J, Bailey, E, Browne, V, Cox, G & Hooper, C. Raising the bar for youth suicide prevention, Orygen, the National Centre of Excellence in Youth Mental Health, 2016

// TIPS FOR PARENTS

Every child needs different things from their family and every relationship is unique. You can show them support by:
- Focusing on the love that you have for your child or loved one;
- Learning all you can about the LGBTIQ+ community; networks, support groups and issues relating to people;
- Researching social groups for LGBTIQ+ people that you may like to suggest your child or loved one attend;
- Educating yourself and your child or loved one about safe sex HIV/AIDS and other STIs;
- Admitting when you do not know something, or if you are uncomfortable – but do not blame your child;
- Take the time to get comfortable. Find a counsellor if you need to;
- Deal with your disappointments and issues as exactly that – yours;
- Using the language that your child or loved one uses e.g. lesbian, dyke or gay;
- Respecting who and when they are ready to tell – do not out anyone before they are ready;
- Encourage them to introduce you to their friends and/or their partner;
- Treat their friends and partners exactly as you would if they were heterosexual;
- Encourage them to talk to you about their experiences; listen without judging; and
- If you know of an adult LGBTIQ+ person that you like and trust, see if they are open to being a sounding board for you and/or a role model for your child.

PFLAG

// WHERE TO GET HELP

NATIONAL LGBTI HEALTH ALLIANCE
Information and support // www.lgbtihealth.org.au

PFLAG
Keeping Families Together booklet //
www.pflagaustralia.org.au

QLIFE
Online chat // www.qlife.org.au or 1800 184 527

TRANSCEND
Parent-led peer support network and information for transgender children and their families //
www.transcendsupport.com.au

REACHOUT
Relationships and sexuality information for young people // www.reachout.com

More support services // Page 35

// DEFINITIONS

GENDER DIVERSE // Gender expression or identity differs from the sex assigned at birth or society's expectations.
GENDER IDENTITY // A person's sense of being masculine or feminine, or both or neither.
HETEROSEXISM // Views or behaviours that assume everyone is, or should be, heterosexual and other sexualities/gender identities are unnatural or not as good.
INTERSEX // Born with natural variations in genital, chromosomal or other physical characteristics that differ from stereotypical ideas of female or male.
SAME-SEX ATTRACTED // Feelings of sexual and/or emotional attraction to the same sex.
SISTERGIRLS/BROTHERBOYS // Aboriginal, Torres Strait Islander and South Sea Islander terminology for someone assigned female or male who identifies or lives partly or fully as another gender.
TRANSGENDER // Umbrella term for people whose gender identity is different from that assigned at birth.

PERSONALITY DISORDERS

Complex and often not diagnosed in young people, signs of emerging personality disorders need to be carefully assessed by a clinician, usually a psychiatrist.

Personality disorders are extremes of the normal personality spectrum. They are the expression of a person's characteristic pattern of thinking, behaving and relating to others. The resulting behaviours are deeply ingrained and maladaptive.

The behaviour of young people with a personality disorder, such as narcissistic, antisocial or borderline, can vary considerably. Factors such as upbringing and life experiences can affect how the disorder manifests and how seriously. The person has often experienced trauma as a young child that can contribute to the development of their condition. They can struggle with emotional regulation, possibly due to being abandoned or rejected at a pivotal time in their development. This can be particularly true of borderline personality disorder.

Someone with a personality disorder often lacks empathy, but they can change their behaviour by making a conscious effort, possibly with the help of a trained psychologist or psychiatrist.

IS A PERSONALITY DISORDER A MENTAL ILLNESS?[1]

A mental illness significantly impairs a person's mental functioning and judgment, including their perceptions of reality and what is right and wrong. Most legal definitions describe it as a clinically significant medical condition that significantly impairs (temporarily or permanently) the person's mental functioning and judgment and strongly indicates that they need care, treatment and/or control.

Mental illnesses, such as schizophrenia and bipolar disorder, are more likely to be, at least in part, influenced by a biological dysfunction for which medical treatments can be effective. Personality disorders are defined as a mental illness in the DSM 5, but on their own may not involve such impaired mental functioning.

However, people with personality disorders can also develop those symptoms and may need treatment. Early intervention is critical to help develop skills to emotionally regulate themselves.

WHAT IS THE DSM 5?

The fifth edition of the *Diagnostic and Statistical Manual of Mental Disorders* (DSM 5) is the American Psychiatric Association's classification and diagnostic tool for psychiatric diagnoses. It is the universal bible for diagnosing mental-health disorders, including mental illnesses and personality disorders.
Visit // **psychiatry.org**

FIND OUT MORE
Spectrum Personality Disorder Service for Victoria //
www.spectrumbpd.com.au or 03 8833 3050
Australian BPD Foundation Limited //
www.bpdfoundation.org.au or 03 8803 5588

// SOME TYPES OF PERSONALITY DISORDERS

NARCISSISTIC PERSONALITY DISORDER
- A need for admiration.
- Inflated views of oneself not backed up by reality.
- Exploitation of others.
- A strong sense of entitlement.
- Marked arrogance.

They see themselves in a class of their own for looks and ability and entitled to the best of everything.

BORDERLINE PERSONALITY DISORDER
- Poor emotional regulation that appears as extremes in reactions, feeling and relationships.
- Intense fear of rejection.
- Impulsive behaviours.

Its severity is strongly connected to experiences of violence and abuse in childhood.

ANTISOCIAL PERSONALITY DISORDER
A pervasive pattern of disregard for and violation of the rights of others since age 15 years. Typical patterns may include:
- Deceit;
- Manipulation;
- Impulsivity;
- Irresponsibility;
- Lack of remorse; and
- Maybe aggression.

They can be relatively fearless and are often described as psychopaths and sociopaths.

AVOIDANT PERSONALITY DISORDER
- A pervasive pattern of social inhibition and lack of social confidence.
- Feelings of inadequacy.
- Hypersensitivity to negative evaluation.

Other personality disorders include obsessive-compulsive, schizotypal, dependent, histrionic and paranoid.

[1] DSM 5, APA, 2013

REMOTE AREAS

Children living in isolated areas may need extra support.

A major Royal Flying Doctor Service mental-health report found suicide and self-harm rates were higher in remote and rural Australia than in major cities. Those in very remote areas were twice as likely to die from suicide as city residents.

The report found that each year, about one in five, or around 960,000, remote and rural Australians experience a mental-health disorder. The overall prevalence was the same as that in major cities, but suicide and self-harm rates were higher in remote and rural Australia than in major cities.

Residents in remote areas were twice as likely to die from suicide as city residents. Several factors exacerbated mental health acuity in remote and rural Australia. They included:
- Poor access to primary and acute care;
- Limited mental-health services and mental health professionals;
- Reluctance to seek help;
- Concerns about stigma;
- Distance and cost; and
- Cultural barriers in service access.

Rural residents faced universal mental-health risk factors such as family history, stressful events, physical health problems, substance use, personality factors, and changes in the brain. But they also faced factors that heightened suicide risk such as economic hardship, easier access to means of death, social isolation, seeking help less and reduced access to support services.

"With poorer service access that results in people in very remote areas accessing mental-health services at about one-fifth of the rate of people in major cities, remote and rural health services are less able to intervene in response to signs of known risk factors," the report found.

SUICIDE RISK FACTORS

Farmers, young men, older people and indigenous Australians in remote areas are at greatest risk of completing suicide. In 2015, those living outside greater capital cities (16.2 deaths per 100,000 population) were 1.5 times as likely as residents of capital cities (10.8) to die from suicide (ABS, 2016). The difference was greatest in very remote areas.

A Royal Flying Doctor Service report found that risk factors included financial hardship, easier access to means such as firearms and pesticides, social isolation, less help-seeking and fewer support services.

Young males aged 15 to 29 in remote and rural areas are almost twice as likely as those in major cities to complete suicide. Risk factors include high use of drugs and alcohol, pressure to conform, pessimism, unemployment, relationship issues, a sense of having nothing to do, greater availability of lethal means, social isolation and a lack of available services.

// INDIGENOUS MENTAL HEALTH

Young Aboriginal Australians, particularly those living in remote areas, face higher rates of mental illness than non-indigenous young people.

A Mission Australia report found that in 2016, more than three in 10 (31.6 per cent) Aboriginal and Torres Strait Islander respondents had a probable serious mental illness, compared to 22.2 per cent of non-Aboriginal or Torres Strait Islander respondents.

The Royal Flying Doctor Service mental-health report found farmers, young men, older people, and Aboriginal and Torres Strait Islander Australians faced the greatest risk of suicide.

Indigenous Australians were 1.2 times more likely to die from mental-health disorders than non-Indigenous Australians and 1.7 times more likely to have hospital treatment for mental health disorders.

Indigenous young people aged 12-24 were three times more likely to need hospital treatment for a mental-health disorder than their non-indigenous peers.

Indigenous Australians of all age groups were between 3.5 and 40.6 times more likely to be retrieved by the Royal Flying Doctor Service for a mental health disorder.

The rate was highest in indigenous Australians aged 35-39 (3.25 per 1,000 population), followed by 25-29 (2.57) and 30-34 (2.24).

Rates for non-Indigenous Australians ranged from less than 0.01 retrievals per 1000 people (non-indigenous children under 10) to 0.12 (20-24 years, 30-34 years and 40-44 years).

WHAT WORRIES YOUNG ABORIGINAL PEOPLE

Aboriginal and Torres Strait Islander young people have similar concerns to others their age.

The Mission Australia Youth Survey Report 2016 found coping with stress was their main concern, with 38 per cent either extremely concerned (20.9 per cent) or very concerned (17.1 per cent) about it.

School or study problems were a major concern for 33 per cent.

Body image was also an important issue of concern for 31.6 per cent.

Just under three in 10 Aboriginal and Torres Strait Islander respondents were extremely concerned or very concerned about family conflict and depression.

Bishop, L., Ransom, A., Laverty, M., & Gale, L. (2017). *Mental health in remote and rural communities*. Canberra: Royal Flying Doctor Service of Australia. © 2017 Royal Flying Doctor Service of Australia

The Mission Australia Youth Mental Health Report / Youth Survey 2012-2016.

INTERNATIONAL STUDENTS

Cultural differences and expectations can lead to problems.

"For most students the transition to a new learning environment such as a new school or a university is a challenge bringing with it the need to fit in, to make friends and to meet the demands of academic standards and family expectations. In the case of international students all of these issues are amplified. For international students, the issue of 'settling in' is made more complicated by the key challenges of having to adjust to different cultural norms, different teaching and learning styles to their native country and different perceptions about help-seeking and mental health issues. There is a correlation between stress, loneliness/isolation and poor mental health so international students are particularly at risk.

"Students moving from one culture to another face new unwritten/unspoken rules which they have to figure out. This frequently occurs in the context of being far from their family and friends and at a time in their lives where a sense of social belonging is so important to their identity. As a result, especially in the first year of this transition they may feel isolated, experience a lack of personal control and uncertainty or inadequacy.

"Western culture tends to emphasise students drawing on different sources of information to come up with their own ideas, however, many Eastern cultures tend to have a far more teacher-centred model of learning where hierarchy is much more explicit. So students coming from these countries may find the new learning environment lacks clear cues as to their role as students, which can lead to general confusion about what to do and how to get information. This brings anxiety and sometimes avoidance of class, teachers and peers. Even for students born in Australia to parents educated overseas, there can be a disconnect and lack of relating between parents and young people. Young people often report how parents do not understand what it is like trying to complete study, part-time work and other social stressors.

"As well as having to adjust at many levels to an unfamiliar environment, there are the financial stressors associated with moving to a new country to live, and many describe a strong sense of obligation and pressure to succeed in order to make their families proud.

"With the unique combination of challenges and stressors that international students face, it is important that support is offered in an explicit and proactive way. There can be strong cultural beliefs that seeing a counsellor is only for the seriously mentally ill, or that to seek help may bring shame upon themselves and family. To remove these blocks to support it is important to normalise and validate help seeking. Counsellors/psychologists working within educational settings need to be accessible, approachable, and open to the challenges faced by international students.

"Having fellow international students share their own experiences and encourage the use of supports such as counselling or additional language help is critical. Peer mentoring programs which provide ongoing support to new students by older or more experienced students, are a proactive and prosocial way to help students transition to new schools/universities."

> "There is a correlation between stress, loneliness/isolation and poor mental health"

// John Coburn is a psychologist and works at Deakin University in the Health and Wellbeing Service.

// CRISIS ASSESSMENT AND TREATMENT (CAT) TEAM

A Crisis Assessment and Treatment (CAT) Team supports people experiencing a mental health crisis. The team is made up of health professionals with different areas of expertise, including psychiatric nurses, social workers, psychiatrists and psychologists.

The CAT Team responds to mental-health crises 24 hours a day. Crises can include but are not limited to psychotic episodes, self-harm and people feeling suicidal.

The CAT Team can be called by the family or friends of someone experiencing a mental-health crisis, or by the person experiencing the crisis themselves. Police, GPs and other treating health professionals can also call a CAT Team.

The CAT Team carries out a psychiatric assessment of the person's mental state and reviews their psychiatric history and available social supports. In some cases, hospital treatment will be required or, where possible, intensive treatment and care can be provided at home.

In some cases, the intervention of the CAT Team will lead to a treatment order under the Mental Health Act 2016 where a registered mental-health professional or a doctor requests an authorised psychiatrist to examine the person in crisis. The treatment order may then be upheld and which may require an admission to a psychiatric unit.

After the crisis has been managed, CAT Team members may refer the patient and their family to community services that can provide appropriate ongoing care.

ASSISTANCE

// EMERGENCIES

Ambulance/Fire/Police // 000

Lifeline, 24-hour counselling // 13 11 14

Suicide Call Back Service // 1300 659 467 or www.suicidecallbackservice.org.au

// WHERE TO FIND HELP

Anxiety Recovery Centre Victoria (has links to other states) // www.arcvic.org.au

Australian Institute of Family Studies // www.aifs.gov.au
More detail can be found at // aifs.gov.au/cfca/topics/mental-health-and-illness // aifs.gov.au/cfca/publications/helplines-and-telephone-counselling-services-children-young-people-and-pare

Australian Psychological Society find a psychologist // www.psychology.org.au/FindaPsychologist

beyondblue // 1300 22 4636 or healthyfamilies.beyondblue.org.au

Black Dog Institute // www.blackdoginstitute.org.au

CAT Teams // www.health.vic.gov.au/mentalhealthservices/adult/

headspace // 1800 650 890 or www.headspace.org.au or www.eheadspace.org.au

Health Direct services directory // www.healthdirect.gov.au

Health on the Net. Health information // www.healthonnet.org

Kids Helpline // 1800 55 1800 or www.kidshelpline.com.au

Lifeline // 13 11 14 or www.lifeline.org.au

MensLine Australia // 1300 789 978

Mind Australia // 1300 286 463 or www.mindaustralia.org.au

Mind Health Connect parenting help // www.mindhealthconnect.org.au/parenting

Mind Matters // www.mindmatters.edu.au

Minus18 // minus18.org.au

National LGBTI Health Alliance // www.lgbtihealth.org.au

QLife // 1800 184 527 or www.qlife.org.au

ReachOut // www.reachout.com

Royal Australian College and New Zealand College of Psychiatrists find a psychiatrist // www.yourhealthinmind.org/find-a-psychiatrist

Safe Schools Coalition Australia // www.safeschoolscoalition.org.au

Sane Australia // 1800 18 7263 or www.sane.org

Transcend (transgender support) // www.transcendsupport.com.au

// PARENT HELP LINES

NSW // 1300 1300 52

Victoria // 13 22 89

South Australia // 1300 364 100

Queensland: 1300 301 300

Northern Territory: 1300 301 300

Tasmania: 1300 808 178

ACT: (02) 6287 3833

Western Australia: 1800 654 432

// APPS AND ONLINE TOOLS

MOOD DISORDER APPS VIA REACHOUT
au.professionals.reachout.com/apps-and-online-tools/mood-disorders

ANXIETY DISORDER APPS VIA REACHOUT
au.professionals.reachout.com/apps-and-online-tools/anxiety-disorders

TOOLS FOR GENERAL WELL-BEING VIA REACHOUT
au.professionals.reachout.com/apps-and-online-tools/wellbeing-apps-and-tools

REACHOUT WELL-BEING TOOLBOX
au.reachout.com/sites/thetoolbox

REACHOUT APPS FOR OTHER MENTAL HEALTH ISSUES
au.professionals.reachout.com/apps-and-online-tools/other-mental-health-issues

BEACON 2.0. PORTAL FOR ONLINE MENTAL AND PHYSICAL DISORDER APPLICATIONS
www.beacon.anu.edu.au

// MEDICARE

A treatment plan lets you claim for up to 10 sessions each calendar year with a mental health professional registered with Medicare. If your health professional decides you're eligible, you can have an extra 10 group sessions.
Health professionals set their own fees, so Medicare may only cover some of the cost. If they bulk bill, you don't pay anything. If you have private health insurance, you may get some money back.
   At first, your doctor or psychiatrist will refer you for up to 6 sessions at a time. If you need more, they can refer you for more. Plans must be regularly reviewed.

For information contact Medicare Australia // 132 011 or www.humanservices.gov.au/individuals/medicare

RESPECT 101

It's time we talked

Cover story

WHAT IT MEANS TO US

WHAT IS RESPECT?
Respect is fundamental to any community. Without it we cannot successfully live, play or work together.

Respect involves positive feelings or actions towards someone held in high regard, and involves expressing admiration for them, caring for them and/or considering their needs or feelings.

In many cases, we respect people we admire because of their abilities, qualities or achievements. Acting respectfully says a lot about your character. Even if you disagree with a person's views and opinions, you can still engage respectfully with them.

RESPECT IN AUSTRALIA
Australia has long been known for its values of mateship and a fair go for all.

But we are also known for refusing to respect authority if we don't like those in charge, and rejecting those deemed "too big for their boots".

The way we demonstrate respect – or lack thereof – has also changed markedly in the age of social media.

Most Australians now have a public profile, so their views and actions are no longer confined to family, friends or work colleagues.

Our thoughts may be shared by thousands online, which makes it more important than ever to be respectful.

Online or off, modern parents and carers face a big challenge in ensuring their digital native children do the same.

DISRESPECTFUL BEHAVIOUR
Are we becoming more disrespectful as a society?

Recent political events in the USA and Australia may have diminished the respect many people had for some politicians and the political process.

The rude and belligerent behaviour of leaders, such as US president Donald Trump, can filter down and enable extreme elements to mimic the disdainful way those who disagree with their views are treated.

In Australia, public figures, media personalities and social media influencers can contribute to the "normalising" of negative talk about certain groups, such as asylum seekers. Parents and carers can help to counter this by modelling respectful behaviour and explaining why the inappropriate behaviour of others is unacceptable.

MODELLING RESPECT
How can parents and carers create an environment that encourages their children to respect others?

Modelling respectful behaviour and instilling values that promote empathy, equality, the acceptance of differences and the value of diversity are important. Racism, prejudice, homophobia, stereotypes and sexism must also be discouraged and called out.

No one is perfect. If you slip up, admit it. Explain why what you did or said was wrong and resolve not to do it again.

> ## // EXPERT TIPS
> Australian National University Research School of Psychology Research Fellow Dr Diana Grace says parents should teach children to critically evaluate social expectation and social media influence.
> - There are good and bad stereotypes, good and bad social expectations, and good and bad media influences.
> - Talking about these issues encourages them to be discerning and allows you to discuss your (and their) values.
> - Ask them how they would portray an attitude or belief if they were behind the advertising or other media influence.
> - Such discussions provide opportunities to learn they are valued, have choices and should value and respect themselves and others.

What is respect and what does it mean to us? Regardless of how it is defined and how that definition may change over time, respect is the cornerstone of a civilised society.

HOW RESPECT WORKS
The two-way interaction of respect between individuals has a ripple effect into the wider community

QUOTABLE

WE DON'T CHANGE // PINK
"Do you see me growing my hair?"
She said, "No, mama."
I said, "Do you see me changing my body?"
"No, mama."
"Do you see me changing the way I present myself to the world?"
"No, mama."
"Do you see me selling out arenas all over the world?"
"Yes, Mama."
"OK! So, baby girl. We don't change. We take the gravel and the shell and we make a pearl. And we help other people to change so they can see more kinds of beauty."
Pink's VMA's Speech About Body Image and Her Daughter (2018) // time.com/4918579/pink-vma-speech-daughter-transcript/

GENDER EQUALITY // MARY CROOKS
"You are more likely to respect another if you don't feel superior to them or feel the desire to dominate. You are not likely to hit or abuse another if you hold them in genuine regard. This is why the data now show that the countries with greater degrees of gender equality have less violence and abuse."
Executive Director, Victorian Women's Trust

GOOD SPORTS
Sporting organisations are encouraging respect in their athletes and families.

In 2018, Tennis Australia implemented a "handshake challenge" at many junior events. It means competitors shake hands with opponents and officials before each match. Parents/guardians, coaches and other spectators are also invited to participate.

In the lead-up to the 2019 Australian Open, Tennis Australia also held a Sporting Parents conference to help parents and guardians deal with the challenges for families involved in elite tennis.

The AFL has a Respect and Responsibility Policy that promotes gender equality and "a workplace culture that is inclusive regardless of gender, sexual orientation, gender identity or intersex status".

Such policies encourage respect and have consequences for those who breach them.

FOCUS ON RESPECT

Parent Guides wanted to know what young people think.

HERE'S WHAT THEY SAID

YOUNG PEOPLE AND RESPECT
What does respect mean to children and teenagers? The first *Parent Guides* focus group asked 24 young Australians aged 9-19 what they thought about it and how it should be demonstrated.

THE FOCUS GROUP PROCESS
Participants were asked about the Australian Government's *Stop it at the Start* campaign (www.respect.gov.au), their perceptions of respectful relationships, their motivations and behaviour, and the *Parent Guides*' focus of "let's start a conversation" between parents and adolescents. Each student was encouraged to contribute, have a voice and test our material.

WHAT THEY REVEALED
The qualitative process revealed that young people see bullying as a big issue and are sensitive to some language but don't have a problem being open once they feel comfortable.

One participant acknowledged that their grandparents were racist, another was surprised that his father was sexist towards his sister, and the teenagers said they wanted "hard" boundaries.

A female teenager was angry that her father did not want her to go for a job because she was younger and "the boys wouldn't respect her", even though she was qualified.

Interestingly, racism with name calling was sometimes seen as acceptable within peer groups and family members.

TAKE-HOME MESSAGE – BE A PARENT NOT A FRIEND
The take-home message from young people is that there is a lot more that unites us than divides us. However, racism and sexism are cultural norms in some families.

The teenagers were a lot more accepting of cultural difference than we give them credit for and did not believe media headlines they considered to be fearmongering.

They were more influenced by peers than their parents and noticed when parents gave siblings contradictory messages. There was also a gap between children and parents when it came to social media. Young people also wanted their parents to be parents.

1 STOP IT AT THE START TELEVISION COMMERCIAL – *DETENTION* 30 SEC

STUDENTS WERE ASKED TO WATCH A VIDEO …
Participants watched a *Stop it at the Start* advertisement, where a father dismisses his son getting detention for flicking up a girl's skirt only to hear his daughter say she will be harassed or abused one day too.

WHAT THE STUDENTS SAID …
Asked for their reactions, the students said it made them feel sad and that the father had taught his son the wrong message, although it was felt he did realise this in the end.

Other words and phrases included "not all boys are boys", "unfair", "disrespectful to the girl", "misogyny values", "tone of voice", "equality", "daughter is too accepting", and "dad is a problem as he will pass this onto the kids".

It was also noted that such behaviour has become normalised by society.

Watch it here // www.respect.gov.au/the-campaign/campaign-materials

2 BREAK-UP TEXT MESSAGE

> but I'm breaking up with u
>
> what?
>
> I'm sorry. Its just that I don't feel the same way about you anymore
>
> I think u have the wrong number
>
> Oh wow I'm sorry how awkward lol. But do you think that's a bad way to tell them?

THE STUDENTS DISCUSSED A BREAK-UP MESSAGE SENT BY TEXT

The students discussed whether a break-up text was disrespectful and why. They also talked about whether communicating via text had caused conflict with an adult, teacher or parent.

All agreed it was unacceptable to send disrespectful texts and, as there is no tone in text messages, lots of miscommunication had resulted. However, they were starting to master this.

Sixteen of the students took their phone to bed, two didn't, two had their phones on silent and four did not have phones. Four had experienced trolling.

GENERAL COMMENTS INCLUDED:
- Hate having "helicopter" parents.
- FOMO (Fear of Missing Out) is who we are as a generation.
- Phones are an addiction.
- "Keyboard warriors" hide behind phones.
- All agreed disrespectful texts are unacceptable.
- Parents are sceptical and don't understand social media.

3 IN THE MEDIA

WHAT DOES RACISM LOOK LIKE?

Anti Semitic incidents in Australia up nearly 10% over year, study says
THE GUARDIAN 27/11/2017

Gillian Triggs tells of alarm over 'demonising' of Muslims in Australia
THE GUARDIAN 11/05/2017

The Prime Minister and Opposition leader agree that racism persists.
SMH 28/05/2016

Students were asked what racism looks like in Australia, what they saw when they saw racism, and the first thing they noticed about a person.

THEIR RESPONSES INCLUDED:
- The media takes things out of proportion.
- Sensationalises and stereotypes people.
- Sensational and confronting stories.
- Not all racism happens everywhere.
- Older people don't have filters, especially grandparents about African gangs.
- Sexism is not gender based. Can be against men, e.g. "men don't cry".
- Things are taken to the extreme.
- Racism = don't believe the headlines i.e. African does not mean bad.
- A Muslim friend would not wear hijab because of bullying.
- Religious freedom is good but not if it violates the religious beliefs of others.
- Friendly racist banter is OK.
- Stereotyping is a reverse racism, e.g. "Asian = being smart". Alternatively: "white people = powerful + wealthy".

Continues // Page 8

// WHAT DID YOU LEARN BY ATTENDING THIS FOCUS GROUP?

Sam // 17
I found that many thoughts portrayed by other students were centred around similar morals as my own."

Polly // 14
"I was fascinated at how similar the other students' definitions of respect were."

Gianluca // 9
"I learned to respect women and people of different races, and also I learned not to let people bully me or anyone else."

Zalia // 14
"I enjoyed how interactive the group was and how safe it was to share our opinions ... which were valued."

Thank you // Piper, Lauryn, Liam, Laura, Despina, Nikki, Josie, Noah, Kyle, Liam, Caroline, Luca, Patrick, Alex, Judy, Mia, Jess, Fin, Chantel and Molly.

4 RESPECTFUL & DISRESPECTFUL

Photo: Adobe Stock / chege

WHAT DO RESPECT AND DISRESPECT MEAN TO YOU?

The students were asked about language and phrases they had heard that allow people to behave badly and disrespectfully. They also brainstormed words associated with respect and disrespect.

These are some of the words and phrases they came up with:

SYMBOLS OF RESPECT
* love heart • equal sign * holding hands * hands clasped in handshake • world globe • cross • scales of justice • Yin/Yang • circle connecting all people/genders • smiley face • word signs • groups of people • justice league symbol * heart and hands together.

RESPECT MEANS
• validation • positive • great work • equality
• encouragement • support • accepting difference
• open-mindedness • consideration • empathy
• fairness • listening • trust • encouragement in sport
• engagement • kindness • manners.

DISRESPECT MEANS
• ignorance • racism • prejudice • having a go (criticising someone) • disregarding viewpoints based on age and gender • desensitisation • swearing • normalising bad behaviour • normalising terms such as "spaso" and "nerd" • faggot jokes that reinforce racial stereotypes • bullying put-downs • jokes within a family because of mixed ethnic background.

5 SEXISM

THE STUDENTS ALSO DISCUSSED SEXISM AND AMONG OTHER THINGS MADE THE FOLLOWING POINTS:

* Sexism is not gender based.
  Can be against men, e.g. "men don't cry".
* Men don't like raging feminists; a lot seen in the media.
* Sexism = The Liberal Party.
* Verbals = patriarchal system, e.g. boys go first; make the decisions.
* Gender = boys + girls – "ladies go first" = signal for a weaker sex.
* Equal pay in sport = progress in tennis/AFLW, but not enough.

Adobe Stock: nastia1983

HELPING *PARENT GUIDES* TO INFORM

This qualitative evaluation was an important opportunity to assess and validate the information, format and design built into *Respect 101*.

Participants enjoyed the process, describing it as fun and educational.

* The focus group was conducted by *Parent Guides* CEO Yvonne Lockwood, editor Eileen Berry and Kildare Ministries Executive Director Erica Pegorer. Thanks go to Kildare Ministries for providing their facilities and making the room neutral, and to the adolescents' parents for entrusting them to our care.

// HOW THE COVER OF RESPECT 101 WAS DECIDED*

At the end of our focus group, mock-ups of suggested covers were put before the students. The graphic with a love heart and holding hands = symbols of respect was picked as the clear winner. In this case, the editor was happy to be "overruled".

First Person

When I was a child, I was encouraged to use the adage "sticks and stones" against anyone teasing me. I remember trying it a few times, but I wasn't impressed with the results. I'm not sure whether it would have been any more effective, but I recall thinking that a swift kick in the shins would have been a lot more satisfying.

Today, the expression "sticks and stones" feels about as relevant as the idea of prescribing smoking as a cure for a persistent cough. Because we now know that verbal bullying can have a real impact on our health and self-esteem.

As a result of this awareness, bullying has become a hot topic. It's a perennial subject for everything from tabloid TV shows to think pieces pondering how we can encourage and nurture respectful

THE CASUAL CRUELTIES OF CHILDHOOD

What we say can have an impact on others, writes Monica Dux.

relationships. For parents, the threat of online bullying looms large, all the more terrifying because it can be so invisible – until it is too late. Yet, as has been pointed out, there is a danger that the term "bullying" might be overused as a go-to term for any and all poor behaviour.

I was thinking recently about a girl in my class in primary school who, over the years, endured relentless name-calling. I often wonder about what impact that might have had on her life.

I'm certain many of the kids I went to school with would at times have been victimised, humiliated or denigrated by their peers – made to feel different, wrong or ugly. Comparing those experiences with what that girl in my class endured would be an insult because there is a huge difference between persistent bullying and people simply being unpleasant to one another. Failing to acknowledge that distinction runs the risk of devaluing the profound, life-changing impact that real bullying can have.

Still, even the little barbs, the unkind comments and the casual cruelties that most of us endure as children can shape us, affecting how we see ourselves, our bodies and our place in the world. There are also some insults that have an impact on everyone who hears them, not just the victim.

My children occasionally report on the social dynamics of their schoolyard. It's usually standard stuff, as pecking orders are formed and maintained, alliances made and broken. But sprinkled in with these anodyne reports, I also get a taste of the banter that modern children exchange, and I'm horrified to discover how little it has changed.

Children are still mocked for being "fat", as if carrying a bit of extra body weight is an unforgivable sin. The term "gay" is widely and casually used as an insult, and then there's that vile word "retard". These are insults that carry a message, to everyone who hears them, about what kind of person is acceptable – about who is valuable, and who isn't.

Most adults wouldn't put up with such banter from our peers and, if we did, it would be evidence that something was deeply wrong in that relationship. Yet there is a tacit acceptance when these insults are hurled by kids, a blithe acknowledgement that children are inevitably going to be cruel to one another and that there is nothing we can do to change that.

We cannot insulate our children from everything hurtful or unpleasant, and childhood should be a time of freedom and discovery without being subject to the same consequences, or the same rules, as adults. Kids, though, are not born homophobic, racist or with an innate disgust at bodily difference. The specific vocabulary of childhood cruelty is something that is learned and, if it is learned, then someone is teaching it.

No decent, well-socialised adult would use repugnant slurs such as "retard" or "fatty". At least not openly. But in the privacy of our homes things seem to be different because anyone who has children knows that they soak up everything they hear and often repeat it at the most inopportune moment. Similarly, when children express views that are fat-phobic, racist, homophobic or ableist, they are almost certainly regurgitating attitudes that they heard expressed by their parents. Those attitudes don't need to be overt. Kids are smart enough to read between your lines, to discern that fat is bad, even if you never speak those exact words.

Children can be cruel, but maybe that's because we all are. Perhaps the only real difference is that they don't censor themselves when they leave the house.

// Copyright permission granted by Monica Dux, *The Age*, 4 October 2018. @monicadux

Growing & learning

RESPECT YOURSELF

Before we can respect others, we must respect ourselves. This can be a challenge for teenagers struggling with peer pressure, social media and mental health issues.

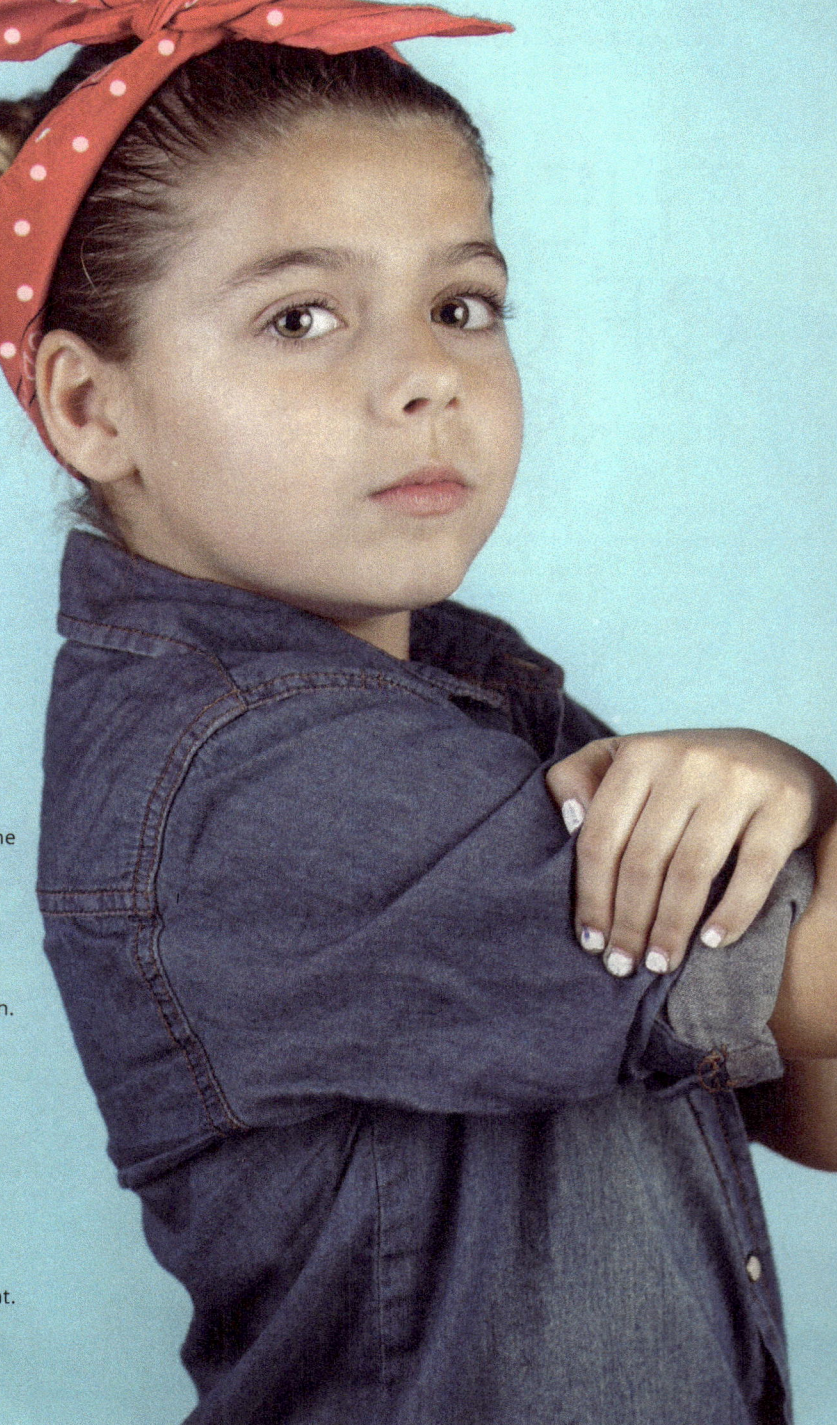

BUILDING RESILIENCE

Instilling strong values, helping to build resilience and providing support when needed is critical in helping children to develop self-confidence.

This is equally important for girls and boys.

Resilience is about being realistic, thinking rationally, looking on the bright side, finding the positives, expecting things to go well and moving forward, even when things seem bad.

Those who demonstrate resilience cope better with life's ups and downs. We do our children no favours when we solve all their problems for them.

RESILIENCE IN TEENAGERS

- Self-respect grows out of setting standards for behaviour.
- Facing difficult emotions will help your child grow stronger.
- Social skills and connections (e.g. community groups, sport) can help to build resilience.
- Encourage empathy, respect for others, kindness, fairness, honesty and cooperation.
- Have a strong, loving relationship and stay connected with them.
- Keep things in perspective when they are upset.
- Encourage positive self-talk.
- Explain that difficult times are part of life, but things will improve.
- Have strategies for low moods, such as watching TV, time with friends, making a kind gesture, physical activity, looking on the bright side, reliving fond memories.
- Foster skills in planning, organisation, self-discipline, hard work and resourcefulness.
- Work with your child on solutions to problems.
- Let them try to fight their own battles before stepping in.
- Model positive and optimistic behaviour.

Source: raisingchildren.net.au – the Australian parenting website.

ROSIE ADVICE

Girls (and boys) can learn more about respect and self-esteem on the **Rosie website**, a national harm prevention initiative by the Dugdale Trust for Women & Girls.

Rosie has objective and research-based information on themes such as body and mind, work and study, relationships, activism, gender issues and the environment. It also contains tips and case studies.

See more // www.rosie.org.au

// PROMOTING SELF-CONFIDENCE

A key to respecting yourself is having confidence in yourself. As parents, we play a pivotal role in developing our children's self-confidence. Self-confidence can be encouraged at home through the acceptance of who a child is as a person and by promoting healthy eating alongside appropriate physical and mental activity. Help is also out there if needed. Many organisations work to reduce bullying and mental health issues that can affect the self-esteem of children and teenagers. Beyond Blue (www.youthbeyondblue.com) has a youth program and The Alannah and Madeline Foundation (www.amf.org.au) and the national Office of the eSafety Commissioner work to reduce bullying.

// WHAT YOUNG PEOPLE WANT TO KNOW

- Puberty and how the body works
- Healthy and respectful relationships
- Sexual feelings
- Sexual pleasure
- Personal values and beliefs about sexual relationships
- Gender roles
- Sexually transmitted infections (STIs)
- Safe sex (such as using condoms)
- Contraception, including emergency contraception (the "morning after pill")
- Intimacy without sexual intercourse
- Sexual problems
- Sexual orientation
- How to say "no" to unwanted sex and what to do if it happens
- What to do in a pregnancy
- How to have conversations with a partner, e.g. about condoms
- Sex, the law and consent

Source: Family Planning Victoria, www.fpv.org.au

BEING YOURSELF
Openly supporting diversity will help your child accept who they are, regardless of their sexuality or gender identity.

RAISING BOYS
Traditional gender roles have changed but society still often considers it a sign of weakness if a boy shows emotion.

It is crucial that boys (and girls) learn about empathy, expression and mental health strategies. They need to know it is OK to cry, how to articulate fears and anxieties, and to seek help if they need it. Programs such as The Man Cave offer advice and programs that facilitate healthy masculinity.

Find out more // www.themancave.life

RAISING GIRLS
Some teen girls still hear messages about what they can or cannot do, or how they are to blame for bad experiences, such as sexual harassment.

Teaching them that they can reject gender stereotypes and control their destiny can help boost their confidence.

RAISING CHILDREN
Self-respect is a great building block for resilience, says Associate Professor Julie Green, the Executive Director at **raisingchildren.net.au**.

"Teens can build self-respect by setting their standards for behaviour," she says. **"If your teen has self-respect, they believe they matter and should be treated respectfully by others."**

Associate Professor Green says parents and carers are role models, so their teen should see and hear outlooks that are positive and optimistic.

"One way to do this is by thanking other people for their support by saying something like, 'things will get better soon, and I can cope with this', and showing you expect good things are possible."

Good, honest communication is crucial. Tackling difficult conversations with your child indicates a healthy relationship.

"If you're warm, accepting, non-judgmental and uncritical, and also open to negotiating and setting limits, your child is likely to feel more connected to you," Associate Professor Green says.

If potential mental health issues arise, Associate Professor Green recommends talking to them and seeing a health professional together. This will also reassure them that they are not alone.

"You could start by talking to your GP, your child's school counsellor, teacher or other school staff. GPs and other health professionals can suggest strategies and give advice," she says. "Family members, friends and other adults that your child is close to might be able to help and support you and your child. Remember that support for your whole family can be just as important as help for your child."

SEXUALITY
Education and communication are key in helping young people embrace their sexuality, and to respect that of others.

Family Planning Victoria recommends parents and carers educate themselves and clarify their values and messages before talking openly and honestly with their young person.

It is also important to support their right to develop healthy, respectful and consensual sexual relationships and not assume everyone is opposite-sex attracted or the gender assigned at birth.

Accept that young people may have different views to yours and take a positive approach that acknowledges that sexual activity and experimentation can be a healthy part of adolescence.

Everyday moments, such as watching TV news or other shows, can be good starting points from which to ask your young person what they are thinking or feeling.

Photo: Adobe Stock / esthermm

Respecting others

DO UNTO OTHERS

Can we teach young people to respect others? It is a tricky age, but teenagers will respond to a message they can relate to.

RESPECTING OTHERS

Children who learn to respect others are well placed to do the same when they attend school, develop friendships and establish romantic relationships.

A solid foundation in moral and ethical behaviour will help them to develop and maintain respectful connections with others throughout their lives.

Parents and carers play a crucial role through modelling behaviour and providing advice and boundaries. They also need to respect themselves if they want their children to follow suit.

FRIENDSHIP

Feeling socially connected is critical to emotional and physical wellbeing throughout our lives, says Australian National University Research School of Psychology Research Fellow, Dr Diana Grace.

Diana says friendships provide children with social support and context to explore behaviours, such as being nice or not, and their consequences outside the family.

"For example, parents may put up with behaviours that friends wouldn't," she says. "This includes simple things such as not helping prepare a meal or simply being rude."

Diana says it's natural for parents to worry about their children's friends as most want them to be good, responsible human beings with similar friends.

She says most children do make friends with those who are similar in some way, so if they are nasty it is important to look at your child's behaviour.

RESPECTFUL RELATIONSHIPS

What is a respectful relationship? Dr Diana Grace says it simply has respect at its heart.

"Having respect for others involves valuing people for who they are, looking for the good in people, and not expecting others to be exactly like yourself, or others for that matter," she says.

"It is about working out what is important, for example having friends you can trust rather than the most … 'likes' on Instagram."

Diana says a respectful relationship sees each person being valued, contributing and having responsibilities.

"A respectful relationship is one in which people feel safe," she says. "It is OK to be nice to people. Indeed, a simple thing to remember in a respectful relationship is to be kind."

If parents truly value their children and model good relationship behaviours, Diana says it is easier for young people to recognise a bad situation if it arises.

"Children who grow up in respectful environments are more likely to recognise lack of respect, but not always," she says.

"Many people (young and old) stay in abusive relationships because they believe they don't deserve better, or because they perceive that is the way relationships are."

Photo: Adobe Stock / Drobot Dean

SAFER SEX

Using condoms is a really important part of safe sex, but it does not stop there.

Parents and carers need to ensure their teenagers know that safe sex is about having sex when they are ready and having sex that's enjoyable, respectful and protected.

This means:
- having sex when the couple both feel ready
- having the kind of sex the couple both want and enjoy
- having sex at a time and place that both are happy with
- having sex that both feel good about afterwards.

It also means doing the things that need to be done to keep the people involved healthy.

This includes:
- protecting against sexually transmitted infections (STIs) and blood borne viruses (BBVs) by using barriers, such as condoms, having sexual health check-ups and being vaccinated against STIs and BBVs
- using contraception to avoid a pregnancy
- having strategies in place to respond when feeling pressured or unsure.

Source: Family Planning Victoria, www.fpv.org.au

BUSTING STEREOTYPES

Societal expectations and stereotypes, such as narrow expectations about gender roles, appearance and behaviour, can weigh heavily on the minds of children and teenagers.

Peer pressure can also encourage bullying or other disrespectful behaviour, such as sledging on the sporting field. Dealing with these issues starts at home, but resources are available if help is needed.

Groups such as Good Sports (**www.goodsports.com.au**), which works with sports clubs to reduce reliance on alcohol and other drugs, can help.

Campaigns such as *This Girl Can* aim to bust stereotypes and boost confidence for girls.

Find out more // www.vichealth.vic.gov.au

CONSENT

- Consent is mutual – everyone involved must agree to be involved or present for the sexual activity.
- Consent can be withdrawn at any time.
- Consent is never automatic.
- Sometimes consent can't be given, such as if a person is drunk or high, asleep, can't understand what is being consented to, or is feeling pressured.
- If there is an uneven power balance in the sexual relationship, e.g., if the partner was the young person's teacher, sports coach or doctor, consent may not be able to be given.
- A lack of no does not mean yes.
- No consent means STOP!

* Source: 'Rosie', a Dugdale Trust for Women & Girls national harm prevention initiative www.rosie.org.au

// UNDERSTANDING ENTHUSIASTIC CONSENT

Playing Right was developed in response to the Australian Human Rights Commission's *Change the Course: National Report on Sexual Assault and Sexual Harassment at Australian Universities*. Published in 2017, it found that in 2015-16, one in five students were sexually harassed and 6.9 per cent were sexually assaulted on campus or at university events.

The program is tailored to school leavers and people in their late teens. Research suggests they receive a lot of information on the biology of sexual relationships, such as disease prevention and birth control, but not so much about the emotional and social issues of sexual relationships.

One of our key messages is "it's not a yes unless it's a hell yes", which is based on the idea of enthusiastic consent. Often young people haven't found their voice and aren't sure how to communicate consent, or to understand if consent has been given.

We emphasise that unless a person you are engaging in a sexual encounter with is enthusiastically wanting to be there, assume they don't want to be there. Young people are often scared to say no, or feel pressured into doing things they may not want to do. It's important to teach what consent is and what it looks or sounds like. It's more enjoyable for everyone if they understand the rules of the game and play the game with someone else who wants to be there.

We teach students basic things like checking in – and that can be repeating the question "is this OK?" If you keep asking that question during a sexual encounter, and the person you are with keeps saying "yes", then you can be sure they want to be there. There is no "grey" area in consent. There's an enthusiastic "yes" and everything else is a no.

We also show a simple way for parents to start the conversation about consent. We also emphasise that a "yes" cannot be given by someone under 16, if they are under 18 and with someone in a position of power, or if they are intoxicated. The absence of a no doesn't mean a yes, either.

The program also empowers bystanders to be active. After discussing consent, people are more likely to say or do something because they understand it is not all right.

We want sexual relationships to be enjoyable and nourishing for young people. The more we talk about concepts like consent and empower them to understand and play by the rules, the more we can help that happen.

// Isabel Fox leads a consent education and sexual assault prevention program, *Playing Right*, at Charles Sturt University

Watch // www.youtube.com/watch?v=h3nhM9UlJjc

Families

ALL IN THE FAMILY

Respect starts in the home, where Australian families continue to evolve.

Young people are shaped by many forces, including friends, classmates, teachers, the wider community and social media.

But the home is where children experience their first role models and learn how to behave.

The importance of parents and carers providing a respectful environment and modelling respectful behaviour cannot be overemphasised.

What parents do and say, such as how they eat, exercise and treat others, influences their children. A child's home is their reality.

The **raisingchildren.net.au** says parents influence their child's basic values, such as religious values, and issues related to their future, such as educational choices. The stronger your relationship with your child, the more influence you'll have.

Your child's friends are more likely to influence everyday behaviour, such as the music they listen to, the clothes they wear and whether they pick on or bully someone.

// IT'S OK TO DISAGREE, BUT ...

- Model respectful behaviour.
- Treat siblings and partners equally, regardless of gender.
- Set boundaries with consequences for breaking them.
- Be consistent.
- It's OK to disagree, but use respectful language.
- Don't criticise ex-partners in front of children.
- Minimise swearing and acknowledge inevitable slip-ups.
- Don't generalise about groups such as LGBTIQ+ or those with disabilities.
- Tell your children you love them regardless of their sexuality or gender identity.
- Don't call anyone useless, unattractive or too fat.
- Pull others up if they speak disrespectfully and explain why.
- Never use violence or aggression to make a point.

Photo: Adobe Stock / martialred

Raising Children Network // raisingchildren.net.au

MODELLING GOOD BEHAVIOUR

It starts with creating a respectful and nurturing environment where all family members are respected, regardless of marital status, family composition, or gender or sexual identity.

This includes families with parents who no longer live together.

Language is crucial, and words matter. Children notice what adults say and how they say it. Disrespectful talk and actions teach children that this is how people treat each other.

Modelling respectful behaviour, having boundaries and calling out disrespectful behaviour all help children learn the importance of respecting others and how it can make a difference.

We all make mistakes. If you do, admit you've done the wrong thing and explain why.

TIPS FOR ROLE-MODELLING*

- Include your child in family discussions and allow them to give input into family decisions, rules and expectations.
- Try to practise what you preach. Teenagers can and do notice when you don't!
- Work towards a healthy lifestyle by eating well and exercising regularly.
- Avoid making negative comments about your body – and other people's.
- Show that you enjoy education and learning. If you make it seem interesting and enjoyable, your child is more likely to be positive about school.
- Keep a positive attitude. Think, act and talk in an optimistic way.
- Take responsibility by admitting your mistakes and talking about how you can correct them. Try not to blame everything on others or circumstances.
- Use problem-solving skills to deal with challenges or conflicts in a calm and productive way.
- Show kindness and respect to others.

Source: raisingchildren.net.au, the Australian parenting website.

// SIBLING RIVALRY

Siblings don't choose each other, which can mean personality clashes, disagreements and sibling rivalry. While we cannot expect them to be best friends, siblings should be taught to respect each other.

BY THE NUMBERS

THE MODERN AUSTRALIAN FAMILY COMPOSITION

 **1/6** — The "average" Australian family still includes Mum, Dad and a couple of kids, but many families have single and same-sex parents. One in six has a sole parent.

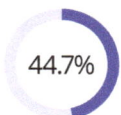 **44.7%** — Families includes couples with children (44.7), couples without children (37.8 per cent), single parent (15.8) and other (1.7).

 **81.8%** — Of the 900,000 single parents, 81.8 per cent are female and 18.2 per cent male.

 **15%** — The 2016 Census counted 46,800 same-sex couples. Fifteen per cent have children, including one in four female couples and 4.5 per cent of male couples.

 **29.6%** — Australians are becoming less religious, with 29.6 telling the 2016 Census they had no religion, up from 19 per cent in 2006 and more than any single religion.

 **52%** — Christianity remains the most common religious affiliation (52 per cent), followed by Islam (2.6 per cent) and Buddhism (2.4 per cent).

Source: Australian Bureau of Statistics 2016 Census (abs.gov.au)

Graphic: Adobe Stock / HURCA!

Family Violence

VIOLENCE OF ALL KINDS IS WRONG

No relationship is perfect. But physical and/or emotional abuse are never OK and can be devastating.

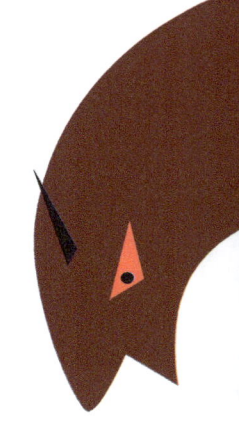

// WAYS TO IMPROVE YOUR RELATIONSHUP

1. Work to **REDUCE STRESS** that might be straining your relationship.

2. Discuss life stresses and how to manage them together. **SUPPORT EACH OTHER** in difficult times.

3. Try to make **POSITIVE INTERACTIONS** outweigh the negative, by five to one. Show appreciation, gratitude and care.

4. **SHARE YOUR VIEWS, IDEAS AND EMOTIONS.** Try to express frustration, disappointment and anger openly and constructively.

5. **CONSIDER YOUR PARTNER'S VIEW** and try to empathise with their thoughts, feelings and actions.

6. **ESTABLISH SHARED VALUES**, expectations and standards, and work to live by those important to you.

7. **REMAIN RESPECTFUL DURING CONFLICT.** Keep calm during any discussions. Ensure you both work to repair any hurt caused.

8. **APPRECIATE EACH OTHER'S ROLES**, the goals that link you, and how each of you contributes to and influences each other.

9. **ENCOURAGE YOUR PARTNER'S WORK**, friendships and activities. Celebrate successes.

10. **KEEP YOUR SENSE OF PLAYFULNESS**, affection and positive humour.

Source: Australian Psychological Society, psychology.org.au

Experts say a ratio of five positive interactions to every negative one indicates a relationship is functioning well *(www.psychology.org.au).*

When interactions involve disrespect, defensiveness or stonewalling, a family may be in crisis.

Recognising this can be difficult and those outside a relationship may not notice if it is well hidden.

A perceived need to control a partner, sexist attitudes and lack of self-control can increase the likelihood of abusive behaviour. Pregnancy can also trigger or worsen abuse.

Research has shown that domestic violence increases during big sporting events, such as the soccer World Cup, and, while alcohol can be a trigger, it is rarely the cause.

Any form of violence can lead to trauma. Trauma can have a debilitating, life-long impact on a person. In some cases impeding cognitive ability and social and emotional functioning.

RECOGNISING FAMILY VIOLENCE

Family violence is complex, insidious and involves much more than physical abuse.

Physical Assault // punching, kicking, slapping, choking or using weapons.

Sexual Assault // any non-consenting sexual act or behaviour, unwanted or disrespectful sexual touch, rape, forced compliance in sexual acts, indecent assault, and forced viewing of pornography.

// HELP

Support is available for families experiencing physical or emotional abuse.
Page 33 lists organisations that can help with counselling and referral to specialist services.

1800 RESPECT
Those affected by family violence can access 24/7 confidential information, counselling and support services through
1800 RESPECT // 1800 737 732
// www.1800respect.org.au

Coercion and threats // telling the person she/he, the children, pets or property will be hurt or taken away.
Intimidation // making a person afraid by using looks, actions or gestures.
Psychological/emotional/verbal abuse // using words and other strategies to insult, threaten, degrade, abuse or denigrate the victim.
Using children // threatening to take them, or to report the partner to child protection authorities.
Control // preventing the partner from making or keeping connections with family, friends or culture; controlling what the partner does.
Economic abuse // controlling and withholding access to family resources.

FAMILY VIOLENCE HURTS EVERYONE

Children who are exposed to family violence experience significant trauma and are at high risk of psychological and emotional damage, says Domestic Violence NSW.

Lifelong impacts can include psychological and behavioural issues, depression, risk taking, abusing their own children, homelessness and health and wellbeing issues.

Domestic Violence NSW Policy and Research Manager Gayatri Nair says seeking help for family violence can be difficult and some women return numerous times before leaving. "Recognising it and being able to talk about it is important and the first step in addressing it," she says.

// WHEN CHILDREN ARE VIOLENT

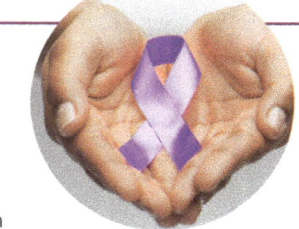

Some families have children who physically abuse parents. Psychologist, social worker and family therapist Eddie Gallagher has worked with more than 500 affected families and says people often unfairly blame the parents.

Eddie estimates that five per cent of children cross the line from misbehaviour to abuse that can involve repeated swearing, threats, intimidation, slapping and punching.

His book, *Who's in Charge* (Austin Macauley), deals with this complex issue and claims it has worsened over the past 20 years, partly because of western culture's lack of respect for authority and age, indulgent parenting and adult domestic violence (DV).

"The physical stuff ... goes hand in hand with a lot of verbal abuse and other forms of intimidation and attempts at control," Eddie says. "Sometimes it gets very serious, so don't let it escalate. If they're swearing and yelling at you at 11, don't wait until they're 15."

Eddie says it is important to seek help early. "If you've done your best you have no reason to feel guilty, even if it didn't work out as you'd hoped," he says.

If needed, a psychologist can help. Eddie also runs *Who's in Charge?* parenting groups in Australia and England.

// DEALING WITH ABUSIVE CHILDREN

- Take disrespect seriously.
- Producing feelings of entitlement in your child makes it easy for them to be abusive.
- Find someone to talk to. Yes, it's embarrassing, and you may be blamed, but ignoring it won't help.
- Have consequences for serious misbehaviour (e.g. any violence, swearing at you).

Source: Psychologist Eddie Gallagher, www.eddiegallagher.com.au

IF FAMILY VIOLENCE AFFECTS YOU#

- Disclose to a support service, friend or relative you can call if things escalate.
- Talk to someone, such as a trusted neighbour who would be able to call police, and create safety plans.
- Make an escape plan, e.g. pack a bag with key documents.
- Leave keys and important papers with a confidant.
- Plan and rehearse the fastest way to leave.
- Keep a record of all violence.
- Download the Daisy app (**www.1800respect.org.au/daisy**) to connect to local services, and stay in touch with them.
- 24/7 Family violence response phone line 1800 015 188.
- In an emergency call 000.
- For support call 1800RESPECT (1800 737 732).

Watch // The ChildTrauma Academy Channel (anything by Bruce Perry) on YouTube.

// Relationships Australia www.relationships.org.au   **# Source** Domestic Violence NSW, www.dvnsw.org.au

Sexism & Equality

TWO SEXES ON ONE LEVEL

Since a bold group of women founded Australia's first female trade union in 1882 – The Tailoresses' Association of Melbourne – women have fought for equality with men. They have achieved it in many areas.

Women are no longer forced to give up their jobs or financial independence when they marry and are generally supported in juggling their career and family.

We even have a national AFL Women's competition.

Yet women still earn less than men and are at significantly higher risk of sexual harassment and family violence.

Women and girls continue to face hurdles at home and work, says Victorian Women's Trust executive director Mary Crooks AO.

Mary quotes a 2017 survey of more than 1700 Australian girls, The Dream Gap, which found that those aged 10–17 dreamed of being equal but knew they weren't in sport, the media, at school and at home. "Moreover, as they get older, their confidence decreases," she says.

Mary urges families to empower girls while working to improve equality in politics, workplaces and homes. Men also need to speak out against wage inequity, sexism and violence.

"The major roadblock is that our society is still imprinted with stubborn hallmarks of patriarchal social organisation," she says. "Men still hold most economic and political power."

TO REDUCE SEXISM AND INEQUALITY, WE MUST ...
- promote equality at home
- challenge assumptions about gender roles
- enhance support systems for girls and women
- teach boys and men to understand male privilege
- shun toxic masculinity at home and in the community
- encourage men to condemn sexual aggression and the degradation of women
- embrace equality and diversity
- recognise structures and systems that promote patriarchy
- eliminate inequity in political, legal and wage systems.

Source: Victorian Women's Trust executive director Mary Crooks, www.vwt.org.au

MISOGYNY SPEECH
In 2012, Australia's first female Prime Minister, Julia Gillard *(pictured)*, made global headlines with a speech in which she decried misogyny in politics.

Directed largely at then Opposition Leader Tony Abbott, the speech sparked global discussion about women in politics and the workplace.

"I will not be lectured about sexism and misogyny by this man, I will not," she said of Mr Abbott. "And the Government will not be lectured about sexism and misogyny by this man.

"The Leader of the Opposition says that people who hold sexist views and who are misogynists are not appropriate for high office. Well, I hope the Leader of the Opposition has got a piece of paper and he is writing out his resignation."

The speech can still be found on YouTube.

Sexism is still an issue for many women, despite the gains made over many years.

THE 'ME TOO' MOVEMENT

The "Me too" movement has empowered many women to speak out about sexual harassment and assault. It originated in 2006 when New York-raised Tarana Burke (metoomvmt.org) used the phrase in her work with low-income women of colour who had experienced sexual violence. *The New Yorker* magazine sparked global discussion with Ronan Farrow's award-winning 2017 investigation about the alleged offenses of movie producer Harvey Weinstein. Actor Alyssa Milano is widely credited with popularising the #MeToo hashtag as debate about sexual harassment and violence exploded online and in the media. Many high-profile offenders have been named, shamed and in some cases charged. Women have gained some closure and, in some cases, justice in the legal system. Education about what "crosses the line" has also improved.

BY THE NUMBERS

THE GENDER PAY GAP

14-19% LESS PAY
FEMALE

Australian women still earn less than men. The Workplace Gender Equality Agency's August 2018 report found Australia's national gender pay gap has hovered between 14 and 19 per cent since 1998. Over the past 20 years, the gap peaked at 18.5 per cent in November 2014 and was lowest in May 2018 – 14.6 per cent. The May 2018 figure was higher in the private sector (18.4 per cent) than the public sector (10.5 per cent).

WOMEN IN LEADERSHIP

16.5% CEOs

Latest results from the Agency's 2016-17 dataset show: Women hold 13.7 per cent of chair positions and 24.9 per cent of directorships, and represent 16.5 per cent of CEOs and 29.7 per cent of key management personnel.

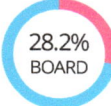
28.2% BOARD

Real-time statistics from the AICD reveal: 28.2 per cent of directors in the ASX 200 are women (July 2018). Women comprised 50 per cent of new appointments to ASX 200 boards in 2018 (as at 31 July).

Source: Workplace Gender Equality Agency. www.wgea.gov.au

// A SPORTING CHANCE

Women have made progress in elite sport, earning the same as men in tennis Grand Slam tournaments and horse racing prize money, but there is still a long way to go.
Women tennis players still earn less overall than men and most professional sports have a large gender pay gap.

SPORT	MEN	WOMEN
AFL \ AFLW *Latest available information.*	2018 average wage was $362,471 (22 games plus possible finals) *The minimum AFLW player payment is relative to the minimum male footballer payment pro rata*	Average 2020 wages: $22,209.75 (8 games plus possible finals). The total finals prize pool for 2020 will be $232,000.
TENNIS	\multicolumn{2}{c}{**EQUAL AUSTRALIAN OPEN GRAND SLAM PRIZES OF $4.1 MILLION (2019)** But 71 of the top 100 men earn more per tournament than women of the same ranking (January-July 2018) + Men & Women compete against each other in mixed doubles}	
BASKETBALL	**NBL** 2019/2020 salary cap was $1.43 million *Teams can exceed the soft cap and pay a new 'luxury tax' imposed at marginal, incremental rates.*	**WNBL** Minimum wage $13,000 (for 2019/20 and 2020/21)
SOCCER Australian team	\multicolumn{2}{c}{In late 2019, a landmark pay deal saw Football Federation Australia announce that the Matildas would earn the same as the Socceroos. It also made Australia the first country in world football to guarantee an equal share of commercial revenue with the men.}	
CRICKET Australian team	In 2021/22 the minimum retainer for a national men's cricketer will be $313,004.	In 2021/22, the minimum retainer for a national women's cricketer will be $87,609.
	\multicolumn{2}{c}{**Cricket Australia agreed to top up any women's earnings in the 2020 T20 World Cup to ensure parity with the men.*}	
SURFING World Surf League	\multicolumn{2}{c}{The World Surf League introduced parity for WSL men's and women's events from 2019}	

© Parenting Guides Ltd

Racism & Xenophobia

AUSTRALIA FAIR?

Modelling empathy and inclusiveness can help reduce racism and bigotry. Calling out racist behaviour is also important.

Australia has long been a multicultural country and has an even longer Indigenous history. Since Europeans first settled here 230 years ago, waves of migrants have followed from all continents.

With them have come new foods, drinks, literature, art and cultural celebrations that have made Australia what it is today – a thriving multicultural society.

Yet racism is still a problem, with issues such as the treatment of asylum seekers and crimes committed by a small percentage of Sudanese refugees reigniting debate.

WHAT IS RACISM?

Racism shows a lack of respect for racial differences. It can offend and cause great harm.

The Australian Human Rights Commission says racism takes many forms, including race-based jokes or negative comments, name calling, verbal abuse, bullying or intimidation. It may involve graffiti, offensive comments, exclusion from groups, physical abuse and ignoring job applications. Systemic racism may see people forced to fill out forms in a language they don't speak.

About one in five Australians say they have experienced racist verbal abuse or name-calling. More than one in 20 have been physically attacked because of their race.

Indigenous Australians also report continued incidents of casual and direct racism.

// WHAT CAN WE DO?

Strategies and tips from Western Sydney University's *Challenging Racism Project* to reduce racism include:
- Alert people to the damage racist language can do and discourage them from using it.
- Consider anti-racism initiatives when celebrating cultural diversity at festivals and events.
- Provide accurate information to dispel false beliefs.
- Encourage people to discuss racism and treat others respectfully.
- Encourage empathy.
- Address issues of differences as well as commonalities.
- Use contact between different groups, where appropriate, to help break down barriers.
- Reflect upon your identity and, if relevant, white privilege.
- Intervene if you witness racism and reassure the victim that they have done nothing wrong.
- Hold organisations and others to account on racism.
- Use social media to send positive messages about diversity.

* Source: Challenging Racism Project / www.westernsydney.edu.au/challengingracism

Racism: It stops with me is a campaign launched by the Australian Human Rights Commission // itstopswithme.humanrights.gov.au
The Scanlon Foundation researches social cohesion // www.scanlonfoundation.org.au

// POLITICAL CORRECTNESS

In the literal sense, political correctness is doing the right thing by others. It describes language, policies or measures intended to avoid offence or disadvantage certain groups. Political correctness generally avoids language or behaviour that can be seen to exclude, marginalise or insult groups, such as the LGBTIQ+ community or members of a certain race or religion.

WHAT IS RACIAL DISCRIMINATION?[1]

Direct racial discrimination happens when a person is treated less favourably than another in a similar situation because of their race, colour, descent, national or ethnic origin or immigrant status.

For example, a real estate agent may refuse to rent a house to a person because of their racial background or skin colour.

Indirect racial discrimination happens when rules or policies have an unfair effect on people of a particular race, colour, descent, national or ethnic origin or immigrant status.

For example, a company ban on wearing hats or other headwear at work would have an unfair effect on people from some racial/ethnic backgrounds.

// CALLING OUT RACISM

Australia's first female Muslim senator, the Greens' Mehreen Faruqi, who migrated to Australia from Pakistan in 1992, called out a resurgence in racism in her maiden parliamentary speech in 2018.

"While I did feel welcomed when we arrived here, migrants coming to our shores today would not be able to say the same," she said.

"The last 26 years have seen governments erode support for newcomers as bigotry and xenophobia has been allowed to flourish.

"The existence of racism, sexism and other discrimination is not new but what has changed is its legitimisation, normalisation and encouragement in the media and in politics.

"We can build a future for each and every one of us, no matter where we come from, no matter the colour of our skin, our religion, our gender or sexuality, our bank balance or our postcode."

// TRUE PATRIOTISM

On his depature as Race Discrimination Commissioner at Western Sydney University's Whitlam Centre in 2018, Dr Tim Soutphommasane decried the return of race politics in Australia.

"We must remain vigilant because race politics is back," he said. "When politicians resort to using race in advancing their agendas, they inevitably excite racial anxiety and stir up social division. They end up damaging our racial tolerance and multicultural harmony.

"Just as there was in the 1980s and 1990s, there is panic about migrants and minorities.

"The consequences are all too real. Within Sudanese-Australian communities, there are many people who are fearful about leaving their homes, and who are sheltering from society.

"This is how racism works. It creates doubts and divisions, and it drives its targets into retreat.

"Where the seeds of racism are planted in political speech, they will bear bitter fruit in society."

Dr Soutphommasane called for the restoration of some standards, proportion and perspective into the public debate and discussed what it means to be anti-racist.

"This is a commitment that reflects the highest form of patriotism – the desire to see our country live up to its very best," he said.

"We reject racism because it is an assault on our values and our fellow citizens. We reject racism because it diminishes our nation. That is why we fight racism.

"It's because we think so highly of our nation in the first place. It's because we want to see our country do better. It's because we are committed to equality and it's because we have a responsibility to uphold our values."

Read the full speech at // www.humanrights.gov.au/news/speeches/confronting-return-race-politics

WHAT IS RACIAL HATRED?

It is illegal to do something in public, which is likely to offend, insult, humiliate or intimidate, based on the race, colour, national or ethnic origin of a person or group of people.

RACIAL HATRED EXAMPLES MAY INCLUDE:[1]

- racially offensive material online, including eforums, blogs, social networking and video sharing sites
- racially offensive comments or images in a newspaper, magazine or other publication such as a leaflet or flyer
- racially offensive speeches at a public rally
- racially abusive comments in a public place, such as a shop, workplace, park, on public transport or at school
- racially abusive comments at sporting events by players, spectators, coaches or officials.

1 Source: Australian Human Rights Commission, www.humanrights.gov.au

LGBTIQ+

VIVE LA DIFFERENCE

Support for diversity is crucial for the health and wellbeing of LGBTIQ+ young people.

Parents should encourage their children to respect all people and model respectful behaviours, including gender and sexually diverse individuals. LGBTIQ+ children need to feel safe and included. Parents also need to be conscious of the fact that sometimes they may not be aware that they have a child who is LGBTIQ+ or questioning their sexuality or gender identity. These (often private) struggles can be incredibly difficult to discuss in an environment that is perceived to be hostile or not open to a lifestyle that is different to the mainstream or may be inconsistent with a community's religious and cultural beliefs.

Australians voted to introduce marriage equality in 2017, and a growing number of mainstream and specialist services work with LGBTIQ+ young people. Many, though, still face poorer mental health outcomes than the general population.

This is not helped by divisive debates about marriage equality, Safe Schools and whether faith-based independent schools should retain the right to discriminate against LGBTIQ+ teachers and students.

A national LGBTI Health Alliance report outlines poor mental health outcomes of many in the LGBTIQ+ communities compared to others. It underlines the positive power of inclusiveness.

"There is a growing body of work that demonstrates the positive impact of social connection and participation on people's mental health, and the extent to which this may mitigate the trauma associated with experiences of harassment and discrimination," the report says.

"The WHO (World Health Organization) has identified several protective factors for the recurrence or onset of mental ill-health. These include a sense of belonging, supportive social networks and supportive relationships."[1]

THE POWER OF INCLUSION

Inclusive language, safe spaces and education can help LGBTIQ+ young people feel more confident about being themselves.

LGBTIQ+ young people, which includes lesbian, gay, bisexual, transgender, intersex and queer/questioning, need to know they are valued and accepted.

For parents and carers, educating children about sexuality, gender, and body diversity in a non-judgmental way can help them feel more comfortable with who they are.

It is also helpful to role model inclusive language and behaviours, for example using the correct pronoun for transgender and gender diverse people.

CREATING SAFE SPACES

LGBTIQ+ young people can access social and support programs at school and in the communities.

Many schools and universities have groups for LGBTIQ+ students and their allies. Numerous youth groups also welcome and support LGBTIQ+ young people, and radio programs such as Joy FM's *Unicorn Youth* give them a voice.

Safe Schools Coalition Australia was a national initiative to help schools be safe and more inclusive for same-sex attracted, intersex and gender diverse students, staff and families.

It provided a range of free support for school staff, including professional learning, advice and resources. The program has completed, with some resources still available at **studentwellbeinghub.edu.au**.

They include curriculum-aligned resources on contemporary issues that affect student wellbeing and a fact sheet for parents.

Visit // safeschoolscoalition.org.au

Graphic: Adobe Stock / martialred

1 Going upstream: A framework for promoting the mental health of lesbian, gay, bisexual, transgender and intersex (LGBTI) people (National LGBTI Health Alliance)

// WHEN I CAME OUT ...
Marcus // 19 // gay

Q. HOW WAS YOUR EXPERIENCE OF COMING OUT?
Such an anticlimax! After expecting the world to cave in, it was actually no big deal, and I was super thankful for that. I told my best mate at the time, and he was fine.

Q. WHEN DID YOU FIRST BEGIN TO RECOGNISE YOU MIGHT BE HOMOSEXUAL?
At puberty, when I was about 12 or 13. I totally freaked out. It was really hard to accept things were going to be different for me. I thought I'd get married and have kids.

Q. WAS YOUR MENTAL HEALTH AFFECTED?
Absolutely. I became more and more depressed and desperately tried to think of ways that I could possibly change my orientation. I was self-harming at this stage.

Q. WHAT HELPED YOU GET THROUGH IT?
I think I'm lucky to have been born at a time when people can live openly.

Q. WAS IT DIFFICULT TELLING YOUR FAMILY?
I was so worried that I'd disappoint them. Family is the most important thing to me and to lose that would be devastating. When I did tell them, when I was 13, it was such a relief that I could be myself around them.

Q. HOW DID THEY REACT?
Initially they had doubt ... I can understand where they were coming from. But soon they were like: "When are you going to bring a boy around?"

THE SEXUAL ATTRACTION QUESTION FOR STUDENTS

*People are different in their sexual attraction to other people. Which best describes your feelings?***

Only attracted to females

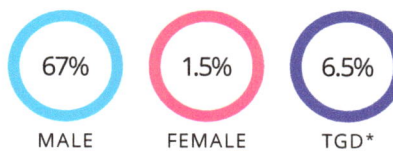

| 67% | 1.5% | 6.5% |
| MALE | FEMALE | TGD* |

Only attracted to males

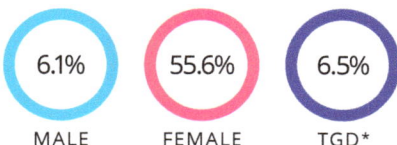

| 6.1% | 55.6% | 6.5% |
| MALE | FEMALE | TGD* |

Equally attracted to females and males

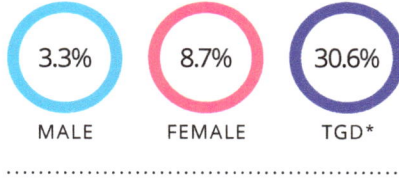

| 3.3% | 8.7% | 30.6% |
| MALE | FEMALE | TGD* |

Not sure

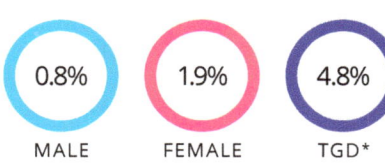

| 0.8% | 1.9% | 4.8% |
| MALE | FEMALE | TGD* |

Base: Sexually active students.
*Trans and gender diverse
** Source: Australian Research Centre in Sex, Health and Society, La Trobe University:
The sixth National Survey of Secondary Students and Sexual Health 2018.

// RESPECT TIPS

Every child needs different things from family and every relationship is unique. You can give support by:
- Focusing on the love that you have for your child or loved one.
- Learning all you can about the LGBTIQ+ community: networks, support groups and issues.
- Researching social groups for LGBTIQ+ people that you may like to suggest your child or loved one attend.
- Educating yourself and your child or loved one about safe sex HIV/AIDS and other STIs.
- Admitting when you do not know something, or if you are uncomfortable – but without blaming your child.
- Taking the time to get comfortable. Find a counsellor if you need to.
- Dealing with your issues and disappointments as yours.
- Using the language that your child or loved one uses, e.g. lesbian, dyke or gay.
- Respecting who and when they are ready to tell – do not out anyone before they are ready.
- Encouraging them to introduce their friends and/or partner and not treating them differently.
- Encouraging them to talk of their experiences, without judging.
- If there is a LGBTIQ+ person you like and trust, getting them to be a sounding board for you and/or a role model for your child.

★ PFLAG www.pflagaustralia.org.au

MORE SAME-SEX COUPLES IDENTIFIED // More Australian couples are identifying as same-sex attracted.

- The 2016 Census counted almost 46,800 same-sex couples living together in Australia, up 39 per cent on 2011. Since this data was first collected in 1996, the number has more than quadrupled.
- The Australian Bureau of Statistics says this may in part reflect greater willingness by people to identify themselves in a same-sex relationship and improved rights for same-sex couples.
- Younger people accounted for most the 2011-2016 increase. Half of the increase was for those aged 20-29 years, with another 35 per cent for those aged 30-39.

Indigenous culture

FIRST AUSTRALIANS

Learning about Australia's rich Indigenous culture is a great way to demonstrate respect for it.

Indigenous culture is an important part of Australian history. It pre-dates white settlement by at least 65,000 years, and it is important to respect and acknowledge this.

For example, we must acknowledge practices such as not publicly naming those who have died and respecting sacred sites, such as Uluru.

// SBS.com.au has a guide that explains some of these cultural sensitivities.

VISITING THE LAND

As the traditional owners of the land, Aboriginal and Torres Strait Island peoples perform a **Welcome to Country** when visitors wish to enter or have permission to enter their traditional country. It may involve singing, dancing, smoking ceremonies or a speech in traditional language or English.

An **Acknowledgement of Country** can be performed by Indigenous or non-Indigenous persons and recognises the Traditional Custodians of the land on which a gathering is held.

The wording usually acknowledges the land's traditional custodians and pays respects to elders, past and present, and Aboriginal and Torres Strait Island peoples attending.

The federal Department of Foreign Affairs and Trade has details at dfat.gov.au and Reconciliation Australia has guidelines at reconciliation.org.au.

A PROUD HERITAGE

From Sydney AFL star Adam Goodes' *Australian of the Year* speech, 2014.

"I believe we are all connected, whether we like it or not. We are all equal and the same in so many ways. My hope is that we, as a nation, can break down the silos between races, break down those stereotypes of minority populations, Indigenous populations, and all the other minority groups.

"I hope we can be proud of our heritage, regardless of the colour of our skin, and be proud to be Australian.

"I'm not here to tell you what to think or how to act or raise your children. All I'm here to do is tell you about my experiences and hope you choose to be aware of your actions and interactions so that together, we can eliminate racism."

// PREFERRED TERMINOLOGY

ABORIGINAL AND TORRES STRAIT ISLANDER (adjective) refers to Aboriginal peoples and Torres Strait Islanders, and related topics.

INDIGENOUS (capital I) refers to the Aboriginal and/or Torres Strait Islander peoples of Australia, and related topics. Some dislike this term. You may prefer Aboriginal, or Torres Strait Islander, or both.

ABORIGINAL (adjective, capital A) is extensively used and widely accepted when referring to Aboriginal peoples and topics.

ABORIGINAL (noun, capital A) is less preferred. Consider "Matthew is an Aboriginal person from Yass", rather than "Matthew is an Aboriginal from Yass".

ABORIGINAL (adjective, no capital) Some groups refer to themselves as "aboriginal" or "Aboriginal", such as in Canada and Taiwan.

NON-ABORIGINAL There is some dissatisfaction with "non-Aboriginal".

ABORIGINE (capital A) or **aborigine** (no capital). This is not recommended, partly because of the historical negative references associated.

PART-ABORIGINAL or **HALF-ABORIGINAL** is often considered offensive to an Aboriginal person.

TORRES STRAIT ISLANDER (adjective, capitals) is extensively used throughout Australia when referring to Torres Strait Islander peoples and topics.

TSI should not be used to describe Torres Strait Islander peoples and topics.

ISLANDER(S) should not be used. This generic term does not adequately describe Torres Strait Islander peoples.

FIRST AUSTRALIANS, "Australia's First Peoples" and "First Nations Australia" (capitals): these terms are growing in acceptance.

*Note terminology preferences will vary across Australia for individuals, communities and agencies. They can also change. It is a good idea to check with relevant individuals and groups.
*Source: Gulanga Good Practice Guide: Preferences in terminology when referring to Aboriginal and/or Torres Strait Islander peoples, www.actcoss.org.au/gulanga-guides.

Timellis09 [CC BY-SA 3.0 (https://creativecommons.org/licenses/by-sa/3.0)], from Wikimedia Commons

// THE ABORIGINAL FLAG

Designed by Harold Thomas, a Luritja man of Central Australia, the Aboriginal flag was first flown on National Aboriginal Day in Adelaide in 1971. Thomas wanted the flag to represent Australia's Aboriginal people, the earth's red ochre colour and a spiritual relation to the land and the sun. In 1972 it became the official flag for the Aboriginal Embassy near Canberra's old Parliament House.

Photo: Adobe Stock \ millenius

Disability

POSITIVELY ENABLING

Everyone, no matter their circumstances, has something to contribute to society.

Those living with a disability do not want to be defined by it. Many are happy to discuss their situation, but it is only part of who they are and what they do.

It is important for parents and carers to discuss these issues with their children, so they are aware of respectful language and other potential sensitivities.

WHAT IS DISABILITY?

The Australian Bureau of Statistics says a person is living with disability if they report a limitation, restriction or impairment that has lasted for at least six months and restricts everyday activities.

"There are many different kinds of disability, usually resulting from accidents, illness or genetic disorders," it says. "Disability may affect a person's mobility, communication or learning. It can also affect their income and participation in education, social activities and the labour force."

RATES OF DISABILITY

- In Australia, 18.3 per cent of people (4.3 million) report living with a disability.
- Most (78.5 per cent) report a physical condition, such as back problems, and 21.5 per cent claim mental or behavioural disorders.
- More than half of those with disability aged 15-64 work (53.4 per cent), compared to 83.2 per cent of those with no disability.

DISABILITY DISCRIMINATION

- Of the 2046 complaints the Australian Human Rights Commission received in 2017-2018, 42 per cent (869) related to the Disability Discrimination Act.
- Most related to goods, services and facilities (36 per cent) and employment (30 per cent). Others related to access to premises, accommodation, superannuation, insurance, education, clubs, associations, laws and programs, sport, qualifying bodies and disability standards.

// INCLUSIVE LANGUAGE

Words matter. It is important to use inclusive and positive language around disability.

- Focus on the person, not the impairment. Use "person with disability" or "people with disability" e.g. "person who is deaf", or "people who have low vision".
- Avoid terms such as "non-disabled" or "able-bodied".
- Avoid language that implies a person is inspirational simply because they experience disability. Implying they are courageous or special just for getting through the day is patronising and offensive.
- Don't represent people with disability as victims or objects of pity. Experiencing a disability does not make someone weak, a victim or to be pitied. Instead of "suffering from...", "struck down by ...", and "afflicted by/with...", use "Paul experiences depression", "Ravi developed multiple sclerosis", or "Katya has epilepsy".
- People are not bound by or confined to wheelchairs – they are enabled and liberated by them. Say "wheelchair user" or "person who uses a wheelchair".
- "Disclosure" of disability can imply secrets and lies. Use "chooses to share information about their disability/impairment".
- Avoid euphemisms and made up words such as "differently abled", "people of all abilities", "disAbility", "diffAbled" and "special needs", which can be considered patronising.
- Change the focus from disability to accessibility. Call it an accessible car park or bathroom, an Accessibility Action Plan or Access and Inclusion Plan, rather than "Disability ...".
- Don't get caught up in semantics. Don't be so afraid of saying the wrong thing that you don't say anything. Relax, be willing to communicate, and listen.

Source: This is an edited version of a guide published by the Australian Network on Disability www.and.org.au

// **Source:** Australian Bureau of Statistics 2015 figures, www.abs.gov.au

Social Media

Online communication can be a positive force in the lives of young people, connecting them to each other, educational materials and the world.

But there can be pitfalls, such as addiction to screen time, bullying (as a victim or perpetrator) and reduced in-person interaction with family and friends.

The internet has also opened a whole new world of pornography, online gambling and access to extreme political views.

The key for parents is to know what children are doing on the internet and communicate with them.

You may not see exactly what they are doing, but you can help to guide them and control their use.

BUILDING A BRAND

Young people can build a positive individual online "brand" through their words and actions, such as supporting social causes and promoting awareness.

The brand they build, whether it be social activist, movie critic, fashion influencer, marketer, creative artist, music performer or even a troll, could stay with them for life. They must also be aware that future employers may check their online profile before hiring them.

If parents and schools have instilled good values, these values may influence the way a child interacts online.

Having rules and boundaries at home can help, especially when children are younger.

IMAGE-BASED ABUSE

Image-based abuse is when someone shares, or threatens to share, intimate or sexual photos or videos of a person without that person's consent.

This includes photos or videos of a person nude or showing their breasts or genitals, engaged in a sex act and/or showering or bathing. It also includes "upskirting" and "downblousing" images.

A survey by RMIT and Monash University in 2016 involving more than 4200 people aged 16–49 found that four in five agreed that image-based abuse should be a crime, although many attributed some responsibility to the victims.

Seventy per cent agreed that "people should know better than to take nude selfies ... even if they never send them to anyone".

Six in 10 agreed "if a person sends a nude or sexual image to someone else, then they are at least partly responsible if the image ends up online".

Men (50 per cent) were much more likely than women (30 per cent) to hold attitudes that minimised the harms or blamed the victims.

....

// Australian Institute of Health and Welfare 2018.
Family, domestic and sexual violence in Australia 2018.
Cat. no. FDV 2. Canberra: AIHW.

Most of Gen Z have a greater knowledge of the internet than their parents, so ensuring they use it respectfully is no easy task.

ONLINE REVOLUTION

// SIGNS SOMEONE IS BEING CYBER BULLIED*

- Abnormal withdrawal from social activities, friends and/or family
- Sudden lack of interest in using their mobile phone, computer or other devices
- Disinterest or avoidance in attending school, sports, or other recreational activities
- Nervous or jumpy when a text message or email is received
- Extreme sleeping behaviour (sleeping a lot more or staying awake all night)
- Self-harming behaviours
- Moodiness and abnormal changes in behaviour

// SOCIAL MEDIA SECURITY SETTINGS BIBLE

 FACEBOOK // Click on "Privacy Check-Up" in the top-right corner. Under "Your Posts" select "Friends", "Only Me", or "Custom" to choose who you want to see your posts. Then click "Next Step" and repeat for all categories. When done, select "Finish Up".

 INSTAGRAM // On your smartphone or tablet, click on the Setting Icon. Scroll down and turn on your "Private Account" setting.

 TWITTER // Select the Settings icon. Then select "Your Account" and turn off "Find Me By Email". Turn on "Protect My Tweets" and switch off "Receive Direct Messages From Anyone".

 SNAPCHAT // Head to Settings, click through to "Send Me Snaps" and select "My Friends". Then back in the Settings tab, click through to View "My Stories", click on "My Friends" or "Custom" to choose who sees your images.

// RESPECT TIPS

- You may not be able to stop them, but you should know what your children do online.
- Learn how social media and various online platforms work.
- No one should post anything they wouldn't tell their grandmother.
- Everything posted online is traceable – even if deleted.
- Words matter; think before posting negative comments to or about someone.
- Everyone is subject to defamation laws, which require only two other people to have seen defamatory content.
- Regardless of privacy laws, potential employers may google applicants.
- Some sexting is illegal – know the law in your state.
- Don't make fun of or exploit other people's misfortune on social media.

// A LESSON LEARNED

Greens candidate Joanna Nilson stood down during the 2018 Victorian state election campaign after a journalist found old comments she had made on Facebook.

Joanna became front page news for jokes she made on a closed women's page about shoplifting and minor recreational drug use.

She wrongly – and naively as she later pointed out – thought it was a safe space. Within half an hour of the journalist's call, Joanna decided to stand down to avoid distracting from the Greens' campaign.

The would-be MP later explained that she had come to realise that everyone had said or done something stupid online, which was quite normal.

While admitting she had made a mistake, Joanna said politicians needed to represent their constituents, who came from all walks of life, were not perfect, and like her, made mistakes.

Many would empathise, but social media mishaps can come back to haunt.

Photo: Adobe Stock / Brian

// *Source: 'Rosie', a Dugdale Trust for Women & Girls national harm prevention initiative. www.rosie.org.au

Schools

LEARNED BEHAVIOUR

Schools play an increasingly important role in shaping the character of young people.

Schools should be a safe place for students. Respect towards and by their teachers and peers is a big part of that. Schools set boundaries and work with parents to model and instil respectful attitudes.

Societal attitudes towards disrespectful behaviour have improved, which is reflected in school programs, but bullying and violence are still big issues on campus.

WHAT SCHOOLS ARE TEACHING

Most schools have numerous programs that promote respect among students. Teachers must also meet acceptable standards and model appropriate behaviour.

The Australian Curriculum covers health and personal development in detail up to year 10. Students are supported to keep a positive outlook and evaluate behavioural expectations in different leisure, social, movement and online situations.

Buddy programs are extremely popular in primary schools and usually pair a Year 6 and Prep student. The older child provides support and encouragement to the younger child as they do activities together.

The Safe Schools Coalition Australia provides schools with resources to help make LGBTIQ+ students feel safe and supported.

The Tasmanian Government links to a range of respect-related programs, including Victorian and Western Australian Government programs that offer respectful relationships teaching resources.

The New South Wales Government has a child protection and respectful relationships program that helps students to identify abusive situations and ensure their relationships are as they should be.

The South Australian Government has a Wellbeing for Learning and Life framework to build resilience and wellbeing by engaging, inspiring and empowering students, while the Queensland Government's Creating Healthier Workplaces strategy covers cyber safety, drug education and making smart choices – in schools.

The ACT Government has a range of wellbeing resources and links, and the Northern Territory Government refers teachers to a Safe Schools website and has an Indigenous Education Strategy.

BULLY STOPPERS[1]

The Victorian Department of Education and Training has school mental health programs and a Bully Stoppers website with tools and resources to empower school communities to stop bullying.

It has a section dedicated to students with information on what to do if they are experiencing bullying, or know someone who is.

It also explores cyber safety, provides interactive learning modules and links to helpful resources.

WHAT STUDENTS ARE LEARNING IN YEARS 9 & 10[2]

- alcohol and other drugs;
- food and nutrition;
- health benefits of physical activity;
- mental health and wellbeing;
- relationships and sexuality;
- safety;
- challenge and adventure activities;
- games and sports;
- lifelong physical activities;
- rhythmic and expressive movement activities.

I LIKE, LIKE YOU

Some schools run programs that encourage children and young people to understand what respectful and equal relationships are. Since 2014, Relationships Australia Victoria has provided, *I like, like you*, a program for schools that emphasises the "me", "you" and "us" in relationships.

At the primary level, me focuses on self-awareness, you highlights empathy, and us looks at relationships, including communication, conflict resolution and self understanding.

These concepts are expanded at secondary level to include intimate relationships, emotional and mental health, gender and power, technology use and recognising unsafe relationships.

// MORE at www.rav.org.au/ILLY

// RESPECT TIPS

- Know your school's respect and wellbeing programs.
- Encourage your school to incorporate inclusion/respect programs.
- Be mindful of the challenges teachers face and encourage your child(ren) to do the same.
- Talk to your child about how school is going socially as well as academically.
- Seek help if you think your child has mental health issues, is being bullied or is bullying others.
- Most schools have psychologists and other staff to help if problems arise.

// 1 Source: www.education.vic.gov.au/about/programs/bullystoppers
2 Source: **Australian Curriculum**, *Health and Physical Education, years 9-10*. www.australiancurriculum.edu.au

Photo: Adobe Stock / Holmessu

// CHARACTER STRENGTHS

Appreciation of beauty and excellence // Ability to find, recognise and take pleasure in the existence of goodness.
Humour // Sees the light side of life and helps people to laugh.
Fairness // Treats people fairly and advocates for their rights.
Persistence/Determination // Focuses on goals and works hard to achieve them.
Honesty/Integrity // Speaks truthfully.
Bravery/Courage // Does not hide from challenging or scary situations.
Citizenship/Loyalty // Stays true to family and friends through difficult times.
Wisdom/Perspective // Can see things from different angles.
Social intelligence // Aware of the needs of others.
Hope/Optimism // Expecting a good future.
Generosity/Kindness // Gives freely of their time and possessions.
Enthusiasm/Vitality // Has lots of energy and excitement for life.
Self-control // Controls desires and sticks to decisions.
Creativity // Thinks of many different ways to solve challenges.
Love of learning // Likes to learn new things.
Forgiveness // Can move on and not hold a grudge, giving others a second chance.
Love/Caring // Likes to help others.
Leadership // Helps the group meet their goals.
Humility/Modesty // Not seeing themselves as more special than others.
Prudence/Being careful // Thinks through the best way to do things.
Spirituality // Believes in a higher meaning or purpose.
Gratitude // Is thankful for what they have.
Curiosity // Keen to explore and discover the world.
Open mindedness // Is not biased or judgmental.

* Source: Level 9 and 10 – Resilience, Rights and Respectful Relationships, Published by Department of Education and Training. Melbourne, April 2018. © State of Victoria (Department of Education and Training) 2016

// NATIONAL WELLBEING HUB

The national Student Wellbeing Hub, developed by Education Services Australia for the federal Department of Education and Training, offers help and advice for teachers, parents and students. It covers topics such as healthy minds and bodies, bullying, diversity, relationships, making choices and online safety.
// SEE www.studentwellbeinghub.edu.au

Community

ONE IN, ALL IN

A strong sense of community can help young people feel engaged and supported.

// RESPECT TIPS

ENCOURAGING RESPECTFUL BEHAVIOUR IN TEENAGERS
- Take time to actively listen.
- Set clear rules about behaviour.
- Follow up broken rules calmly, firmly and consistently.
- Encourage self-reflection.
- Try to be a positive role model.
- Choose your battles.
- Take your child seriously.
- Let go of the wheel sometimes.
- Tackle problems in a positive way.
- Praise your child.
- Plan ahead for difficult conversations.
- Keep "topping up" your relationship with fun times and support.
- Share your feelings and be honest.
- Learn to live with mistakes.
- Look for ways to stay connected
- Respect your child's need for privacy.
- Encourage a sense of belonging.
- Keep promises.
- Have realistic expectations.
- Look for the funny side of things.

For more information visit //
raisingchildren.net.au, the Australian parenting website

Young people will always push boundaries, but those boundaries need to be set and enforced.

Adults must also model ethical behaviour, call out bad behaviour and educate children and young people about the importance of respect.

ROLE MODELS

All adults are potential role models for the young people they interact with, whether they are a sports coach, a school teacher or just a neighbour who joins in games of street cricket.

High profile sportspeople are also role models and can set a good example.

For example, the coach of Australian rules football club Collingwood, Nathan Buckley, was widely praised after the 2018 AFL Grand Final for physically comforting his sons and his players following the team's five-point loss.

This sent a message that it was OK to show your emotions and to offer a comforting hug.

BENEFITS OF COMMUNITY

The Australian Government's Head to Health mental health program highlights the benefits of connecting with the community and provides resources to help people become involved. (www.headtohealth.gov.au)

Head to Health quotes research that shows social support can protect the mental wellbeing of children and teenagers.

It has also found that community connection via peer groups leads to fewer behavioural issues.

"Being part of a community can have a positive effect on mental health and emotional wellbeing," it says.

"Community involvement provides a sense of belonging and social connectedness. It can also offer extra meaning and purpose to everyday life."

A study by the University of Sydney's Faculty of Education and Social Work and the Australia Council for the Arts also found that

// Source raisingchildren.net.au, the Australian parenting website

engagement in the arts benefitted students in the classroom and in life.

Students who are involved in the arts had higher school motivation, engagement in class, self-esteem, and life satisfaction. (www.australiacouncil.gov.au)

BREACHING THE STANDARDS

What happens when community leaders behave badly?

Experts have expressed concern that the sort of lying and bullying behaviour practised by US President Donald Trump filters into the community.

Counsellor Rosemary K.M. Sword and psychology expert Philip Zimbardo wrote two articles for *Psychology Today* about President Trump's behaviour (www.psychologytoday.com).

In early 2017, they noted an increase in school bullying because of Trump's rhetoric. By early 2018, this had expanded to include religious and racial bullying by adults as well as misogyny, sexual assault and other socially unacceptable behaviour.

YOUNG PEOPLE ARE ENGAGED

Young people are more politically engaged than people give them credit for, but their contributions are often undervalued, Deakin University research has found.

The study found most young people were not democratically disengaged but engaged in "off the radar" ways such as youth volunteering and social enterprise work.

When they did engage in social protest or unrest, they were often portrayed as democratically deviant and dangerous.

Researcher Dr Rosalyn Black said young Australians tended to shy away from representative bodies and big institutions such as the mainstream political parties.

Instead, they opted for more cause-based or issue-based politics and local engagement.

"There is a desire among many young people to make an active contribution and to have their voices and actions taken seriously by those in power," she says.

"But negative attitudes towards young people's civic engagement are devaluing the scope of their contribution – their desire to take part is being treated tokenistically and dismissed."

TAKING A STAND

Young people locally and globally are taking a stand against sexism, inequality and injustice, with social media giving them a voice to tackle the world's problems.

A high-profile example followed the 2018 shootings at Marjory Stoneman Douglas High School in Parkland, Florida, where a former student killed 17 students and staff and injured 17 others.

Rather than simply grieve, the victims' friends and families got vocal. They founded the *March for our Lives* movement that sparked huge anti-gun protests throughout the USA.

In Australia, young people found their voice in protests against political inaction on climate change that attracted thousands nationally.

Both movements came at a cost, with gun activists attacking the US students' credibility and some even accusing them of being "crisis actors".

In Australia, some criticised the student protesters for skipping school and Prime Minister Scott Morrison said he wanted less activism and more learning in class.

marchforourlives.com

// EMPOWERING YOUNG PEOPLE

By the time he turned 16 in November 2018, Dylan Storer (right) was an accomplished broadcaster, aspiring journalist and the youngest panellist to have appeared on Australia's *Q&A* TV show.

Partly inspired by a grandmother with strong political views, Dylan watched parliamentary *Question Time* on TV at five years old and began making voice recordings after he turned six.

Based in remote Fitzroy Crossing in WA, he is active on social media and has a radio show that covers a range of issues, including politics and the environment.

Dylan's *The Edge* program is broadcast locally via Wangki Yupurnanupurru Radio (www.wangki.org.au) and the Pakam Network (www.pakam.com.au), and through Melbourne-based SYN Nation (syn.org.au/syn-nation/).

He attends Fitzroy Valley District High School, which has a large Indigenous population, and has organised students to have their say on issues involving local authorities, such as the community group Fitzroy Valley Futures.

Dylan, who has three younger sisters, says it is important that young people have opportunities to engage with their community, develop respect for political processes and question them if needed.

Despite politics affecting them directly he says many students his age are politically agnostic, partly because the education system needs to better engage and empower them.

"There might need to be better civics education, so that people really understand things like that," he says.

Dylan's school offers a big picture curriculum centred on student interests, which has enabled him to explore his passion for journalism and political issues. He'd love others to do the same.

"If you can't even have a say over your own education how can you feel empowered?" he asks.

Dylan Storer is on Twitter //
@StorerDylan

Photo: supplied

DYLAN STORER ON ENGAGING YOUNG PEOPLE

- Better civics education.
- Voluntary voting for 16-18-year-olds.
- A "big picture" education that is more relevant to students' lives and interests.
- Giving students more say in their education.
- Engaging students in school and community programs.
- Empowering young people so that they feel they can have a say and make a difference.

Elderly

ELDER ABUSE: A GROWING PROBLEM

As society ages, respecting the elderly is more important than ever.

The abuse of older people is a growing problem and one that many families must face.

Property and elder law specialist Professor Eileen Webb likens elder abuse to domestic violence 20 years ago, before it became a public issue and the true extent was realised.

The University of South Australia Law School professor and Curtin University adjunct professor believes the problem is getting worse.

Eileen says an increasing number of elderly Australians are having experiences of physical, psychological, financial or sexual abuse, and those in institutions are even more vulnerable.

Severe neglect, such as social exclusion and inadequate living conditions, is also a form of abuse.

"This whole issue of social isolation and older people being neglected is a bit of a sleeper issue," Eileen says. "Neglect can have just as severe an impact.

"Part of the problem is the population is growing so quickly. There's more older people, so there's more opportunity for this abuse to occur. There's increased financial stresses on families.

"It's a bit like domestic violence 20 years ago. It's in the family, we don't talk about that, it's none of our business. It even seems to be more of a taboo because everyone thinks 'we all look after our elderly people'."

With many families facing financial and relationship issues, Eileen says it is important to consider the rights of elderly relatives and raise children to respect and empathise with them.

She says friendship and positive communication are important for healthy ageing and can minimise elder abuse. Parents can start by nurturing a child's relationship with elderly relatives and friends.

"It's really important right from when they're little to get these older people into their lives and make them part of their lives," Eileen says. "Spend time talking and learning. It's a two-way street."

> Grandchild: "Grandpa can you croak like a frog?"
> Grandpa: "Why?"
> Grandchild: "Because dad says when you croak we're going to Disneyland."

// ENCOURAGING RESPECT

- Watch yourself; kids watch and learn from your actions.
- Look out for older people. Don't intrude but help if needed e.g. mowing lawns.
- Ensure children spend time with elderly relatives, friends and neighbours.
- Value older people's experience and advice; encourage children to do the same.
- Ask about the past and what life was like when they were younger.
- Emphasise the importance of listening and respecting opinions. You don't have to agree but be polite and respectful.
- Visit nursing homes when it is safe to do so. Having kids there gives residents a real boost.

AVOIDING ELDER ABUSE

- Put the older person's best interests first.
- Remember it is their house and their money.
- Never assume "they don't need it" or "it's going to be mine eventually".
- If you have enduring Power of Attorney, know your responsibilities and abide by them.
- Use legal templates when dealing with financial issues.
- Encourage older people to disclose if they are being treated badly.
- Avoid situations that might financially disadvantage an older person, such as using their money to extend your home but not including them on the title.

ELDER ABUSE EXAMPLES

- An adult child with enduring Power of Attorney sells a parent's house without their consent, controlling the proceeds and forcing them into residential care.
- An elderly person lives with an adult child in substandard conditions, socially isolated and with basic needs neglected.

ASSISTANCE

// EMERGENCIES

Ambulance/Fire/Police // 000

Lifeline 24-hour counselling // 13 11 14

Suicide Call Back Service // 1300 659 467
www.directline.org.au

Kids Helpline // 1800 55 1800
www.kidshelpline.com.au

// PARENT HELP LINES

NSW // 1300 1300 52

Victoria // 13 22 89

South Australia // 1300 364 100

Queensland // 1300 301 300

Northern Territory // 1300 301 300

Tasmania // 1300 808 178

ACT // (02) 6287 3833

Western Australia // 1800 654 432

// FAMILY VIOLENCE

1800 Respect // National sexual assault, domestic family violence counselling service // Call 1800 737 732 // NRS: 1800 555 677 // Interpreter: 13 14 50 // https://www.1800respect.org.au/

ANROWS // Domestic violence resources // ANROWS does not provide emergency assistance or support services // https://www.anrows.org.au/get-support

Centres Against Sexual Assault (CASA) // Victoria // www.casa.org.au // Sexual assault crisis line, free call: 1800 806 292. Email: casa@thewomens.org.au

Domestic Violence Resource Centre // 8346 5200 (OH) // www.dvrcv.org.au

DV Connect // Queensland 24/7 // 1800 811 811 // www.dvconnect.org

Men's Referral Service // Confidential advice for men who may have overstepped the line // 1300 766 491 // www.ntv.org.au

No to Violence // Peak body for those working with men to end family violence in Victoria and New South Wales // www.ntv.org.au

Safe steps // Family violence response centre. Victoria only // safesteps.org.au // 1800 015 188 (24/7)

1800 RESPECT: The Australian Government's *Stop it at the Start* campaign // Aims to stamp out disrespect that can lead to physical and emotional abuse // www.respect.gov.au

The Victorian Government's Ending Family Violence: Delivering Change program // Working to transform the government's approach to family violence. w.www.vic.gov.au/familyviolence

Violent children – advice for parents // South Australian Education Department // www.education.sa.gov.au/parenting-and-child-care/parenting/parenting-sa/parent-easy-guides/violence-towards-parents-parent-easy-guide

// RELATIONSHIPS

Bullying. No Way // Anti-bullying advice // www.bullyingnoway.gov.au

Bursting the Bubble // Family advice "What's OK at home" // www.burstingthebubble.com

Family mediation and Dispute Resolution // Australian Government // https://www.familyrelationships.gov.au/separation/family-mediation-dispute-resolution

Family Relationships Advice Line // Australian Government // 1800 050 321 // www.familyrelationships.gov.au/talk-someone/advice-line

Family Relationship Centres // Australian Government // https://www.familyrelationships.gov.au/document/7201

It's Time We Talked // Advice about porn // www.itstimewetalked.com.au

Love: The good, the bad and the ugly // Relationship advice // www.lovegoodbadugly.com

MensLine Australia // Parenting and relationships 24/7 // Ph. 1300 789 978 // www.mensline.org.au

Relationships Australia counselling services // www.relationships.org.au

Tip sheets // https://www.relationships.org.au/relationship-advice/relationship-advice-sheets

Continues // Page 72

ASSISTANCE

From // **Page 71**

// YOUNG PEOPLE

Alannah & Madeline Foundation // Anti-bullying //
www.amf.org.au

Headspace // Youth mental health //
www.headspace.org.au

Kids Helpline // 1800 55 1800 // www.kidshelpline.com.au

Office of the eSafety Commissioner // www.esafety.gov.au

Mission Australia // Youth services //
www.missionaustralia.com.au

Raising Children Network // Australian parenting website //
raisingchildren.net.au

Rosie // Research-based information for girls //
www.rosie.org.au

ReachOut // Youth mental health and wellbeing //
www.reachout.com

The Line // Relationships advice for young people //
www.theline.org.au

Youth Beyond Blue // Beyond Blue's youth program //
www.youthbeyondblue.com

// LGBTIQ+

Minus18 // www.minus18.org.au

Intersex Human Rights Association // www.ihra.org.au

National LGBTI Health Alliance // www.lgbtihealth.org.au

National LGBTI Health Alliance knowledge hub //
https://lgbtihealth.org.au/hub/

PFLAG // Parents, Family and Friends of Lesbians and Gays //
www.pflagaustralia.org.au

QLife // 1800 184 527 // www.qlife.org.au

Rainbow Network // LGBTIQ youth //
www.rainbownetwork.com.au

Safe Schools Coalition Australia //
www.safeschoolscoalition.org.au

Star Observer // Lists many support services //
www.starobserver.com.au

Transcend // Transgender support //
www.transcendsupport.com.au

The Gender Centre // www.gendercentre.org.au

Transgender Victoria // www.transgendervictoria.com

Zoe Belle Gender Collective // www. zbgc.org.au

// INDIGENOUS

AMS Aboriginal Medical Service and other health services //
http://www.bettertoknow.org.au/AMS.html

Australian Government Indigenous services //
www.indigenous.gov.au

National Aboriginal Community Controlled Health Organisation (NACCHO) // www.naccho.org.au

Relationships Australia // Indigenous services //
https://www.relationships.org.au/what-we-do/services/aboriginal-and-torres-strait-islander-people-and-their-families

// MENTAL HEALTH

Anxiety Recovery Centre Victoria // (has links to other states) //
www.arcvic.org.au

Be You // Beyond Blue // beyou.edu.au

The Black Dog Institute // www.blackdoginstitute.org.au

headspace // 1800 650 890 //
www.headspace.org.au or www.eheadspace.org.au

Mind Australia // 1300 286 463 // www.mindaustralia.org.au

Mind Health Connect // For parents //
www.mindhealthconnect.org.au/parenting

National LGBTI Health Alliance // www.lgbtihealth.org.au

Parent Guides // parentguides.com.au/mental-health-101/

ReachOut // Youth support // www.reachout.com

Sane Australia // Mental health support // 1800 18 7263 //
www.sane.org

// SEXUALITY

Dr Marie (Marie Stopes International) // Reproductive support //
www.mariestopes.org.au // 1300 866 130

Family Planning Victoria // Reproductive support //
www.fpv.org.au

Kotex site for girls // Puberty advice //
www.ubykotex.com.au/puberty

Scarleteen // Sex education // www.scarleteen.com

Melbourne Sexual Health Centre // 9341 6200 // 1800 032 017
www.mshc.org.au

Parent Guides // parentguides.com.au/sex101

ReachOut // Relationships and sexuality information //
www.reachout.com

The Royal Women's Hospital // Sex and sexuality //
www.thewomens.org.au/health-information/sex-sexuality

The Women's Health Information Centre // 1800 442 007 //
8345 3045 // www.thewomens.org.au

// GENERAL ADVICE & INFORMATION

Australian Institute of Family Studies // www.aifs.gov.au

Good Sports // Reducing reliance on alcohol and other drugs in sport // www.goodsports.com.au

Health Direct services directory // www.healthdirect.gov.au

Health on the Net // Health information //
www.healthonnet.org

Law Stuff // Legal advice and responsibilities //
www.lawstuff.org.au

Learning Potential // Helping kids learn //
www.learningpotential.gov.au

Student Wellbeing Hub // Wellbeing advice and information //
www.studentwellbeinghub.edu.au

This girl can // VicHealth participation program //
www.vichealth.vic.gov.au/programs-and-projects/this-girl-can-vic

Victorian Government Better Health Channel //
www.betterhealth.vic.gov.au

Women's and Children's Health Network // www.cyh.com

***PARENT GUIDES* IS A REGISTERED CHARITY**
To purchase booklets or for school bundles contact;
Eileen Berry // 0407 542 655
Or visit // parentguides.com.au
Copyright Parenting Guides Ltd   ABN 786 2129 8093

Parent Guides // Keeping Your Children Safe

Young people have never had so many communication tools, yet communicating with them is as tricky as ever. Our Parent Guide content is transparent, trustworthy and relevant. Talented, like-minded researchers, editors, experts and case studies create evidence-based guides with the latest information. We want to champion change, and minimise and prevent harm.

 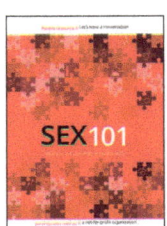

Parent Guide packages for schools // 500 Resources $3,975 // 250 Resources $2,375 // 200 Resources $2,100 // 150 Resources $1,725
Prices are per edition. Contact us for parent events or custom publishing. Parenting Guides Ltd is a not-for-profit organisation.

Website // www.parentguides.com.au   Phone // 0407 542 655   Email // eileen@parentguides.com.au

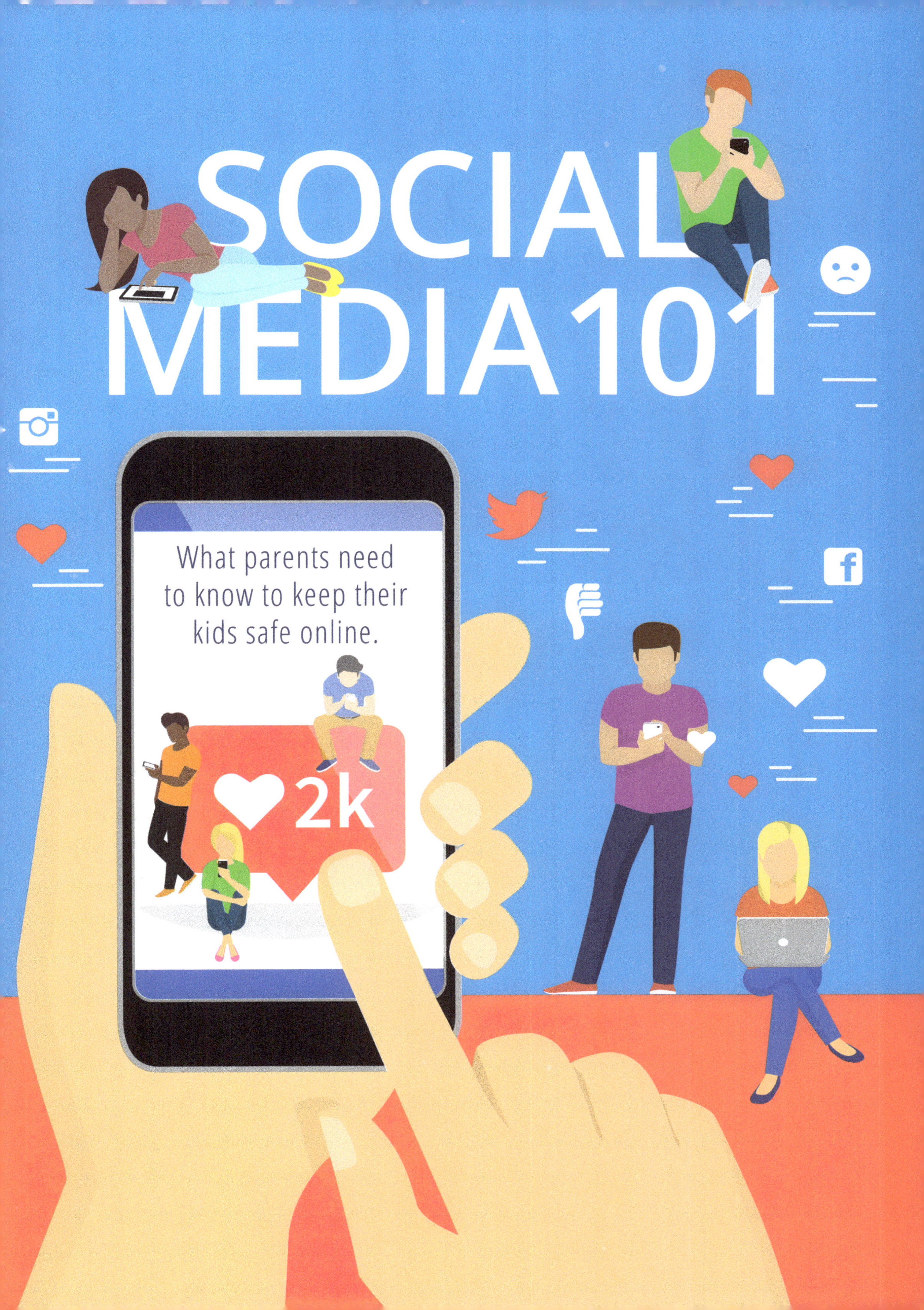
SOCIAL
MEDIA 101
What parents need
to know to keep their
kids safe online.
2k

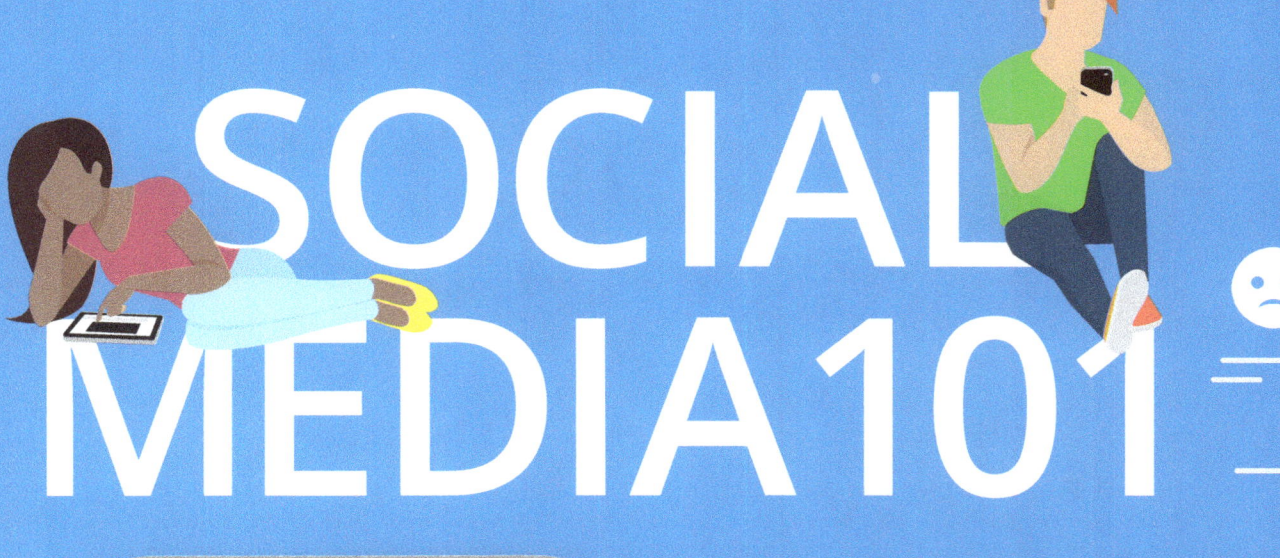

TEEN USE

Young Australians go online to be entertained, to communicate, to search for information and to simply browse.

There's no doubt that teenagers live in a digital and highly connected world. In many households they are online from the moment they wake until they go to bed – or until frustrated parents confiscate their smartphones and tablets.

The latest statistics from the Office of the eSafety Commissioner and the Australian Communications and Media Authority show just how prevalent the online world has become in the day-to-day lives of Aussie teenagers.

The Aussie teens and kids online report found 82 per cent of teenagers had been online in the past four weeks. Teenage girls and teens living in cities were more likely to be using the internet.

Around 83 per cent of teenagers go online at least three times a day and most are using their mobile phone to do so.

They are also streaming videos from YouTube and TV – 64 per cent do this. Research and browsing, sending emails and social networking are also popular online activities. Websites with videos, movies, games or music accounted for 56 per cent of teenagers' online browsing time, the report found.

The facts and figures make for interesting reading – and highlight how important it is for parents to keep an eye on what their children are doing online and where they are hanging out in cyberspace.

SCREEN TIME AND KIDS *****

- Most Australian children across all age groups exceed national screen time guidelines.
- Parents who have high screen use levels are more likely to report having children with high screen-use levels.
- Almost all (94%) Australian teenagers, 67% of primary school-aged children and 36% of pre-schoolers have their own mobile screen-based device.
- Three in four teenagers (78%) and one in six primary school-aged children have social media accounts.
- Almost half of all teenagers (46%) reported using social media every day. They also watched TV and videos (40%), did homework (39%), played electronic games (33%) and did video chat (20%).
- More than a third (37%) of primary school-aged children and 21% of pre-schoolers are playing electronic games almost every day.
- Half of toddlers and pre-schoolers use screen based devices on their own.
- Almost two thirds (62%) of parents report family conflict due to screen-based device use.
- Parents say one in five (19%) of teenagers have experienced online bullying.
- Almost half (43%) of all children regularly use screen-based devices at bedtime and one in four (26%) of them are reported to have screen-related sleep problems.

// WHAT DO TEENAGERS USE THE INTERNET FOR?**

All statistics are percentages for teenagers aged 14 to 17 years.

- ENTERTAINMENT // 90
- COMMUNICATION // 85
- RESEARCH & INFORMATION // 60
- BROWSING & SURFING // 55
- BLOG & ONLINE // 50 Communities
- BUY/SELL/SHOP // 25 Non-transactional
- BANKING/FINANCE // 20 Non-transactional
- BUY/SELL/SHOP // 15 Transactional
- BANKING/FINANCE // 10 Transactional

ENTERTAINMENT VS SHOPPING

Teenagers are more likely to use the internet to entertain themselves – 90 per cent use it for this reason, compared to 75 per cent of adults who go online for entertainment. But adults are more likely than teens to use the internet to carry out transactions such as shopping, selling or banking.

Parents who have high screen use levels are more likely to have kids who do the same

- More than half of parents of teenagers and a third of parents of children aged under six do not limit the amount of time spent or type of content their children access on screens.

---

* Source: Telstra and ACMA Aussie teens and kids online snapshot report, Roy Morgan Australia July 2015 Australian Mobile Owners research, Australian Child Health Poll (The Royal Children's Hospital Melbourne), Office of the eSafety Commissioner ** Source: ACMA Aussie Teens Online report – Nielsen Online Ratings. *** Source: Office of the Children's eSafety Commissioner for period covering April 2015 and Nielsen Online. **** State of play—Youth, kids and digital dangers, Office of the eSafety Commissioner, 2018. ***** Screen time and kids: What's happening in our homes? The Australian Child Health Poll, Royal Children's Hospital, 2017

HOW DO AUSTRALIAN TEENAGERS ACCESS THE INTERNET?**

Teenagers aged 14 to 17 years.

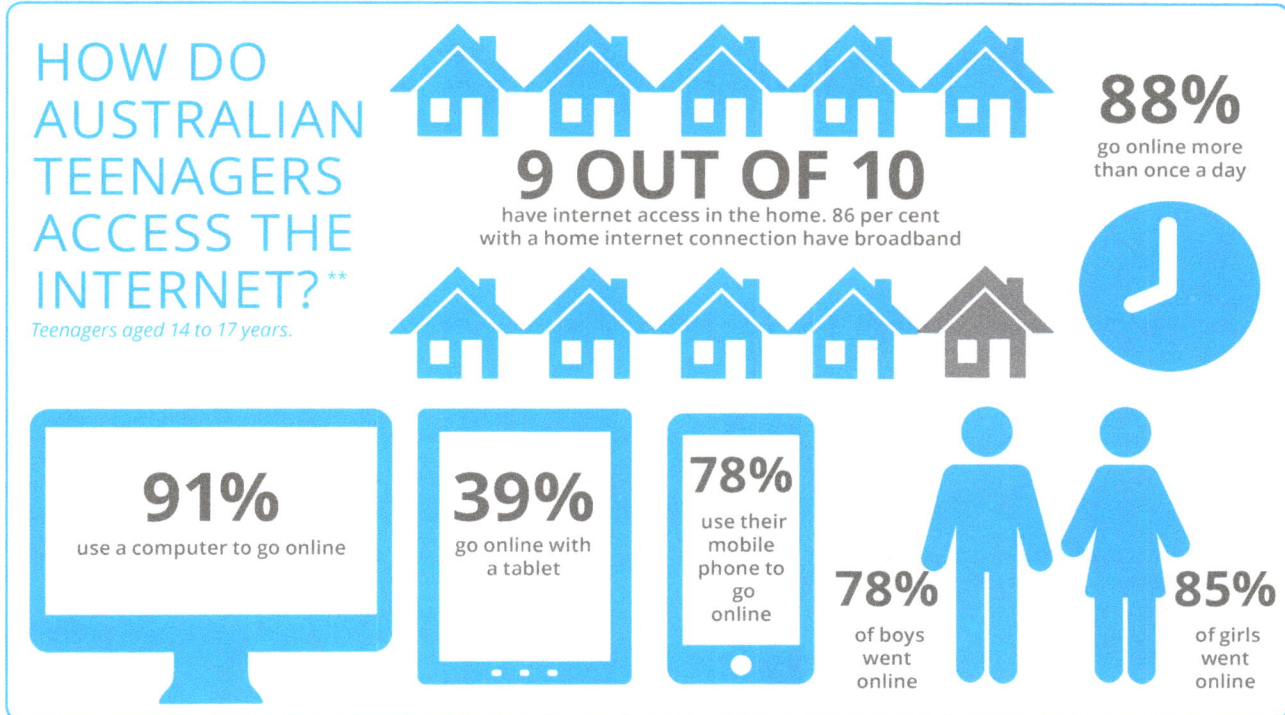

9 OUT OF 10 have internet access in the home. 86 per cent with a home internet connection have broadband

88% go online more than once a day

91% use a computer to go online

39% go online with a tablet

78% use their mobile phone to go online

78% of boys went online

85% of girls went online

// WHAT ONLINE CHANNELS DO TEENAGERS ACCESS AND WHEN?

TOP 5 ONLINE CHANNELS****
Percentage of teenagers who visit online channels.

YOUTUBE	FACEBOOK	INSTAGRAM	SNAPCHAT	*GOOGLE+
86%	**75%**	**70%**	**67%**	**29%**

EACH CHANNEL IS AN UMBRELLA FOR A NUMBER OF SITES

YouTube // User-generated and professional media video content that can be viewed on the website, via apps or embedded in third party content.
Facebook // Facebook platform of profiles, pages, apps, games and associated websites.
Instagram // Social media platform of photos, videos and stories.
Snapchat // Multimedia messaging app.
Google // Google+, Google Search, Gmail, Chrome, Google Maps, Google Earth and other Google services and products.

* *Google+ has since been discontinued in 2019.*

TIME OF DAY ONLINE***
Easy smartphone access means teens are online more often, across a broader range of times. From 2011 to 2015, the percentage online between 10pm and midnight almost doubled, and doubled from midnight to 7am.

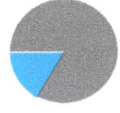
27% 07:00 - 08:59

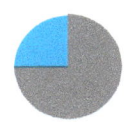
27% 09:00 - 11:59

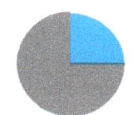
35% 12:00 - 14:59

49% 15:00 - 16:59

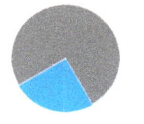
74% 17:00 - 19:59

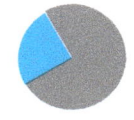
28% 20:00 - 21:59

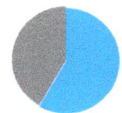
8% 00:00 - 06:59

// RESOURCES

- **Teenagers Who Won't go to Sleep //** Dr Paul Jeffrey
  https://audioboom.com/posts/7347524-teenagers-who-wont-go-to-sleep-dealing-with-difficult-sleep-habits
- **Conversations Podcast //** How the iPhone rewrote the teenage brain // David Gillespie
  https://www.abc.net.au/radio/programs/conversations/david-gillespie-2019/10986686
- **Parental as Anything //** Screen time – how much is too much // Maggie Dent
  https://www.abc.net.au/radio/programs/parental-as-anything-with-maggie-dent/screen-time-how-much-is-too-much/11138188
- **Sleep Shack //** an online self-help program // http://www.sleepshack.com.au/
- **Sleep Health Foundation //** tips and resources // http://www.sleephealthfoundation.org.au

© Parenting Guides Ltd

WEB WEAVERS

Never before have we been so connected ... to our devices.

SOCIAL MEDIA
Young people use Instagram to post photos and videos, follow friends, influencers and celebrities, and message each other. They also enjoy Snapchat (sending temporary content) and TikTok (short form mobile videos). Facebook is largely used for chatting and creating events.

VARIOUS APPS
With apps for almost every aspect of life, teens like to use them for communicating, playing games, listening to music and ordering food, clothes and services such as Uber.

WATCHING YOUTUBE VIDEOS
From funny cats to music clips, pranks and home-made films, YouTube is still a big hit.

STREAMING SERVICES
These are popular for watching TV series and movies.

TEXTING, MESSENGER AND OTHER COMMUNICATION PLATFORMS
Many young people prefer to message each other than talk.

VIDEO CHAT ON FACETIME OR ZOOM
Most apps have a video messaging service, which teenagers use to speak to each other and older relatives.

BUYING STUFF & CONCERT TICKETS
Online shopping is second nature, and many do it on their phones.

CREATING SPOTIFY PLAY LISTS AND LISTENING TO OTHERS'
Spotify play lists are a popular way of sharing and listening to music of all types.

WATCHING eSPORTS
Growing in popularity, eSports involves professional gaming tournaments that are generally live streamed.

GAMING
Most young people play online games, some suitable and others not so suitable, so parents need to keep an eye on them.

GAMBLING
Online gambling is restricted to those over 18, but some access it earlier.

GEN Y & Z DIGITAL HABITS *since 2000*

YEAR	TECH	MEME	NEW JOBS
2000	• USB flash drives • Nokia 3310		
2001	• Wikipedia • iPod		• Digital Records Manager • Sustainability Officer
2003	• Myspace • Skype	Badger video	• Data Visualisation Designer • Blogger
2004		Charlie the Unicorn	• Big Data Analyst
2005	• YouTube	Chuck Norris Facts	
2006	• Facebook opens to the public • Twitter	Potter Puppet Pals	• App Developer • Social Media Marketer
2007	• Dropbox • Apple TV • iPhone	Charlie bit my Finger	
2008	• Spotify	David after Dentist	• Autonomous Vehicle Technical • Medical Nanotechnologist
2009	• WhatsApp	JK Wedding Dance	
2010	• iPad • Instagram • Facetime	Photo-Bombing	
2011	• Siri	Planking	• UX manager • Cyber Security Professional
2012	• 1Billion active Facebook users • GoProHERO3	Gangnam Style	• Blockchain Developer
2013	• 3D printers	The Fox	
2014	• Google Glass	Icebucket Challenge	• Robotics Technician
2015	• Apple Watch	Blue & Black / White & Gold	• JAV Operator
2016	• Tesla Powerwall	Bottle Flip	• Virtual Reality Engineer • Workplace Concierge
2017	• Fidget Spinner • Fortnite	The Dab	
2018	• Smart Speakers • TikTok	Floss Dance	• Professional Organiser • Wellbeing Manager
2019	• Air-Pods	10-year Challenge	

ABS, McCrindle, cb, 2019

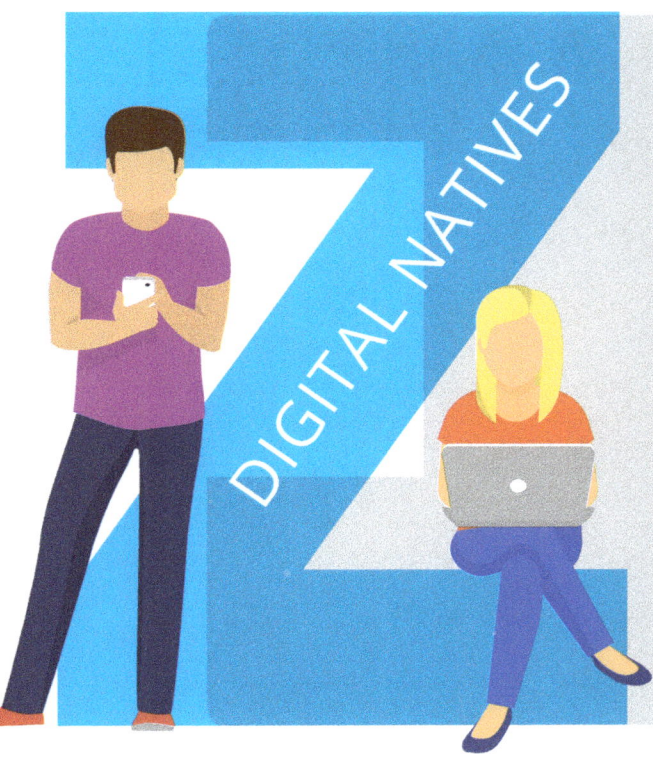

DIGITAL NATIVES

GEN Z ONLINE (BORN 1995-2009)

THE FIVE KEY TRAITS OF GEN Z ARE:
1. Digital **2.** Global **3.** Social **4.** Mobile **5.** Visual

Gen Z are digital integrators, says a 2019 McCrindle Research report.

"They have integrated technology seamlessly into their lives. Having used it from the youngest age, it is almost like the air they breathe, permeating all areas of their lifestyle and relationships.

"Gen Z live in an open-book environment. They are just a few clicks away from any piece of information. They connect in a borderless world – across countries and cultures. They communicate in a post-literate community where visuals and videos get the most cut-through.

"Gen Z are highly intuitive and confident, unaided users of digital technology. They are too young to remember its arrival. They have grown up with and, in many cases, have been significantly socialised by screen-based devices."

Source: Understanding Generation Z, by McCrindle Research Pty Ltd, 2019

TAKING A GAMBLE

Research has found that some teenagers who play gambling-like games online are more likely than others to illegally access gambling sites.

Gambling-like games, where no real money is won or lost, and micro-transactions for chance-based items in popular video games are of increasing concern.

A 2019 Australian Institute of Family Studies paper found that many popular online multiplayer games, such as Overwatch and Counter-Strike, offer a variety of virtual items (e.g. more powerful weapons) on top of standard game features.

"Players can obtain these items either through game play (i.e. winning or scoring), trading them with other players, or via in-game purchases of 'loot boxes' for real or in-game currency (Cleghorn & Griffiths, 2015)," the researchers found.

"The widespread availability of loot boxes in modern video games has led to questions over whether they should be regulated as a form of gambling (Griffith, 2018), especially given findings from recent research that found that the more money an adult video game player spent buying loot boxes, the more likely they were to be classified as experiencing gambling problems (Zendle, McCall, Barnett, & Cairns, 2018)."

Around one in four boys (24%) and one in seven girls (15%) aged 16-17 have played gambling-like games in the past 12 months. Boys played them more often than girls, but only 5% of boys and 2% of girls played weekly or more often.

The percentage of 16–17-year-olds who reported having spent money on at least one gambling activity in the past 12 months was significantly higher among those who had also played gambling-like games during that time.

Three out of 10 boys and one in five girls who had played gambling-like games in the past 12 months had also spent money on gambling during that time.

"These results support the theory that, for teenagers, playing gambling-like games may increase the likelihood of transitioning to commercial gambling in the future," the authors found.

GAMBLING AND 16-17 YEAR OLDS

- Despite being illegal, one in six 16–17-year-olds reported having gambled in the past year.
- More boys than girls reported having gambled on private betting, sports betting and poker.
- Although 65% of parents reported having gambled at least once in the past year, the majority (around 90%) were non-problem gamblers.
- Boys who had either been the victim or perpetrator of bullying at school were more likely to report having gambled.
- At age 16–17, around one in four boys (24%) and one in seven girls (15%) reported having played gambling-like games in the past 12 months.
- Teenagers who engaged in risky behaviours such as smoking and drinking, or had friends who smoked or drank alcohol, were more likely to report having gambled.

Source: Gambling activity among teenagers and their parents, by Diana Warren and Maggie Yu, Australian Institute of Family Studies, 2019.

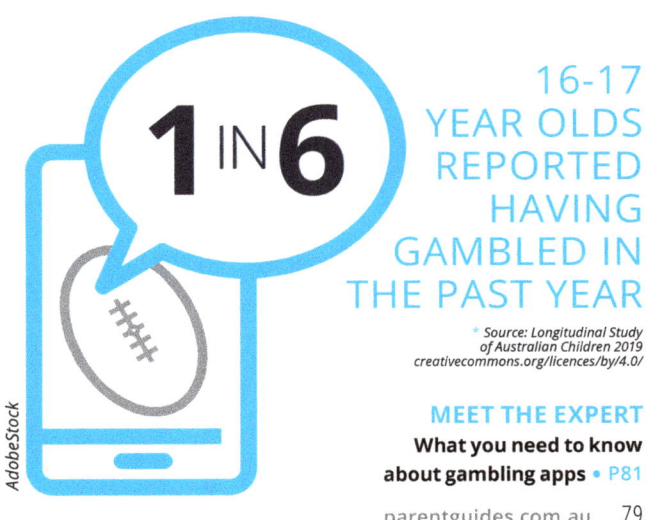

1 IN 6 16-17 YEAR OLDS REPORTED HAVING GAMBLED IN THE PAST YEAR

Source: Longitudinal Study of Australian Children 2019 creativecommons.org/licences/by/4.0/

MEET THE EXPERT
What you need to know about gambling apps • P81

LIFE'S A GAMBLE

A small but worrying number of boys and girls start gambling before they turn 18, and some of them develop problems.

Between 0.2 and 4.4 per cent of Australian adolescents are already problem gamblers.

Research shows that problem gambling risk factors can be related to socio-demographic, personality, psychosocial, substance abuse, gambling, peer, school, and family factors.

Some of these common risk factors include being male, low socio-economic status, extraversion, non-conformity, impulsivity, sensation seeking, undercontrolled temperament, depressive symptoms, anxiety, impaired coping, life stress, ADHD, substance use, risk-taking, antisocial behaviour, violence, exposure to gambling, peer pressure, school difficulties and family problems.

Deakin University School of Psychology Lecturer Dr Stephanie Merkouris says parents and carers can reduce the risk by talking to young people, looking for problems, limiting internet use and thinking about family attitudes towards gambling and gambling-related activities.

Go to // deakin.edu.au
Gamblers Help telephone line // 1800 858 858
Gamblers Help youth telephone line // 1800 262 376
Online support // www.gamblinghelponline.org.au
Raising children // www.raisingchildren.net.au/articles/gambling.html

HOW DO I SPOT GAMBLING PROBLEMS?
- Sudden changes in the amount of money your child has;
- Changes in sleep pattern;
- Changes in mood;
- School absences or falling marks at school;
- Decreased social activities and friends (or complete withdrawal);
- Preoccupation with: sports, internet, odds, video arcades, simulated gambling apps and games;
- Secrecy about gambling or denial.

PROTECTIVE FACTORS FOR YOUTH GAMBLING PROBLEMS
- Female gender;
- Adaptive coping strategies;
- Emotional Intelligence;
- Well-being;
- Self-monitoring;
- Personal competence;
- Resilience;
- Interpersonal skills;
- Social competence;
- Social support;
- Social bonding;
- School connnectedness;
- Understanding of randomness;
- Parental monitoring;
- Family cohesion

// YOUNG PEOPLE & GAMBLING

WHAT ARE THEY GAMBLING ON?

GAMBLING ACTIVITY	Never	At least once	Once a month or more often
Scratch tickets / lottery	52%	43%	3.6%
Card games (home/school)	58%	30%	10.5%
Horse or dog racing (TAB)	78%	19%	1.8%
Sports	81%	14%	3.3%
Horse or dog racing (racetrack)	85%	12%	1.0%
Poker machines	92%	6%	1.0%
Internet	93%	4%	1.8%
Table/cards (casino)	94%	3%	1.1%

WHO ARE THEY GAMBLING WITH?

GAMBLING ACTIVITY	Alone	Parents	Siblings	Other Relatives	Friends
Scratch tickets/lottery	13%	60%	13%	11%	3%
Sports	16%	34%	6%	8%	35%
Horse or dog racing (TAB)	6%	62%	13%	11%	23%
Horse or dog racing (racetrack)	3%	55%	11%	20%	35%
Internet	41%	12%	3%	12%	41%
Table/cards (casino)	12%	4%	16%	4%	52%
Poker machines	3%	24%	16%	8%	57%
Card games (home/school)	7%	20%	25%	20%	67%

Dowling, N., Jackson, A. C., Thomas, S. A., & Frydenberg, E. (2010). Children at risk of developing problem gambling. Melbourne: Gambling Research Australia.

// Dr Stephanie Merkouris is a Lecturer in Psychology at Deakin University School of Psychology

Profile // Dr Wayne Warburton

THE PROFESSOR

Dr Wayne Warburton says statistics suggest that in most high school classrooms in Australia, one teenager would have a gambling problem.

"Studies of Australian youth gambling show 3 to 4 per cent of teenagers have a problem – in adults it's around 0.5 to 1 per cent of the population. Teenagers may be more susceptible to problem gambling because the adolescent brain is still 'under construction', but it's not an obvious problem. Most parents wouldn't know their teenager was having difficulties because teenagers tend to be very reluctant to admit to gambling – it's illegal under the age of 18 and teenagers don't want to get into trouble either for gambling or for the ways they may have obtained the money to gamble. They may also feel ashamed and not want their social network to know just how many people they have borrowed from.

"For many teenagers, a gambling problem begins online with an activity that isn't strictly gambling but gets them in the mindset to gamble. Many video games have a gambling component, and other games that simulate gambling (such as online 'slot machines') are commonly advertised on many social media sites.

"Online gambling games are programmed to make you win – it's almost impossible to lose. They groom you to believe you are going to win a lot of money gambling, that you are skilled at it, and such beliefs can promote gambling behaviour.

"Typically several of the top 10 iPhone gaming apps are casino-style games. You can spend as much as you want, but because they don't involve winning money, they're not 'gambling' so are unregulated. We know that kids access these sites and apps, and also play online video games that have a gambling component. Many games have gambling-like devices to progress, or skins that can be gambled online, or loot boxes that can be purchased. Interestingly, loot boxes were recently shown scientifically to have most of the same characteristics as gambling. Research also suggests that making in-app purchases for gambling-like activities is predictive of developing a gambling problem later.

"Parents need to know about gambling apps and simulated gambling and to realise that for some kids this will be a precursor to developing a gambling problem. And remember, kids can spend lots of money on these games before progressing to actual gambling. It's big money and a big industry.

"For some teenagers, gambling becomes a bigger part of their life and school becomes less and less important. Gambling becomes more important than friendships and family, and teenagers often start to lie about money and what they are doing with their time. Teenagers usually don't have access to large amounts of money so they may steal from parents, buy and sell things illegally, or use a stolen credit card.

"On a practical level, parents can keep internet-connected devices out of bedrooms and in public areas of their home. Use internet blocking devices that block pop-ups and invitations to gamble from coming up on screen. You can also use internet monitoring software, although your teenager won't think that's very cool!

"Because children/teenagers are reluctant to talk about gambling, even when they're in financial difficulty and are scared that their gambling is out of control, parents need to know how to talk with a teenager about it.

"Keep the conversation open. Talk about the traps but don't be judgmental. Explain that playing gambling-like games online and making in-app purchases increases the risk of developing a gambling problem. Educate them about the inflated win-rate of such games and the low chances of success in real gambling – the odds of winning a poker machine jackpot are 9.7 million to one. They have a greater chance of being struck by lightning ('just' 1.6 million to one). Help kids understand that these online games and apps are designed to suck them in – and they do a really good job."

Photo: Supplied

// REMOVE TEMPTATION

POPULAR INTERNET GAMBLING FILTERS
- GamBlock
- Betfilter

INTERNET MONITORING SOFTWARE
- Qustodio
- Norton Family
- Net Nanny
- Surfie (good for mobiles)

BETTING IN SPORT
Psychologist Jo Lamble shares some tips for starting a conversation:
- Make use of stories
- Learn how to listen so your children will talk
- Choose the right time
- Use some humour
- Tailor your message to their interests
- Leave them wanting more

OTHER HELPFUL RESOURCES
Australian Council on Children and the Media app reviews with clearly labelled gambling information //
childrenandmedia.org.au/app-reviews/
KidBet // kidbet.com.au
Gambler's Help Youthline (24/7) // 1800 262 376
Gambling Help Online // www.gamblinghelponline.org.au
Parent resources // www.responsiblegambling.vic.gov.au

// Dr Wayne Warburton is an Associate Professor of Developmental Psychology at Macquarie University.

WHAT YOU NEED TO KNOW ABOUT GAMING

Did you know 97 per cent of Australian homes with children have computer games?

A few years ago, a Russian teenager addicted to online gaming died after developing suspected deep-vein thrombosis. The 17-year-old had spent 22 consecutive days playing popular online game *Defense of the Ancients*.

He collapsed and died after developing a thrombosis, like those that passengers can suffer on long-haul flights. In the 18 months leading up to his death, investigators say the teenager spent about 6.5 hours a day playing online. During the days preceding his death, he had broken away from his computer screen only to eat and nap.

While this case may seem extreme, online games present another potential challenge for teenagers and parents, who need to become familiar with what their child is playing online, and with whom they are playing.

A 2018 report from the Office of the eSafety Commissioner found eight in 10 young people aged eight to 17 played games online in the 12 months to June 2017. The same report found online multiplayer gaming is very popular, with six in 10 young people playing these games.

Many online games include content and themes unsuitable for certain age groups. So games often come with age recommendations or ratings, similar to movie or film classifications. For example, *Call of Duty (CoD)* has an MA 15+ rating and contains strong themes and violence. *Clash of Clans*, a multiplayer game, is recommended for players over the age of 13.

Many games allow players to communicate through forums, chat and messaging services. In the interests of player safety, Activision, creators of *CoD*, recommend young people never share their password or give players they meet online their name, address, email address or school details. Computers and tablets should also have up-to-date security software to protect against viruses.

Supercell, owner of *Clash of Clans*, does not pre-screen or monitor all user content and recommends that players never share their login data or log into their account on someone else's device.

Parents should also be aware that some games allow players to purchase points, different versions of the game and game-related merchandise. The Office of the eSafety Commissioner found around 34 per cent of eight to 17-year-olds made an in-game purchase in the 12 months to June 2017. So find out whether your child is using money to play online.

The Office of the eSafety Commissioner lists a number of games and has comprehensive information on game content, who can play, how to protect personal information, how to report cyber-bullying or abuse and how to block your child spending money while playing online.

Go to // www.esafety.gov.au/esafety-information/games-apps-and-social-networking // www.videogames.org.au // www.instituteofgames.com
Watch // www.abc.net.au/7.30/content/2015/s4472277.htm

RISK FACTORS
- Withdrawn
- Nightmares
- Loss of interest
- Online friends vs real friends
- Anger about not being able to play

Find out more // internetsafeeducation.com // familyzone.com // eSafety.gov.au

// AT A GLANCE

Photo: iStock

GAMING AND YOUNG PEOPLE: A SNAPSHOT

76% of children under 18 play video games.
60% of parents play online games with their children in the same room.
81% of parents are familiar with controls on online games.
84% of parents say they have discussed playing safely online with their children.
48% of parents say they play online games with their children as a way of spending time with them.
77% of parents say they have rules about how long children can play games.
76% of parents have rules about games their child can play.

Digital Australia Report 2018 by Interactive Games & Entertainment Association

WHY KIDS ARE HOOKED ON FORTNITE

This game has been one of the most popular video games for children and young people in recent times.

The free version, *Fortnite: Battle Royale*, operates across Windows and Mac, Xbox and PlayStation. However, while the game itself is free, players can purchase outfits, weapons and other accessories to boost their chances of survival.

Fortnite pits players against other players around the world and the aim is to be the last person standing on a sometimes violent and hostile island inhabited by monsters and enemy figures.

On average, each game can last around 20 minutes, assuming your character doesn't get killed before that.

The Australian Council on Children and the Media says *Fortnite* is not recommended for children 12 years and under. Parental guidance is recommended for children aged 13 to 17.

Profile // Andrew Kinch

INTELLIGENT GAMING

Andrew Kinch is founder of GameAware. He says video games – in the right measure – can help young people meet some important psychological needs.

"Gamers have been stigmatised over the years. There used to be a time when people wouldn't admit to their friends that they played video games. Once an underground subculture, in 2017 these games were a $109 billion industry.

"Gamers often feel the need to become defensive when they're told that their passion is a waste of time. After that, anything that is true about the harms of excessive gaming is completely ignored. It's a polarised debate between those who play and those who blame video games as the cause of gaming disorders. The truth lies somewhere in the middle and is often complex.

"Gaming is a great form of entertainment, but we must be on top of our self-regulation skills, especially when the motivation to play is to escape real life. When gaming becomes a coping mechanism to seek relief from pain, it can become excessive and problematic. People can choose gaming to attempt to meet their needs. When you combine this with easy access and the game mechanics that entice players to keep coming back, you can see how an individual might be motivated to live in the virtual world.

"In my experience, video games hit three motivational needs for young people: competence, autonomy and relatedness.

"Competence is the feeling of mastery. Everyone wants to be good at something and video games allow you to become good at something quickly. If I want to be good at basketball it can take years – with video games, it takes months and you do it without breaking a sweat.

"Secondly, teenagers and children don't have a lot of autonomy in their lives. In a game, they have freedom over their own choices and can express themselves creatively. They can customise their characters and develop a second identity if they choose.

"Every multi-player game meets the third need, which is relatedness or social connection. When you play with other people – in a competitive or collaborative way – you feel part of something bigger than yourself. You are part of a gamer

Photo: Supplied

community. Gaming can allow kids to build self-confidence because the community is accepting of people from all walks of life and any age.

"I'd argue that you can't completely fulfill psychological needs through video games. Real life will always provide us with the opportunity to feel more fulfillment from competence, autonomy and social connection."

THREE THINGS YOU CAN TRY NOW

1 **Do a 10-day gaming challenge – go cold turkey and stay away from games and gaming culture.**
But parents can't just yank the Wi-Fi. It must be something the gamer decides to do to test the commonly spoken phrase – "I could stop if I wanted to, I just don't want to". The challenge is about helping a gamer help themselves. Even if they don't reach 10 days, you get information as to whether they can control themselves. However, three or four days in to the challenge, gaming's grip tends to be loosened!

2 **Parents need to play video games with their kids.**
Get coached and get a better understanding of the nuance in the games your child plays. Be a spectator from time to time to show interest. If you take your child to soccer and watch them play, they feel valued and it's the same if they see you are taking their gaming seriously. Take down defensive walls by getting involved. The conversation about gaming changes when parents are not considered the opposition.

3 **Set up social gaming sessions to be shoulder-to-shoulder with friends.**
When we game in the same room and play the same game, the dynamic is more exciting and provides a level of connection that online gaming isn't quite able to provide.

Andrew Kinch is founder of GameAware and developed Intelligent Gaming strategies to keep gaming healthy. www.gameaware.com.au

eSAFETY TIPS

Whether your child is the victim or the bully, help is never far away.

// FINDING CYBER-SAFETY HELP

Hundreds of websites and organisations offer help and advice for parents. A great starting point is the office of the eSafety Commissioner website – a central portal for cyber-safety information and resources for parents, carers, schools and children. Cybersmart resources, previously available on the Cybersmart website, are available through the eSafety Commissioner website (www.esafety.gov.au), as well as a complaints system to report cyber-bullying material targeted at Australian children.

The eSafety Commissioner also investigates illegal and offensive online material.

Online help and complaint links can be found at // **www.esafety.gov.au** or call Crime Stoppers on 1800 333 000.

HOW MANY KIDS ARE CYBER-BULLIED?

The Office of the eSafety Commissioner says one in 5 Australian young people reported being socially excluded, threatened or abused online. One in 5 (15% of kids, 24% of teens) admitted behaving in a negative way to a peer online — such as calling them names, deliberately excluding them, or spreading lies or rumours.

Resources // **https://www.esafety.gov.au/key-issues/cyberbullying**

WHAT DO GOOD ANTI-CYBER-BULLYING PROGRAMS INCLUDE?

Good school anti-cyber-bullying programs teach social skills and online etiquette with individual learning plans. They keep parents informed of, and involved in, cyber-bullying-prevention policies and prompt effective bystander behaviour by encouraging children to support others being victimised. It is important to establish a common language for discussing bullying and victimisation with young people so it has meaning to them. Involving young people in school policy development that encourages pro-social behaviour and bystander action is more likely to attract their support. Students must also understand that everyone has a right to feel safe at school and home.

COMMON MISTAKES BY PARENTS

Some parents overreact when their child is cyber-bullied and may remove access to technology, which can put children off confiding in them. Research suggests that children are less likely to tell adults about cyber-bullying if they think the adult will make things worse.

Parents should talk to their children about what cyber-bullying looks like before it happens and that it is not OK. They can plan what they will do together if it occurs. Parents should also make it clear that they will not tolerate their child cyber-bullying and encourage them to avoid negative conversations of any kind.

STAYING UP TO SPEED

Parents should learn about the technology that their kids use. They don't need to be experts but must understand what happens on the relevant sites, apps and games, whether the content is appropriate, what safety features they have and complaint mechanisms. Parents should walk through apps and websites with their child, checking age guidelines, looking at content, being honest about their feelings about it and giving the child their say. Open communication can protect against the impact of bullying and help put off potential bullies.

Parents sometimes don't check age guidelines for games, videos, websites and apps. These should be followed, regardless of what other parents allow. Don't be afraid to stand your ground. Many parents of younger children do not limit the Wi-Fi access of the apps and games, leaving children open to contact from others, which they may not be mature enough to manage.

Resources // **www.esafety.gov.au/parents**

> Good school cyber-bullying programs teach social skills and online etiquette with individual learning plans.

Photo: Thinkstock

// WHAT IF YOUR CHILD IS THE BULLY?

Don't overreact, but have consequences. All children make mistakes and need a chance to repair their errors.

A calm conversation is likely to have more impact than a heated argument, even if parents need to wait a day or so until they have calmed down.

It is helpful to raise the target's feelings, to help the perpetrator understand the hurt caused and help prevent a recurrence.

It is important not to become extremely angry with your child, despite your disappointment, as you need to model forgiveness and empathy for them to develop the social skills needed to prevent future bullying.

Photo: Thinkstock

// eSAFETY TIPS FOR PARENTS

YOUNG CHILDREN
- Closely monitor their internet use;
- Know how your child uses the internet and explore it with them;
- Teach them to tell a trusted adult if they feel uncomfortable about something they see;
- Have rules about what sites are appropriate, what is appropriate to post and telling a trusted adult before posting any personal information;
- Teach them online manners and to ignore and report negative messages;
- Consider filters and other tools to manage online access;
- Install and update anti-virus and other esecurity software; and
- Seek professional help if your child shows concerning changes in behaviour or mood.

OLDER CHILDREN
As well as the above general tips ...
- Talk to your child about personal information and how it can be used to locate them. They should never share passwords;
- Keep computers in a shared or visible place;
- If they use social networking, help them sign up safely, use privacy settings and decide how to choose "friends";
- Consider getting them to use avatars or usernames that don't identify them or provoke unwanted attention;
- Encourage them to use the same manners online as they would offline;
- Monitor their use and be alert for signs of overuse;
- Discuss cyber-bullying before it happens and have strategies prepared in case it does;
- Encourage them to report concerns to you;
- Discuss cyber-stalking and online grooming and encourage them to report any concerns to a trusted adult; and
- Educate them about their online reputation, e-security and appropriate downloading.

TEENAGERS
As well as the previous tips ...
- Stay involved with their use of technology and ask them to show you what they use and the sites they visit. If they agree, ask them to help you set up your own accounts to see how the sites work;
- Encourage them to use social-networking site privacy settings so that only their friends see their material;
- Remind them to create screen names that are not sexually provocative and do not reveal their gender, age, name or location;
- Encourage them to think before they post and ask themselves who might see or misread it;
- Ask them to think about images they upload of themselves to ensure they aren't risking or compromising their own or others' privacy;
- Advise them to keep online friends online and not meet unless in a public place during the day, possibly with a trusted adult;
- Encourage them to ignore negative messages, block abusive people, report them to site administrators and tell a trusted adult;
- Help them block and/or report bullies;
- Reassure them that you won't block their internet access if they are bullied;
- Encourage them to support friends involved in cyberbullying; and
- Advise them to check links sent through social media before clicking.

CYBER-BULLYING

Federal and state laws exist to protect potential victims and punish offenders.

Cyber-bullying is illegal, but working out what aspects are covered, and how, can be a challenge. Cyber-bullying and its related offences are covered by a range of state, territory and federal laws. Some jurisdictions have specific anti-bullying laws, while others use existing laws to prosecute cases. Regardless of whether a jurisdiction has specific cyber-bullying laws, related behaviours such as stalking, making threats and physical assault are generally covered by existing state and territory legislation.

// FEDERAL LAW

ENHANCING ONLINE SAFETY FOR CHILDREN ACT 2015

Passed in early 2015, the Enhancing Online Safety for Children Act established a Children's eSafety Commissioner, a complaints system for reporting cyber-bullying material aimed at an Australian child and a two-tiered system for rapid removal of cyber-bullying material from large social-media services.

In 2017 the role was expanded to include all Australians and under the revised Enhancing Online Safety Act 2015 is known as the Office of the eSafety Commissioner. The independent statutory office within the Australian Communications and Media Authority (ACMA) administers cyber-bullying complaints, promotes online safety, co-ordinates relevant Commonwealth department, authority and agency activities, conducts and oversees educational and community awareness programs, makes grants and advises the Communications Minister.

A person can lodge a complaint to the commissioner if they have reported the material to the specific social-media site first and did not receive an outcome. The commissioner has the power to investigate complaints into cyber-bullying and conduct investigations as he or she sees fit.

Among other things, the legislation provides for:
- Setting out the eSafety Commissioner's functions and powers;
- A complaints system for cyber-bullying material;

Photo: Thinkstock

// SOUND ADVICE

Unbullyable by Sue Anderson can be purchased online.
Australia's Youth-Driven Movement Against Bullying //
projectrockit.com.au/about or call 0435 150 280.
Body image movie *Embrace* //
www.youtube.com/watch?v=__2AayArYfs
Reach out // au.reachout.com

- A two-tiered scheme for the rapid removal from large social-media services of cyber-bullying material;
- A mechanism for the commissioner to give end-user notices to require a person who posts cyber-bullying material to remove the material, refrain from posting further material or apologise for posting the material; and
- Enforcement mechanisms.

Laws state by state // Page 88

Parent Guides // Keeping Your Children Safe

Young people have never had so many communication tools, yet communicating with them is as tricky as ever. Our Parent Guide content is transparent, trustworthy and relevant. Talented, like-minded researchers, editors, experts and case studies create evidence-based guides with the latest information. We want to champion change, and minimise and prevent harm.

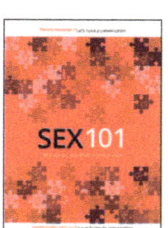

Parent Guide packages for schools // 500 Resources $3,975 // 250 Resources $2,375 // 200 Resources $2,100 // 150 Resources $1,725
Prices are per edition. Contact us for parent events or custom publishing. Parenting Guides Ltd is a not-for-profit organisation.

Website // www.parentguides.com.au Phone // 0407 542 655 Email // eileen@parentguides.com.au

// WHO ENFORCES CYBER-BULLYING LAWS?

Many forms of cyber abuse could be considered illegal under state or federal legislation. For example, under the Commonwealth Criminal Code Act 1995 ('the Act') it is an offence to menace, harass or cause offence, using a 'carriage service'.

It is also an offence under the Act to use a carriage service to make threats to kill or cause serious harm to a person, regardless of whether the person receiving the threat actually fears that the threat would be carried out.

These provisions could capture instances of menacing, harassing or offensive conduct and threats carried out using landlines, mobile phones (e.g. MMS, SMS) and the internet, including emails and social media. For example, using a mobile phone to repeatedly send offensive images to someone.

Most Australian states and territories also have laws covering stalking, blackmail, criminal defamation and various unlawful uses of technology. A number of jurisdictions have also passed laws creating offences for the threat to distribute, or distribution, of intimate images (image-based abuse).
Office of the eSafety Commissioner // **esafety.gov.au**

Photo: Thinkstock

THE PROCESS FOR REPORTING CYBER-BULLYING FOR UNDER-18s
- Collect evidence
- Report to the platform/site in which it occurred
- If not removed within 24 hours, then report to the Office of the eSafety Commissioner

More info // **www.esafety.gov.au/complaints-and-reporting/cyberbullying-complaints/i-want-to-report-cyberbullying**

CYBER-BULLYING AND THE AUSTRALIAN FEDERAL POLICE
- Due to the internet's borderless nature, unwanted contact, harassment or cyber-bullying can occur from anywhere.
- Schools and parents should become involved in the first instance, as they would with most "offline" bullying.
- Schools should have a cyber-bullying policy with sanctions for students who bully others during or outside school hours.
- Serious cyber-bullying or stalking cases can be reported to the Australian Cyber Security Centre's ReportCyber service (cyber.gov.au / cyber.gov.au/report).
- Through initiatives such as ThinkUKnow, the AFP works with state and territory police forces, Neighbourhood Watch Australasia and the private sector to educate about staying safe online.
- The AFP's High Tech Crime Operations Crime Prevention team presents at schools, junior sporting clubs and community groups about online risks and staying safe.

More info // **www.thinkuknow.org.au**

// THE AUSTRALIAN CYBER SECURITY CENTRE

Cybercrime can be quickly and easily reported online. The Australian Cyber Security Centre allows secure online reporting of online crimes through its ReportCyber service.

The Commonwealth, state and territory governments policing initiative also helps people to recognise and avoid common cybercrimes.

The ACSC educates and advises about common cybercrime, such as hacking, online scams, online fraud, identity theft and attacks on computer systems.

It also covers cyber-bullying, which can be reported if the actions are intended to make the victim feel fearful, uncomfortable, offended or harassed. Those being physically stalked or concerned about their safety should report to local police immediately.

Cyber-bullying or stalking involves someone engaging in offensive, menacing or harassing behaviour using technology. It can happen to people at any age, time and often anonymously.

Those being physically stalked or concerned about their safety should report to local police immediately.

Examples include:
- Posting hurtful messages, images or videos online;
- Repeatedly sending unwanted messages online;
- Sending abusive texts and emails;
- Excluding or intimidating others online;
- Creating fake social-networking profiles or websites that are hurtful;
- Nasty online gossip and chat; and
- Any other form of digital communication that is discriminatory, intimidating, intended to cause hurt or make someone fear for their safety.

More info // **www.cyber.gov.au**

STATE BY STATE

States have specific laws to protect their residents.

// VICTORIA

BRODIE'S LAW

Victoria's 2011 anti-bullying laws make serious bullying a crime punishable by up to 10 years in jail. Dubbed "Brodie's Law", they were introduced after Brodie Panlock, 19, suicided in 2006 after being bullied at work.

The move extended provisions in Victoria's Crimes Act 1958 to include behaviour that involves serious bullying. The offence of stalking, and therefore conduct that amounts to serious bullying, carries a maximum penalty of 10 years imprisonment. Brodie's Law applies to bullying anywhere in the community and on the internet.

Bullying can include threats and abusive and offensive words or conduct. Serious bullying may also include conduct or behaviour that is intended, or could reasonably be expected, to cause the victim of the bullying to engage in suicidal thoughts or thoughts or actions that involve self-harm.

> Bullying can include behaviour such as threats and abusive and offensive words or conduct.

SEXTING

In late 2014, Victoria introduced Australia's first "sexting" laws. They created offences of maliciously distributing or threatening to distribute intimate images of another person, and ensured young people engaging in non-exploitative "sexting" did not end up with criminal records or on the sex offenders' register.

The Crimes Amendment (Sexual Offences and Other Matters) Act 2014 created two summary offences of "distribution of an intimate image" and "threat to distribute an intimate image" in circumstances contrary to community standards of acceptable conduct. They cover the distribution of images of anyone aged under 18 and the distribution of images of adults without consent.

The distribution offence carries a penalty of up to two years in prison and the new offence of threatening to distribute carries a penalty of up to one year in prison.

Exceptions will ensure that those aged under 18 are not inappropriately prosecuted or added to the sex offenders' register for consensual, non-exploitative sexting. They do not apply if the image depicts a criminal offence such as a sexual assault, or if the person in the image does not consent to it being sent.

STALKING

Since the Victorian Crimes Act (1958) was widened in 2011 to include a range of bullying acts under the offence of stalking, the number of reported offences has risen. The amendments related to actions such as those expecting to cause mental or self-harm, making threats and using abusive or offensive words.

For more information visit // www.legalaid.vic.gov.au/find-legal-answers/sex-and-law/sexting-and-child-pornography

// SOUTH AUSTRALIA

Cyber-stalking is recognised under stalking in South Australian legislation. However, prosecution is rare. Cyber-bullying may be considered assault if the bully threatens to physically hurt the victim, and either there is a real possibility that the bully will act or is in a position to act and intends to do so. Cyber-bullying and trolling may also be defamatory.

Stalking has occurred when a person, on at least two occasions follows, loiters near the victim's home, interferes with their property, sends them offensive material, publishes offensive material, communicates in a way to make them fearful, keeps them under surveillance or acts in another way reasonably expected to cause apprehension or fear.

These acts must intend to cause serious physical or mental harm, serious apprehension or fear.

The maximum penalty is three years imprisonment for a basic offence and five for an aggravated offence.

STALKING

There has been concern over the inability of the police to intervene where a person "stalks" someone. Legislation has been enacted which makes stalking an offence [Criminal Law Consolidation Act 1935 (SA) s 19AA]. Behaviour defined as stalking includes:

- following another person
- loitering outside the home of another person or a place frequented by the other person
- entering or interfering with property in the possession of another person
- giving or sending offensive material to another person, or leaving it where it will be found by, given to or brought to the attention of the other person
- publishing or transmitting material by means of the internet or some other form of electronic communication in such a way that it will be found by, or brought to the attention of the family member
- communicating with the family member or other members of the family by way of mail, telephone (or associated technology), facsimile transmission or the internet or some other form of electronic communication
- keeping another person under surveillance
- acting in any other way that could reasonably be expected to arouse another person's apprehension or fear.

// QUEENSLAND

Cyber-bullying and sexting are both illegal in Queensland. Cyber-bullying is a crime if it involves using the internet or a mobile phone to make threats, stalk, menace, harass or seriously offend someone. This can include sending offensive messages or making posts that make someone feel extremely angry, outraged, humiliated or disgusted. Threats may include trying to intentionally frighten, intimidate or annoy someone by threatening to hurt them or enter or damage a property,

It is a crime in Queensland to share an intimate image of someone without their consent in a way that could reasonably cause distress to the other person. A person under 16 cannot legally give consent. It is also illegal to threaten to share an intimate image without the pictured person's consent. This applies to threats made to the person in the image, or threats to anyone else. This is the case even if the image doesn't exist.

If the person in the image is under 16, the law says it is never OK to share that image. The maximum penalty for sharing or threatening to share an intimate image without consent is three years in prison. The courts can also order people who share the images – or even threaten to share the images – to take reasonable action to remove, destroy or delete them.

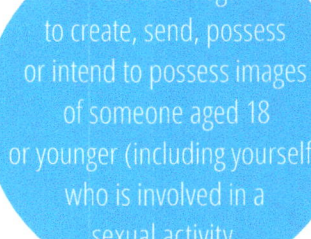

It is also illegal to create, send, possess or intend to possess images of someone aged 18 or younger (including yourself) who is involved in a sexual activity.

Find out more //
legalaid.qld.gov.au.
Queensland sexting laws // **www.qld.gov.au/law/crime-and-police/types-of-crime/naked-pics**

// WESTERN AUSTRALIA

In Western Australia, police urge cyber-bullying victims to contact organisations such as the Australian Communications and Media Authority (**www.acma.gov.au**), ThinkUKnow (**www.thinkuknow.org.au**), and ACORN – The Australian Cybercrime Online Reporting Network. (**www.acorn.gov.au**). All handle complaints about inappropriate online activities.

Sexting is not covered by the criminal code or defined under legislation in Western Australia. As a generic term to describe the act of sending sexually explicit messages or photographs, primarily via mobile phones between adults and teens, sexting between adults is not a criminal offence in WA.

However, sexting involving a child under 16 is covered by offences relating to the production, distribution and possession of child-exploitation material under Chapter 24 of the Criminal Code (WA). These offences are applicable to sexting between children or between a child and an adult. Further electronic communications of a sexual nature, including pictures and live streaming by an adult to the child, attract criminal sanctions under section 204B of the Criminal Code (WA).

Photo: Thinkstock

// TASMANIA

New Tasmanian anti-bullying laws that encompass cyber-bullying were passed in September 2019.

Tasmanian Attorney General Elise Archer says The Criminal Code Amendment (Bullying) Bill 2019 criminalises bullying and expands the existing crime of stalking to address serious bullying behaviour.

"Our Government believes this legislation strikes the right balance between protecting Tasmanians from serious cases of bullying, while also taking due care not to unnecessarily bring people, especially young people, before the courts," Ms Archer says.

"Critically, the decision to prosecute serious cases will always be a matter for the Director of Public Prosecutions.

"We know bullying can occur in almost any social environment and has become a significant issue given rapidly changing technology and the widespread use of social media."
Find out more // **www.justice.tas.gov.au**

// NEW SOUTH WALES

In New South Wales and throughout Australia, cyber-bullies may face criminal charges depending on the seriousness of the offence. For example, it is illegal to use mobile phones or the internet in a way that is menacing, harassing or offensive. Legal Aid NSW says that "menacing" would be threatening to harm someone. Threats are illegal under a number of laws and may be considered assault. (This is a federal crime, so anyone in Australia can be charged with this).

A "harassing" use may include repeatedly bothering someone. An "offensive" use could include sending or sharing a "sexy pic" or nude photo. If you use your mobile or the internet in a way that is likely to really hurt or anger a typical person, you may be committing a crime. The penalty for menacing, harassing or offensive cyber-bullying is up to three years in jail.

Legal Aid NSW has an under-18s youth hotline // 1800 101 810

TERRITORIES LAW

The ACT and Northern Territory use a combination of laws.

// AUSTRALIAN CAPITAL TERRITORY

In the ACT, cyber-stalking is defined as the persistent use of mobile devices and the internet to threaten, intimidate or harass someone. Charges are laid under Section 474.17 of the Criminal Code Act 1995 (Cth) using a Carriage Service to Menace, Harass or Cause Offence. Offences may include:
- Text, voice, or other harassment – the sending of threatening or harassing messages, or posting of offensive content;
- Sexual harassment via digital means (colloquially referred to as "revenge pornography" – the sharing of intimate images without consent); and
- Unauthorised surveillance through hacking into your accounts or installing spyware on your devices to monitor your activity.

ACT POLICE TIPS
- Check mobile device apps and disable geotagging or location services for those that do not require a physical location;
- Delete any apps that appear suspicious;
- Know how to block and report people on the sites, apps and games you use;
- Know who you are talking to online – think of your safety if you meet someone in person you've only spoken to online;
- Have strong passwords and change them regularly. Avoid recycling passwords for different accounts and change them at least twice a year;
- Install and maintain security software on your devices;
- Reconsider having social media "joint accounts";
- Avoid unauthorised access to your wireless by changing the default password on the router and not broadcasting your wireless across a large area; and
- Think before you send – once you send something digitally, you cannot control where it ends up.

Photo: Thinkstock

For more preventative and proactive measures visit //
www.staysmartonline.gov.au
www.wesnet.org.au,
www.thinkuknow.org.au

> Think before you send – once you send something digitally, you cannot control where it ends up.

// NORTHERN TERRITORY

The Northern Territory does not have specific cyber-bullying laws, however in August 2018 a Northern Territory Law Reform Committee report recommended that the NT Government create an offence under the Criminal Code (NT) of intentional and reckless bullying that causes physical or mental harm.

It also recommended that offenders aged under 18 be counselled or directed to an education campaign rather than charged with an offence.

In the meantime, the NT uses related laws in the Commonwealth Criminal Code Act, which details offences depending on the specific alleged incident. They include:
- Using a carriage service to make a threat or for a hoax threat;
- Using a carriage service to menace, harass or cause offence;
- Using a carriage service for suicide-related material;
- Using a carriage service for child pornography material; and
- Possessing, controlling, producing, supplying or obtaining suicide-related material for use through a carriage service.

Existing Northern Territory legislation can also be used to proffer a charge relating to cyber-bullying:
- Threats to Kill;
- Threats;
- Unlawful Stalking; and
- Offensive Conduct.

Northern Territory Police also play a community education and enforcement role around cyber-bullying instances and issues. The NT Police partners with the ThinkUKnow Program, which educates parents and caregivers about cyber safety.
Visit // **www.thinkuknow.org.au**

Profile // Jocelyn Brewer

DIGITAL NUTRITION

What is 'digital nutrition'? Jocelyn Brewer says we can take the same approach to our intake of digital content as we do when considering what and how we eat food.

// "We talk a lot about digital addiction and digital detoxing – terms that are very negatively framed. That doesn't sit well with me because the future is going to involve technology. We need to embrace the kinds of skills we need to use technology in a clever way.

"I coined 'Digital Nutrition' as a response to the idea that technology is toxic. There are decades of research and public education on healthy food and eating choices and Digital Nutrition borrows from that. It emphasises the importance of balance in the way we use technology but also in considering evidence of its impacts.

"When you have the basics of a healthy, balanced relationship with technology, you don't need to force yourself offline to find peace. If it's school holidays and it's raining, your kids are more likely to spend more time online. At Christmas, we eat and do things in excess and in January we make resolutions about eating healthy again.

"Some research says playing things like Candy Crush for 20 minutes at the end of the day is a great circuit breaker – it helps people chill out and decompress after a day's work. But that is different to playing for 90 minutes when you haven't had a conversation ... it's about context.

"And Digital Nutrition is positive about the opportunities that technology offers modern communities.

"We get obsessed with 'digital calorie counting' – we're stuck on measuring screen time and using that as a measurement of impact. But we need to look beyond that to what people are consuming.

"Young people may be looking at Instagram but is that content making them think 'I'm not pretty/good/smart enough' – or are they on Instagram following inspiring and aspirational people?

"If there was a nutritional label on technology and games and apps, what would be the vitamins and mineral content, and what would be the fats and sugars? Look for virtual vitamins, like Vitamin E for empathy.

"When kids play a certain game, are they sharing the experience of the other person in the game? Are they seeing new perspectives? Look for games and apps with plenty of Vitamin C for Creativity – do they create and contribute something, rather than consuming, consuming, consuming?

"Because these nutritional labels don't exist, parents need to play the games and use the apps and social media that their children are using. And teens and kids need help to think about whether they want a particular app or game to be a snack or a sometimes food, rather than their main digital meal. As in real life, you don't want to eat hot chips all the time ...

"If you are someone who loves chocolate and can't have it in the fridge because you'll eat it all, be aware of this temptation

"Playing things like Candy Crush for 20 minutes at the end of the day is a great circuit breaker."

Photo: Supplied

THE THREE Ms OF DIGITAL NUTRITION

Mindful // Pause and think more broadly about how what you do, say, click on and scroll through affects your overall wellbeing.
Meaningful // Have a sense of purpose and clarity in what you read, comment on or participate in.
Moderate // Use technology in moderation. Also consider moderating what you say and how you react to things that show up in your online world.

from a digital perspective, too. Just like not being able to stop at one or two squares of chocolate, if you dip into something online do you then lose a sense of time? If so, maybe you need to take that app off your phone, just like not keeping chocolate in the fridge."

....

// Jocelyn Brewer is a psychologist and former high school teacher who developed the concept of Digital Nutrition. She is part of Australia's first formal cyber-psychology research group at the University of Sydney. www.digitalnutrition.com.au

Profile // Simon Fogarty

THE POLICEMAN

Simon Fogarty's working day is dedicated to reducing cybercrime, including the grooming and sexual exploitation of children via the internet.

"Generally, there are two types of offenders. There's the offender who has a scattergun approach who doesn't necessarily care about the age of the person they talk to via social media. They'll ask where someone lives, what they're wearing and then do they want to meet up for sex? Children may not be targeted specifically, but unfortunately they do get caught up in this.

"Then there is the offender who targets kids because of their age, and that is when we see the longer-term grooming process. Conversations start through social-networking sites, then offenders take kids to more private sites where they can have one-on-one engagement and develop a relationship.

"They start to get control over the child and usually convince a child to send pictures of themselves in various naked poses. When they have those pictures they use those photos to blackmail the child to send more pictures, or to meet up with them for sexual activity. That's known unofficially as 'sextortion'.

"Police do a lot of work within social-media sites. We identify who the offenders are, what they are doing online, and investigators then arrest and prosecute them. We do a lot of work with counterpart agencies interstate and overseas and we spend a lot of time researching where kids are accessing social-network sites and identifying child victims. It's a priority to find kids who are being exploited online and to rescue them.

"These kinds of social-media crimes are a growth area and they are under-reported. Kids can be unlikely to report an incident because they're worried about losing access to the internet or they're afraid or embarrassed.

"Our children need to understand that they wouldn't walk down a street with photos of themselves and hand out those and their phone number to strangers."

"We've got to pull our heads out of the sand and realise this is happening to kids from all backgrounds. Parents need to take an interest in what their children are doing online and to talk to them about where they hang out and what is happening online. Build your child's confidence so they can approach you if they get into harm online because kids don't have the capacity to know how to get themselves out of danger.

"If your child does have problems online, call Crime Stoppers or go to your local police station. Contact the appropriate website administrator and make a report. There are also Sexual Offences and Child Abuse Investigation teams who we work closely with to investigate these types of crimes.

"We are interested in finding out what has happened online even if someone doesn't want to pursue an incident. Keep messages and images and a copy of the chat between your child and the potential offender. We may need access to your child's social network profiles – we only need their login details and can access their account at the police station.

"Look at the apps your child is using and learn how they work. You don't have to be experts but look at your child's iPad or mobile and see what they're doing online. But of course children need some privacy, particularly when they are older, and it's important they learn how to engage through social networks because that's the way of the world now. They may talk to each other in ways that parents think are a little inappropriate and we have to be flexible. But that has to be balanced with appropriate behaviour and your child's online safety.

"Our children need to understand that they wouldn't walk down a street with photos of themselves and hand out those and their phone number to strangers. Yet they get online and provide personal information to people they don't know."

For parents, carers and teachers //
www.thinkuknow.org.au/site/

Photo: Supplied

// Simon Fogarty is a tactical intelligence officer with the Joint Anti Child Exploitation Team (JACET) – a Victoria Police initiative.

Profile // Brett Lee

THE CYBER EXPERT

Are all teenagers sexting? No, says Brett Lee, who investigated child exploitation for 16 years, and says it is vital to understand that most teens do not sext.

Photo: Supplied

"If a young person believes everybody else is sexting – and they're not – then they think they are missing out on something, that there must be something wrong with them, and if everyone else is doing it, it must be OK. A young person doesn't have the knowledge to allow them to make an informed decision that best protects them.

"Don't assume most teenagers are sexting. It's not 'normal' behaviour. But between the ages of 12 and 17 young people are looking for their identity and exploring where they fit and there can be a need or vulnerability. They want to be accepted – can't wait to grow up – and they may have someone in their life and think they must do this otherwise they'll lose them. Young people don't get involved in sexting for sinister reasons.

"In most instances, when young people sext, they are committing criminal offences and it can lead to embarrassment, humiliation, depression, fear, loss of dignity and blackmail – 'I'll make sure everyone at your school sees this photo unless you do this or that'.

"Parents don't have to know everything about the technology. Real world analogies are more important. I use an example of picturing yourself in a mall with thousands of people around. As you look through the crowd, you see someone you like – maybe you know them, maybe you don't. You push your way through the crowd, walk up to that person and take off all your clothes. Or that person says, 'take off your clothes' and you do that.

"When I watch the students' reaction I know they're thinking 'why would you do that? I'd never do that!' But sexting is similar. They take a photograph of themselves in a split second, share it in another split second, and it goes into a community of 3 billion people for the rest of their lives.

"Have conversations about the internet being public and discussions about whether your child would be happy for other people to see them naked. Ask them, 'if you send one of those photos and it became public, would you want to take it back if you could? How would you feel if your grandma saw it? What if you sent that photo to a friend and they left their phone on the kitchen bench, and your friend's Mum or Dad picked it up?' Verbalise real world outcomes so your child can consider them and it can sit in the back of their mind.

"A parent will be repaid for the rest of their life if they develop a culture of communication with their child about this. So your child knows you are interested and a source of support if something happens. If you think something is not right, step in and ask questions. Maybe you need to remove your child's device for a while until a situation is fixed – some parents feel it is a birthright for their child to have possession of their personal device. It is not. Technology is way down the list when it comes to what is best for our children."

> A parent will be repaid for the rest of their life if they develop a culture of communication.

BRETT'S FIVE SAFEGUARDS

1. **Set rules and boundaries.** These are not optional.
2. **Stay current.** Increase your knowledge base as needed.
3. **Take charge.** You are the one who controls technology and makes the final decisions.
4. **Use management controls.** Parents have a right to know where their children go and whom they communicate with.
5. **Communicate.** Create an environment of openness about technology and talk about it with your kids.

www.internetsafeeducation.com
www.internetsafeeducation.com/blog/sexting-and-children/

// Former Queensland police officer Brett Lee is the founder of Internet Safe Education. www.internetsafeeducation.com

APPS & SITES

Do you know Houseparty from TikTok? Or Snapchat from Instagram?

While there is talk of Facebook losing some of its appeal for teenagers – mostly because they feel too many parents have invaded the social media site – it's still the most popular online meeting place site for teenagers.

About 71 per cent of them share photos and use Facebook to find out what friends, and friends of friends, are doing.

Instagram and Snapchat are also popular channels for today's teenagers and their user numbers are on the rise. They're the place to share candid moments, share videos and photographs, make a statement or send quick messages.

YouTube is also a long-time favourite of children and has more than a billion users worldwide. Year on year, the number of hours people spend watching YouTube content increases by 50 per cent and 300 hours of video are uploaded to the site every minute.

Here we give you a brief summary of the most popular social media apps that you have probably heard of, and some that you may not be as familiar with.

// POPULAR APPLICATIONS

SOCIAL NETWORKING

Facebook is a social networking website where users create a profile, upload photos and videos and send messages.

About 1.56 billion people use Facebook every day. About 15 million Australians check in each month (Social Media News, May 2019) and around 940,000 are aged between 13 and 17.

Facebook has ramped up its "community standards" content monitoring, focusing on adult nudity and sexual activity, bullying, harassment, child nudity, sexual exploitation of children, fake accounts, hate speech, regulated goods, spam, global terrorist propaganda and violence and graphic content.

The latest metrics from May 2019 suggest that for every 10,000 times people viewed content on Facebook, 11 to 14 views contained content that violated the company's adult nudity and sexual activity policy, and 25 violated its violence and graphic content policy.

Children should check their privacy settings so they know who is seeing their content. They should click Account at the top of any page and then Privacy Settings in the dropdown menu. This means they can control who sees their posts, limit the audience of posts they share with friends of friends, and limit who can send them a friend request.

It's important to control who can see your profile contact info. Go to your profile and click the Update Info button. Look for the Contact Info section and then click Edit.

Use the audience selector at the right of each piece of contact information to adjust who it is shared with.

Facebook has a Family Safety Center with safety resources and general safety information // www.facebook.com/help/

Hot tip from Project Rockit //
Challenge online hate in risk-free ways. For example, write a "counter-comment", i.e. type 'dislike' and use your status to take the power back // @projectrockit

♂ JAMES // 19

WHAT ARE YOUR FAVOURITE APPS?
Spotify, Instagram and Snapchat

WHAT DO YOU LIKE ABOUT THEM?
I like Spotify because it has the latest up-to-date music. I like Instagram to see what is going on around the world. Snapchat lets me see what people I know are doing.

WHAT APP DON'T YOU LIKE AND WHY?
iMusic – I prefer to listen to music on Spotify.

WHAT OTHER APPS DO YOU LIKE TO USE?
Netflix – they have a good selection of movies and documentaries.

// TIPS FOR PARENTS

ConnectSafely.org is a US-based not-for-profit organisation that aims to educate people about how to use technology safely.

The website has lots of safety tips, research and guides for parents on how to keep children safe when they surf the internet and use social media.

Useful guides that can be downloaded include
* A Parents' Guide to Mobile Phones
* A Parents' Guide to Instagram
* A Parents' Guide to Cyberbullying
* A Parents' Guide to Cybersecurity

Go to // www.connectsafely.org to download the guides and for practical safety tips.

 # Houseparty

VIDEO CALLS WITH GAMES & QUIZZES

AGE 13+ Houseparty enables people to connect anywhere and anytime. This proved popular during the COVID-19 social isolation with many friends and family using it to stay in touch.

Houseparty has rules that ban nudity, threats, bullying, trolling and impersonation. It also allows users to unfriend or block someone they don't like.

Rumours emerged of safety issues, which Houseparty denied. It insisted its data was secure and there had been no data breaches or exposure of customer data or third-party accounts.
Go to // **houseparty.com**
Guidelines // **https://houseparty.com/guidelines/**

PHOTO SHARING

AGE 13+ Instagram is all about sharing photos and short videos. It also has other functions such as Instagram TV and shopping. People can upload their own material, share it with friends, view images and post comments on material shared by their friends and people they follow. About 95 million photos are shared every day, and about nine million Australians a month use Instagram, according to Social Media Statistics Australia (December 2018).

Instagram's default setting for all photos makes them available for viewing by anyone using Instagram. It's a good idea for children to create a private account instead, so only people who follow them, and whom they know, can see their images.

A Help Center with a Privacy and Safety section has instructions on how to ensure photos and videos can only be seen by people approved by your child to follow them. It also shows how to block people.

Instagram has an Add to Photo Map feature where a location can be added to a photo and reveal where it was taken. This is usually turned off but once it is turned on, it stays on until it is turned off again. Encourage teenagers to think carefully about sharing details of where they are – especially if their account settings are public.

A comprehensive Tips for Parents section at Instagram Help Centre is at **help.instagram.com**
For help, go to // **parents.au.reachout.com/landing/parents-insta-guide**

Hot tip from Project Rockit // Use the DM (direct message) feature to support someone having a tough time // **@projectrockit**
Read // **https://www.abc.net.au/life/talking-to-daughter-about-body-editing-apps-instagram/9771928**

 # iTunes

MEDIA MANAGEMENT

AGE 13+ iTunes was recently replaced with new Mac apps for music, videos, podcasts and audiobooks.

With macOS Catalina, your music, videos, podcasts and audiobooks are organised into their own dedicated apps – the Apple Music app, Apple TV app, Apple Podcasts app and Apple Books app. You can also access your iTunes Store purchases in these apps.

If you have a PC, you can continue to use iTunes for Windows to manage your media library, make purchases and manually sync and manage your iPhone, iPad or iPod touch.

Use Finder to sync and manage your iPhone, iPad and iPod touch.

Finder is the new place to back up, update or restore your iPhone, iPad and iPod touch.

Just connect your device to your Mac and it appears in the Finder sidebar. And you can easily drag and drop files to your device. Use Finder to manage your devices.

Upgrade your iTunes library
After you update to macOS Catalina, just open the Apple Music app or Apple TV app to use your iTunes library in the new apps. Have multiple iTunes libraries? Learn how to switch between them in macOS Catalina.
If you open the Apple Podcasts app or Apple Books app first, you won't see any of your media until you open the Apple Music app or Apple TV app.
Go to // **https://support.apple.com/en-au/HT210200**
Family sharing // **www.apple.com/au/icloud/family-sharing**

SOCIAL NETWORKING

AGE 13+ Pinterest started in 2010 as a place for people to collect ideas they found around the internet. It's about getting inspiration from other people's ideas and what they share. Pinterest now has an international community of more than 250 million people and is home to more than 200 billion ideas.

The Help Center has information on how to best manage an account and to maintain privacy. For example, if you want to block a Pinterest user, open the profile of the person you want to block. Then click on the flag symbol. Click block and then OK to confirm. To unblock an account, open the profile of the person and then click unblock. **help.pinterest.com**

MORE POPULAR APPS & SITES • P96

APPS & SITES

CONTINUED FROM • P95

SOCIAL NEWS

Google is a search engine that scours the Internet for information. Reddit's tagline is "Conversation starts here" and the social news internet site is used by millions of people worldwide who share comments, views and interests.

The most interesting posts and comments are "upvoted" to the top of the pile or the "Hot" pages.

About 330 million people use it every month and take part in chats and forums that match their interests – called subreddits. Subreddits range from Parenting and Politics to Comics, "Today I Learned" and Gaming.

Reddit recently raised $300 million in investments which will be used to improve and streamline the website.

PHOTO MESSAGING

Snapchat is a media-sharing and chat app. The text, photos and videos your child sends automatically disappear between 1 and 10 seconds after posting.

Over 180 million people use Snapchat every day, and about 6.4 million Australians use it each month. While "Snaps" are supposed to be momentary, they can be screenshot, which may leave images open to being used or shared in a way your child didn't intend. Talk to teenagers about ensuring that any images they share won't embarrass them or get them into trouble.

Look at Privacy Settings to make sure teenagers only receive images from people they know.

- Filter who can send you Snaps by tapping the ghost icon at the top of the camera screen to access your profile.
- Then tap the gear icon in the upper-right corner to reach the settings menu.
- When you see "Who Can Send me Snaps", choose 'My Friends'.

Inappropriate content can be reported. Press and hold on the Snap, then tap the Button with the flag emblem.

For help, go to // **support.snapchat.com/a/privacy-settings**
Go to // **support.snapchat.com** for safety advice and how to report concerns and abuse.
Snapchat lets you to block someone from sending you Snaps // **support.snapchat.com/a/block-friends**

You can delete your teenager's account at **accounts.snapchat.com/accounts/delete_account** You need the username and password. If a teenager won't reveal them, parents can file a deletion request at **tiny.cc/5fsj8y**

VIDEO SHARING

TikTok is described as "the world's leading destination for short-form mobile videos". Using smartphones, people capture and share moments of their everyday life. In 2018, TikTok was one of the world's most downloaded apps.

TikTok produces a Community Well-Being series with information on how users can make the most of various safety and privacy tools. Some of the key tools are being able to keep your list of liked videos private by going to Privacy and Settings – click on the three dots in the top right corner. Then go to "Who Can See the Videos I've Liked" and choose between All or Me.

Users can keep the videos they make themselves private by choosing "Private" on the video posting page where it asks, "Who Can View This Video".

By default, initially TikTok accounts are public – so you need to actively switch to a private account. Parents can get advice on safety for children on TikTok at **support.tiktok.com**

MICRO BLOGGING

The Tumblr app is a blogging platform where people can post short texts, photos, quotes, links, music and videos. About 3.7 million Australians use Tumblr.

In December 2018, Tumblr introduced new Community Guidelines around the type of content that can be shown on the site. Content flagged as "adult" is no longer allowed.

Tumblr defines adult content as photos, videos or GIFs that show real-life human genitals or female-presenting nipples, and any content – including photos, videos, GIFs and illustrations – that depicts sex acts.

Tumblr accounts are generally public and, according to antivirus and security company McAfee, a primary Tumblr account is always public.

But you can start a secondary blog or account and protect it with a password to be more private.

Tumblr also has an "ignore" feature that blocks people you don't want to communicate with from being able to see your blog posts.

Nor can they send you messages or follow your blog and your blog won't appear in their search results.

To block someone, open your blog, go to the user menu and select "Block".

For help with security concerns about Tumblr, go to // **www.tumblr.com/help** or visit **support.tumblr.com**

MESSAGING SERVICE

AGE 13+

Twitter keeps people in touch with short messages, photos, videos and links. Posts or "Tweets" are sent to followers once you click the "Tweet" button.

Twitter sees free expression as a human right and aims to give everyone a voice. But Tweets cannot be abusive or threatening and the company has a suite of features to keep Twitter safe. About 4.7 million Australians use Twitter each month.

You can mute an account to stop seeing Tweets from someone without blocking them and you can block words, hashtags and phrases. You can instantly block an account and opt out of images that you don't want to see. Parents can use the "safe search" function to remove potentially sensitive content by default. **@TwitterSafety** keeps users up to date with the latest safety updates and tools.

Go to // **help.twitter.com**

PHONE MESSAGING

AGE 16+

WhatsApp is officially described as a "cross-platform mobile messaging app". Essentially, it allows you to send and receive messages without paying SMS fees. More than one billion people in more than 180 countries, including around seven million Australians, use WhatsApp.

Users can set up groups to receive messages from each other and to send images, video and audio messages. There is a block facility, so messages sent from a blocked contact won't be delivered. Your online information and status message updates won't be seen by blocked contacts either. But blocking someone won't remove their contact from your WhatsApp list. To delete them you must delete the contact from your phone's address book.

Go to // **www.whatsapp.com/faq** for details about the app and safety options.

 SOPHIA // 12

WHAT ARE YOUR FAVOURITE APPS?
Instagram and Snapchat.

WHAT DO YOU LIKE ABOUT THEM?
I like Instagram and Snapchat because they allow me to talk to my friends and I can see what they are doing when we are not at school.
I can also share what I am doing with them.

WHAT APP DON'T YOU LIKE AND WHY?
Call of Duty. I don't like it because it's violent and hard to play. If I do play it, I get frustrated so I avoid it.

WHAT OTHER APPS DO YOU LIKE TO USE?
TikTok because it makes me laugh and I can view my friend's videos and there are a range of video genres to choose from.

VIDEO SHARING

AGE 13+

At its most basic level, YouTube is a video-sharing website. It is designed for users aged 13 or older. YouTube has over one billion users.

Every day people watch over a billion hours of video and generate billions of views. 15 million Australians use YouTube each month according to Social Media Statistics Australia from (April 2019).

YouTube does set out some basic rules for users. Videos featuring nudity or sexual content should not be posted, nor should violent and graphic content be shared. There is a flagging feature on video and if you see content that is offensive or concerning, you can flag the video and submit it to YouTube staff for review. That content may then be removed.

Go to YouTube and log on to the Safety Center for parent resources. This provides information about what kind of content is not allowed, reporting and includes tips and tools on how to stay safe and screen out disturbing content **support.google.com/youtube**

You can also visit your child's channel to see what they are posting and what they are watching on YouTube.

Go to // **www.youtube.com/yt/about/policies/#community-guidelines**

VIDEO CONFERENCING

AGE 16

Zoom allows video conferencing and messaging across any device and grew in popularity among all age groups during the 2020 COVID-19 pandemic. Zoom has some similarities to **Skype\Facetime** but its functionality is slightly different. Meetings can be recorded, and password protected. Multiple participants can share their screens simultaneously and choose a virtual background.

Younger people can also use Zoom Chat and create private or public groups. The recommended age for use is 16, unless through a school subscription. Go to // **zoom.us**

STAY IN CONTROL

A range of tools can help parents control their child's use of social media.

To the uninitiated, cyberspace can be a bewildering world. And at first glance, the social-media landscape can be an unfamiliar and unfriendly place where parents seem to have little ability to monitor and control how their teenager operates.

So where do parents start if they want to gain a better understanding of what their children are doing online? What effective and easy-to-use resources are available to support concerned families? What actual tools can parents use right now, and what practical steps can they take to become informed about how their children are using social media?

The good news is that parents aren't powerless when it comes to having influence over their child's social-media use and experiences. The resources and tools available to parents can help them control how often and how much time their children spend using social media, and what kind of online content teenagers access. And parents don't have to become IT experts either.

// FAMILY FRIENDLY FILTERS

The Communications Alliance, a communications industry forum in Australia, recommends Family Friendly Filters.

To be classified as a Family Friendly Filter, a filter undergoes independent testing to ensure it is effective, easy to use and that it is updated as and when required by the office of the eSafety Commissioner.

For example, if it determines that a specific website is prohibited under Australian law, a Family Friendly Filter will be updated by the filter company to block access to that website. All internet service providers must offer a Family Friendly Filter.

The office of the eSafety Commissioner has a series of filter classification codes to help parents decide what level or category of filter is appropriate for their household:

Unclassified – These filters block websites on the eSafety Commissioner's prohibited URL filter (PUF) list, and are recommended for 18-plus years of age
Class 1 – recommended for children over 15 years;
Class 2 – recommended for children between 10 and 15 years;
Class 3 – recommended for children under 10 years.

CURRENT APPROVED FAMILY FRIENDLY FILTERS ARE:

Norton Family Premier // **Version: 3.6.4.71**
Manufacturer: Symantec.
Class of accreditation: Recommended for children over 15 years of age (accreditation class 1).

Family Zone
Manufacturer: Family Zone.
Class of accreditation: Recommended for children under 10 years of age and older (accreditation class 3).

Australian Private Networks
Manufacturer: Australian Private Networks.
Class of accreditation: Recommended for children over 15 years of age (accreditation class 1).

Go to // **www.commsalliance.com.au/Activities/ispi/fff**

// PARENTAL-CONTROL SOFTWARE

WHAT ARE PARENTAL CONTROLS?

Parental-control tools help parents to monitor and limit what their children do and see online. There are many tools available and they offer different functions, such as allowing parents to limit the amount of time children spend on certain websites or games.

Currently, there are more effective tools for use with PCs and Macs than with mobile, tablet devices and game consoles. The important thing to remember is that no tool is 100 per cent effective at blocking access to inappropriate content online.

WHAT DO PARENTAL CONTROLS DO?

Most control tools allow parents to block children from accessing specific websites or apps, and they filter inappropriate material, such as sexual or violent content.

Most parental controls also allow parents to monitor their child's online activities by reporting on the sites that children access, the length of time spent on those sites and how often your child accesses them.

Parents can use controls to set time limits and so block their child's access to game sites or to social-media sites after a set period. Additionally, many parental control tools allow parents to change the "tool settings" according to a child's age, i.e. you can control who sees your child's posts on Facebook, who can see their images and profile, and control and tighten their privacy settings.

Photo: Thinkstock

DO THEY BLOCK ALL THE BAD STUFF?

- Parental controls aren't a silver bullet and they won't block all inappropriate content, but they can reduce the chances of your child being exposed to something they shouldn't see.
- Currently, parental-control tools are more efficient at blocking "adult" or sexual content than content that may promote self-harm, eating disorders, violence, drugs, gambling, racism and terrorism.
- While new control tools are being developed every few months, at the moment some may have difficulty filtering content within social-media sites and messaging services, including video-messaging services such as Skype.
- Parental-control tools are improving on game consoles, mobiles and tablets.
- Parents still need to keep talking to children about what social-media sites, games and apps they are using, who they are communicating with and what kinds of material they are accessing.

// CHOOSING THE BEST PARENTAL-CONTROL TOOL

So how do you decide what tool is best to help protect your child online?

Parental-control tools are developed and updated regularly, but the most effective tools are the ones that are easy to install and use. User reviews are a good guide to helping you find the right tool. Look for a tool that:

- Allows you to monitor your kids' online behaviour and has the ability to schedule monitoring times and password access;
- Blocks content and websites. Blocking and filtering elements may include application blocking, chat blocking, search-engine filtering and social-network blocking;
- Offers good reports on which websites have been accessed and computer use. This should include screenshots, keyboard strokes and online searches. Some products can capture usernames and passwords for sites such as Facebook;
- The best parental-control software will capture screenshots and send you emails about activity on your child's computer so that you stay informed, even if you are far away;
- Is automatically updated to ensure new websites and content are blocked;
- Can be used remotely – handy if your child is doing a school project and the tool is over-blocking content, or if children are home alone and you want to know which websites they are visiting; and
- Is compatible. In a household it is likely that you will want to monitor a number of computers and phones with different operating systems. The best parental-control software is compatible with a range of phones and operating systems.

FINDING THE BEST TOOL FOR YOU

Look at recent reviews on trusted consumer review sites and technology review sites such as TopTenReviews, TopConsumerReviews, *PC Magazine* and *Laptop* magazine. You can also search for the latest reviews on parental-control tools, content filters and internet filters.

Remember that parental controls don't provide software or hardware security. For this you need firewalls to block access by unauthorised systems and anti-virus to block programs that seek to steal or destroy data. And these tools must be automatically updated, as new viruses are released every day.

Profile // Katie Miller

THE LAWYER

If your son or daughter does something offensive on social media, what's the potential legal fallout? Katie Miller highlights some of the legal issues.

Photo: Supplied

"The key thing to remember about social media is the same rules apply in the online world as apply in the offline world. So the same kinds of things that get children into trouble offline get them into trouble online.

"But social media and the online world have changed the game by making everyone more connected, and so allowing potentially problematic situations and actions to happen more quickly. For example, bullying that would happen at school over a term can now happen 24 hours a day, seven days a week. So the groundswell can build more quickly and the effects can be longer lasting.

"But we wouldn't accept our kids being bullied or bullying offline. And while bullying online may cause psychological rather than physical harm, that doesn't mean it's acceptable. If your child is saying nasty things about someone else online, theoretically that could be defamation.

"When it comes to the online world, know what your kids are doing online and talk about their responsibilities. It's not a lawless world. Just as there are rules in the physical world, there are rules to comply with in the online world.

"Explain to kids that often rules on social-media websites are about protecting them and so many sites state that children should be over the age of 13 to join. But parents sign up younger kids because kids pester parents that all their friends use that particular site and parents relent. But when you sign up your 10-year-old to a social-media site that's for children aged 13-plus you're sending the message to your child that online rules don't matter.

"When it comes to mobile phones, children under 18 can't sign a mobile-phone contract, so when you sign that contract for your child you have an important role to play in ensuring your child understands the boundaries of the law and how to use their mobile responsibly.

"Sexting is a key issue that parents need to know about. Sexting generally starts between two consenting teenagers as an extension of flirting behaviour. The problem can arise when that relationship goes bad. Then one person decides to distribute intimate photos of their ex, or in some cases a person uses intimate photos of another person to intimidate and threaten them.

"Until very recently, teens who took intimate photos of another person, even when they were engaging in consensual sexting, could be considered by law to be creating child pornography.

> "When you sign up your 10-year-old to a social-media site that's for children aged 13-plus you're sending the message to your child that online rules don't matter."

That's a problem, because if you're found guilty of creating child pornography you become a registered sex offender.

"In Victoria the law recently changed to ensure that young people who engage in non-exploitative 'sexting' don't end up with a criminal record on the sex offenders' register. But if your teenager distributes intimate photos of another person without their consent, i.e. the wounded boyfriend sends intimate photos of his ex-girlfriend as revenge, then they are committing a crime.

"Ultimately, if you have confidential information from someone – an intimate photo or something they've told you online – and you spread it further than the sender intended, that could also be a breach of privacy.

"Always remember that you sign the mobile-phone contract for your child. So if you suspect that your child is using their phone inappropriately you can talk with them about that, but at the end of the day if they don't listen then you pay for the phone, you sign the contract, you own it – and you have options.

"Keep reminding children that there is nothing special or different about the online world and the real world. Talk to them about what is right and wrong and what rules apply, and make it clear that if they break the rules there are consequences within the family, at school, and perhaps with the police and the courts.

"Look at your own behaviour with social media, too. How do you treat rules online? Children copy their parents, and if they see you treating online rules as flexible and breakable, don't be surprised when they do the same thing."

// Katie Miller is a past president of the Law Institute of Victoria.

Profile // Dr Suelette Dreyfus

THE PRIVACY EXPERT

Dr Suelette Dreyfus says while parents need to stay in touch with how their children use the internet and social media, making the right decisions online is a skill.

// I had a conversation about children and their online presence years ago with Julian Assange, my co-author of Australia's first mainstream book about computer hacking, who was also a father. He said if you tell your teenage boy 'you can't have free run on the internet because there are bad things out there and you might see those things', the first thing he will do is hunt down the 'forbidden fruit'.

"His point was that parents are often better off explaining and reasoning with their teenager rather than just forbidding access to information. His approach at the time could be described as 'I trust you to be responsible using the internet. Yes, there are some bad things online, but there is also a big, bright world at the other end of that ethernet cable. If you want to do something interesting and valuable with your life, explore that world'.

"Parents need to work out where their child sits on the spectrum of freedom versus constraints, wisdom and maturity. If a teenager is generally truthful, have regular discussions with them about what they're doing online and set parameters with them. But you don't need a heavy-handed 'sniffing of the network to monitor all their traffic' approach because reading every text message is unrealistic. The minute you take off that harness, they may lash out. You also don't want them to live a double life you don't know about because they feel constrained.

"The kind of rule that is sensible is that their circle on social media needs to be closed. I've put constraints on my children that it only includes friends they know face to face – not friends of friends and tenth cousins once removed! There must be a relationship in the real world that generates accountability that improves behaviour online.

"If teenagers are spending a lot of time alone in their room, it's reasonable to ask to see their messages. Explain that it's not so much about the content but finding out what is eating at your teenager emotionally. Seeing what they are doing online is not only about protecting them from creepy people – just as serious is recognising depression.

"Technology allows children to isolate themselves more. If you get enough information about what is worrying them, go online and find resources. A great gift of the internet is that people who would otherwise be outsiders can find a community of people just like them. Helping them make appropriate use of specialist communities can make a teenager feel less isolated in their awkward years.

"In terms of what they place online, ask your child to remember how incredibly uncool they were in grade 5. That's how they are going to feel in year 12 if they do stupid things online today. You can talk about it hurting their chances with employers later, but they won't get that – but they understand embarrassment.

"People don't necessarily want privacy because they are doing anything wrong – they want privacy because it's a kind of autonomy. It allows us to make mature choices in deciding how much information about ourselves we are going to give someone else.

"That decision-making and recognition that there are different pieces of ourselves that we do or don't want to share is part of becoming independent. Parents need to give their teenagers a chance to practise that. We don't hand the keys of an undriven car to an 18-year-old who has never been behind the wheel and say, 'Off you go! Good luck!' We do an awful lot of test driving first, and it's the same with learning to manage privacy.

"Privacy is a basic human right, and if your child knows this they feel they have some power. This lets them own the outcome of your discussions so they are more likely to abide by it.

"Finally, if you think your child will never find out that you're monitoring them online, think again. If and when they find out, that breaks their trust in you."

> "Ask your child to remember how incredibly uncool they were in grade 5. That's how they are going to feel in year 12 if they do stupid things online today."

Photo: Supplied

// Dr Suelette Dreyfus is a lecturer in the Department of Computing and Information Systems at the University of Melbourne. Her research interest is in privacy and anonymity.

Profile // Steve Biddulph

THE AUTHOR

Steve Biddulph is a parent educator, psychologist and author. His books include *10 Things Girls Need Most*, *Raising Boys*, *Raising Girls* and *The New Manhood*.

Q. HOW IS MODERN LIFE MAKING THINGS MORE CHALLENGING FOR YOUNG PEOPLE TODAY?

A "We've put them in this frantic life with the hurry of our lives, the competitive nature of schooling and the way they see the world – it's just the contest. It's not just doing well at school, you have to look amazing and you have to be out there and switched on and then there's the 24/7 saturation of the internet … It's a perfect storm."

HOW DO PARENTS TALK ABOUT SEXTING AND SOME OF THE SEXUALISED IMAGERY CHILDREN SEE ON PHONES AND THE INTERNET?

A "Let kids know that you know about some of the things that they're encountering. Say, 'look, I'm sure people have shown you stuff on phones and pictures on the net that are pretty yucky looking, and I want to let you know that love and sex – that's not what it's really like. It's a really great part of life and we'll talk to you about that as time goes on and I'm always happy to talk about it'. Make those openings, so when some idiot holds a picture up in the playground that's gross, your daughter thinks 'mum knows about that so I don't have to keep that secret from her'. When kids are older you'd say something like what they need to know about pornography is that it's different – people in real life talk to each other and they're kind and not mean when they're having sex."

"We can easily overreact or not know what to do because maybe we had parents who yelled at us and were cold and difficult."

WHAT DO PARENTS NEED TO BE AWARE OF ABOUT THEIR OWN BELIEFS AND EXPERIENCES WHEN DISCUSSING SENSITIVE TOPICS WITH CHILDREN?

A "What brings us unstuck as parents are the things we're just not quite aware of. So if a child is experiencing a little bit of bullying and we had bullying in our past, it's very hard to come to that in a steady, balanced way. We can easily overreact or not know what to do because maybe we had parents who yelled at us and were cold and difficult. Or perhaps you can say to yourself, 'my parents never helped me with sexuality so I'm going to have to get a bit of support for this and I want to do it differently'."

YOU HAVE WRITTEN EXTENSIVELY ABOUT BOYS AND THEIR HEALTH, WHAT ARE YOUR CONCERNS FOR GIRLS?

A "There may be people who've got daughters who are relaxed and confident and spirited into their mid-teens. They may have loyal friends and are treated respectfully by boys … but for about two girls out of five, that's just not so. They're massively anxious and currently across the Western world one in five teenage girls is on anxiety medication… Anxiety then drives the other things like self-harm and eating disorders and alcohol over-use and risky sex – but anxiety we think is the core."

HOW DO WE SUPPORT YOUNG PEOPLE, PARTICULARLY GIRLS, WHEN THEY FACE PROBLEMS WITH SOCIAL MEDIA?

A "Mothers and fathers have to wield a sword, and that might mean saying we don't have phones on after 7pm in our house, or we don't just leave the TV on all the time because our daughters will get this wash of completely unconscious imagery that if you're female you have to be thin and hot and sexy and young."

WHAT IS ONE THING PARENTS CAN DO TODAY TO TRY TO TACKLE THE SOCIAL MEDIA TSUNAMI THAT THEIR CHILDREN ARE EXPOSED TO?

A "Maybe have one night a week when you just hang out without a television – kids will just love it."

// STEVE BIDDULPH'S BOOKS

- 10 Things Girls Need Most
- Raising Girls
- Raising Boys
- The New Manhood
- Raising a Happy Child – in the precious years from birth to six
- Raising Babies
- The Making of Love
- Love Laughter and Parenting
- Stories of Manhood

// This is an edited interview conducted by Clare Bowditch with psychologist and author Steve Biddulph on ABC Radio Melbourne.
www.stevebiddulph.com

FAMILY TECHNOLOGY USER AGREEMENT

I WILL KEEP MYSELF SAFE
- I will not give out any personal information, such as my age, last name, address or phone number, or meet someone I've met online, without my parents' permission.
- I will not put myself at risk by posting or sending inappropriate photos of myself or others.
- I will block creepy messages from people I don't know and inform my parents.
- I will tell my parents or an adult I trust if anything happens online that makes me feel uncomfortable, upset or sad.
- I will not share my password with anyone other than my parents, even my best friend.
- I will set privacy controls and always discuss with my parents when I want to create a social networking profile.

I WILL THINK FIRST
- I agree that not all apps, TV shows, movies, games, music and websites are right for me. I will talk to my parents if I am not sure what's appropriate.
- I will discuss ratings with my parents and agree to follow my family's agreed ratings.

The agreed ratings are:

_____

_____

- I know that not everything I read or see is true, and I will think about whether a source is credible.
- I agree not to download anything or fill out surveys without my parents' permission.
- I know that the pictures and videos I post online, and everything that I write about myself and my friends, will likely be online forever. Therefore I will not put anything on my profile that I wouldn't want my parents, teachers, or future employees to see.

I WILL BE A GOOD DIGITAL CITIZEN
- I agree not to bully anyone online by sending pictures or sharing videos without the permission of the person(s) in the photo/video, or by spreading gossip, setting up fake profiles or saying cruel things about people.
- I agree not to use technology to cheat on schoolwork and always cite the sources of information.
- I agree to flag and report content that is inappropriate and be an upstander against bullies by reporting incidents to trusted adults

I WILL KEEP A HEALTHY BALANCE
- Even though I love media, there are other things in my life that I'm interested in. So I will help my parents set time limits that make sense and then I will follow them.
- I will help my parents understand why media is so important to me by sharing my online experiences, but I also recognise that my safety is more important to them than anything else.
- The agreed charging time for all devices on a school night is 8pm.
- Our house will have a technology-free time for an hour each night for dinner.

The agreed time limits are:

_____

_____

_____

_____

IN EXCHANGE, MY PARENTS AGREE TO
- Recognise that media is a big part of my life, even if they don't always understand why.
- Before saying "no", talk with me about what worries them and why.
- Embrace my world: understand downloads, IM, online games and the sites that I like.

// SIGN SETUP

ME

....

MY PARENTS

....

// Kindly supplied by Firbank Grammar School.
© Parenting Guides Ltd

FREE DOWNLOAD YOUR FAMILY TECHNOLOGY USER AGREEMENT FROM parentguides.com.au

ASSISTANCE

There are many places to get information and help.

// CYBER HELP

Office of the eSafety Commissioner
esafety.gov.au

Parent resources
www.esafety.gov.au/parents

Cyber help
www.staysmartonline.gov.au

Project Rockit
www.projectrockit.com.au

ThinkUKnow online advice
www.thinkuknow.org.au

Australian Cyber Security Centre ReportCyber crime reporting
cyber.gov.au/report

Gaming resources
www.videogames.org.au

Gaming workshops
www.instituteofgames.com

Internet Safe Education
www.internetsafeeducation.com

EMERGENCIES
Ambulance/Fire/Police // **000**
Lifeline, 24-hour counselling
13 11 14 // www.lifeline.org.au

Protecting kids online
www.familyzone.com

Australian Council on Children and the Media app reviews
childrenandmedia.org.au/app-reviews

GameAware
www.gameaware.com.au

Family friendly filters
www.commsalliance.com.au/Activities/ispi/fff

Connect Safely
www.connectsafely.org

Internet safety
www.wesnet.org.au

Parent Guides
parentguides.com.au/social-media-101

// SOCIAL MEDIA LAWS

ACT // www.thinkuknow.org.au

Northern Territory //
www.thinkuknow.org.au

NSW // Legal Aid NSW under-18s youth hotline
1800 101 810

Queensland //
Queensland sexting laws
www.qld.gov.au/law/crime-and-police/types-of-crime/naked-pics //
www.legalaid.qld.gov.au

Tasmania // www.justice.tas.gov.au

Victoria // sexting laws
www.legalaid.vic.gov.au/find-legal-answers/sex-and-law/sexting-and-child-pornography

// GENERAL HELP

Anxiety Recovery Centre Victoria (has links to other states)
www.arcvic.org.au

Australian Psychological Society find a psychologist
www.psychology.org.au/FindaPsychologist

Beyond Blue
1300 22 4636
healthyfamilies.beyondblue.org.au

Black Dog Institute
www.blackdoginstitute.org.au

CAT Teams
www.health.vic.gov.au/mentalhealthservices/adult/

Health Direct services directory
www.healthdirect.gov.au

Mind Australia
1300 286 463
www.mindaustralia.org.au

Mind Matters
www.mindmatters.edu.au

Royal Australian College and New Zealand College of Psychiatrists
www.yourhealthinmind.org/mental-illnesses-disorders

Raising Children Network //
Australian parenting website
raisingchildren.net.au

Safe Schools Coalition Australia
www.safeschoolscoalition.org.au

Sane Australia
1800 18 7263
www.sane.org

Transcend (transgender support)
www.transcendsupport.com.au

National LGBTI Health Alliance
www.lgbtihealth.org.au

QLife
1800 184 527
www.qlife.org.au

Minus18
minus18.org.au

Suicide Call Back Service
1300 659 467 //
www.suicidecallbackservice.org.au

// PARENT HELP LINES

ACT // (02) 6287 3833

Northern Territory // 1300 301 300

NSW // 1300 1300 52

South Australia // 1300 364 100

Queensland // 1300 301 300

Tasmania // 1300 808 178

Victoria // 13 22 89

Western Australia // 1800 654 432

// GAMBLING

Gambler's Help Youthline (24/7)
1800 262 376

Gambling Help Online
www.gamblinghelponline.org.au

Parent resources
www.responsiblegambling.vic.gov.au

KidBet
kidbet.com.au

// APPS AND ONLINE TOOLS

MOOD DISORDER APPS VIA REACHOUT
au.professionals.reachout.com/apps-and-online-tools/mood-disorders

ANXIETY DISORDER APPS VIA REACHOUT
au.professionals.reachout.com/apps-and-online-tools/anxiety-disorders

TOOLS FOR GENERAL WELL-BEING VIA REACHOUT
au.professionals.reachout.com/apps-and-online-tools/wellbeing-apps-and-tools

REACHOUT WELL-BEING TOOLBOX
au.reachout.com/sites/thetoolbox

BEACON 2.0. PORTAL FOR ONLINE MENTAL AND PHYSICAL DISORDER APPLICATIONS
www.beacon.anu.edu.au

// YOUNG PEOPLE

ReachOut
au.reachout.com

Alannah & Madeline Foundation // Anti-bullying
www.amf.org.au

Headspace // Youth mental health
www.headspace.org.au

Kids Helpline
1800 55 1800
www.kidshelpline.com.au

Rosie // Research-based information for girls
www.rosie.org.au

Youth Beyond Blue // Beyond Blue's youth program
www.youthbeyondblue.com

Instagram resource
parents.au.reachout.com/landing/parents-insta-guide

MY NOTES

....
....
....
....
....
....

FREE DOWNLOAD

YOUR FAMILY TECHNOLOGY USER AGREEMENT FROM
parentguides.com.au

© Parenting Guides Ltd

So you think you know it all?
Think again.

DRUGS 101

YOUTH & DRUGS

Honest and open communication is vital.

// SIGNS OF DRUG USE*

It can be hard to tell if someone is using drugs, and their effects vary greatly from person to person. Signs that appear to be uncharacteristic of the person may require your attention, regardless of whether drugs are involved. These signs include:
- Mood swings, tiredness, explosive outbursts.
- Minimal interaction with family.
- Trouble with the police.
- Changes in eating patterns.
- Frequent absences from school/work, declining school/work performance.
- Sudden changes of friends.
- Unexplained need for money, disappearing money and valuables.
- Impaired memory, poor concentration, withdrawing socially.

*Copyright © Australian Drug Foundation 2015

SHOULD I SEARCH THEIR ROOM?

How you respond to suspicions of drug use is a personal matter. "Some parents feel comfortable searching their kid's room for illicit (drugs), others feel this violates trust," says Family Drug Support founder and CEO Tony Trimingham. "It certainly pays to think this through before doing something you will regret later. Whether or not you decide to search their room, you need to be aware of how your behaviour will model trust in your child's eyes.

"Parents should certainly put an emphasis on communication and simply try asking their children about drugs in a calm non-judgmental way. If your child feels that their honesty will be rewarded with anger, punishment or hysterics, then it will only be natural to lie and conceal their drug use. It is usually far better for your child to feel that you understand them and are willing to help them, even if they are making mistakes."

TIPS TO PARENTS

Tony Trimingham lost a son to heroin overdose in 1997. He says most parents believe their kids won't use drugs, will be truthful if asked and will turn to them if they are in trouble. This is not always the case. Trimingham urges parents to:
- Let them know that if they need help they can come to you and you will support them; you won't kick them out.
- Improve communication.
- Look for cues that they want to talk.
- Discuss drugs and alcohol openly. Listen more than directing or lecturing. Have a view, but accept theirs.
- Accept that they think they know more about drugs than you.
- Be informed and educated. Beware the extremes.
- Promote safety and encourage your children to look after themselves and their friends.
- Ensure they know the dangers of mixing drugs and alcohol and how to get medical help if needed.
- Discourage mixing substances and driving.
- Encourage them to have designated drivers or use public transport.

WHAT ABOUT YOUR DRUG USE?

Parents should be honest about current and past drug use, says Trimingham. "It will demonstrate that you were young and did rebellious things. It will encourage them to open up. You will also be demonstrating that you have changed and no longer need to use. If they believe you are being hypocritical, there will be no chance of your messages about drugs being effective."

// WHAT YOUR KIDS COULD BE BUYING WITH THEIR POCKET MONEY

$5
- Three litres of petrol **$1.20-$1.50 a litre**
- Correction fluid 20mL **$2**
- Extra-strong glue 3mL **$2.50-$3**
- 375mL beer stubby/can **$4**
- 240mL energy drink **$3-$3.50**
- Aerosol deodorant **$2.50-$7.25**
- Four-pack fluoro highlighters **$2-$5.50**
- Cheap wine bottle 750mL **$5**

$10
- Four-litre case of fruity wine **$9.99**
- Glue various sizes and types, up to **$9.90**
- Butane cartridge four-pack, 880 grams from **$9.95**
- Aldi beer six-pack from **$7.99**
- Aldi 4x275mL Vodka Crush **$9.95**

$20
- 1–1.5mL of GHB/GBL **$4-$8**
- One gram of hydroponic cannabis head **$10-$50**
- Basic 20-pack of cigarettes from **$20**
- Ten nitrous oxide whipped-cream charger bulbs from **$14.95 on eBay**
- One-litre all-purpose thinner **$16.90**
- 200mL of popular-brand rum **$17.99**

// PERCENTAGE OF 12 TO 17-YEAR-OLDS WHO HAVE USED THESE DRUGS IN THEIR LIFETIME

Percentage of students surveyed indicating they had used each of the different substances outlined in 2014.

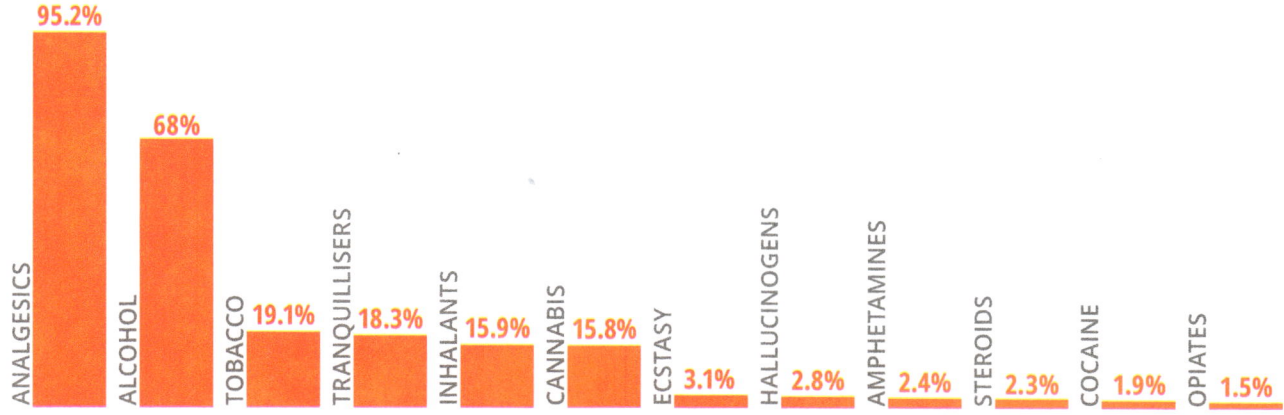

- ANALGESICS 95.2%
- ALCOHOL 68%
- TOBACCO 19.1%
- TRANQUILLISERS 18.3%
- INHALANTS 15.9%
- CANNABIS 15.8%
- ECSTASY 3.1%
- HALLUCINOGENS 2.8%
- AMPHETAMINES 2.4%
- STEROIDS 2.3%
- COCAINE 1.9%
- OPIATES 1.5%

The substance categories, descriptions and examples below are identical to the ones used in the questionnaire provided to students.

ANALGESICS
Pain killers/analgesics such as Disprin, Panadol and Nurofen.

ALCOHOL
Ordinary beer, low-alcohol beer, wine, wine cooler, Champagne or sparkling wine, alcoholic cider, alcoholic sodas, premixed spirits, spirits, or liqueurs.

TOBACCO
Cigarettes.

TRANQUILLISERS
Sleeping tablets, tranquillisers or sedatives such as rohies, Rohypnol, barbs, Valium or Serepax, for non-medical reasons.

INHALANTS
Deliberately sniffed (inhaled) from spray cans or sniffed things such as glue, paint, petrol or thinners in order to get high or for the way it makes you feel.

CANNABIS
Marijuana, grass, hash, cannabis, dope, weed, mull, yarndi, ganga, pot, a bong, or a joint.

ECSTASY
Ecstasy or XTC, E, MDMA, ecci, X, bickies.

HALLUCINOGENS
LSD, acid, trips, magic mushrooms, Datura, Angel's Trumpet.

AMPHETAMINES
Amphetamines or speed, uppers, MDA, goey, dex, Dexies, ox blood dexamphetamine, methamphetamine or ice, other than for medical reasons.

STEROIDS
Steroids, muscle, roids or gear, without a doctor's prescription to make you better at sport, to increase muscle size or to improve your general appearance.

COCAINE
Cocaine.

OPIATES
Heroin, smack, horse, skag, hammer, H, or other opiates (narcotics) such as methadone, morphine or pethidine other than for medical reasons.

Australian secondary school students' use of tobacco, alcohol, and over-the-counter and illicit substances in 2014, prepared for the Australian Government Department of Health Drug Strategy Branch by Victoria White and Tahlia Williams, Cancer Council Victoria Centre for Behavioural Research, October 2016.

$30

- A tab of LSD **$8-$50**
- Basic vodka 700mL **$30**
- Twelve Aldi Vodka Crush 275mL **$29.85**
- Basic 700mL rum bottle **$33**
- Six bottles of 750mL cheap sparkling white wine **$36**
- Basic 40-pack of cigarettes from **$43**

$50

- One MDMA tablet (ecstasy) **$4-$50**
- Basic 50-pack of cigarettes **$60**
- Slab (24 cans) of 375mL beer **$40-$50**
- 0.1-gram amphetamine **$50-$500**
  (WA & Tas data only)

$100 OR MORE

- Basic carton of cigarettes 10 x 20 or 4 x 40 packs from **$220**
- A single 10mL vial of testosterone propionate testosterone **$130-$250**
- A gram of heroin **$100-$700**
- A 10mL vial of anabolic steroid **$150-$250**
- A gram of cocaine **$200-$600**

Prices as of March 2019. Alcohol prices sourced from a bottle shop, cigarette, deodorant, and correction fluid prices from a supermarket/office supplier and glue and paint/paint thinner prices from a hardware store. Illicit drug prices sourced from The Australian Criminal Intelligence Commission Illicit Drug Data Report 2016-17.

ALCOHOL

OTHER NAMES // BOOZE, GROG, PISS, LIQUOR, CHARGE, NIP

Drinking can pose unacceptable risks in young people's formative years.

Parents may think they are doing their children a favour by letting them drink alcohol before they turn 18, particularly if it is supervised. But a growing body of evidence suggests that alcohol can damage developing young brains, which don't mature until we are about 25.

Early drinking can also lead to increased drinking rates and damaging behaviour. The risk of accidents, injuries, violence and self-harm are high among drinkers aged under 18. Young people who drink are also more prone to risky and antisocial behaviour than older drinkers.

National Health and Medical Research Council (NHMRC) guidelines recommend that not drinking alcohol is the best option for those under 18. For those under 15, this is especially important, and for those aged 15-17 drinking should be delayed as long as possible.

Experts also advise parents to discourage their children from abusing alcohol by modelling safe behaviours at home and while socialising. Many parents don't realise the influence their own drinking habits can have on their children and how important it is to model responsible alcohol use. It is important to be informed about the possible risks and to be aware that your child is learning from your behaviour.

> Combining alcohol with caffeine-laced energy drinks or other drugs can result in even more risky behaviour, put the body under great stress and increase the chances of overdosing

ALCOHOL IS NOT HARMLESS

Family Drug Support founder and CEO Tony Trimingham says alcohol should not be regarded as less harmful than other drugs. He says it is responsible for one in five hospital admissions, one in three drownings, one in four motor-vehicle accidents, three in four assaults, one in three divorces, domestic violence, sexual assault, unplanned sex, homelessness and suicide. The later young people start drinking, the less likely they are to develop severe issues.

Trimingham talks at many schools and believes 85 per cent of students have tried alcohol and more than 50 per cent drink regularly and to the point of intoxication. "It is without any question the most damaging drug that we use. Many parents turn a blind eye or even encourage underage drinking. Of course teenagers will use it, but … we should not actively promote it."

WHERE ARE KIDS GETTING IT?

Adolescents aged 12 to 17 are most likely to get alcohol from their parents. A 2014 Australian school student survey found 37.9 per cent of 12 to 17-year-olds received their last alcoholic drink from their parents, compared with 22 per cent from friends, 19 per cent from someone else and 8.7 per cent from siblings. Almost five per cent (4.7) took their last alcoholic drink from home.

// LAST ALCOHOLIC DRINK SUPPLIED BY

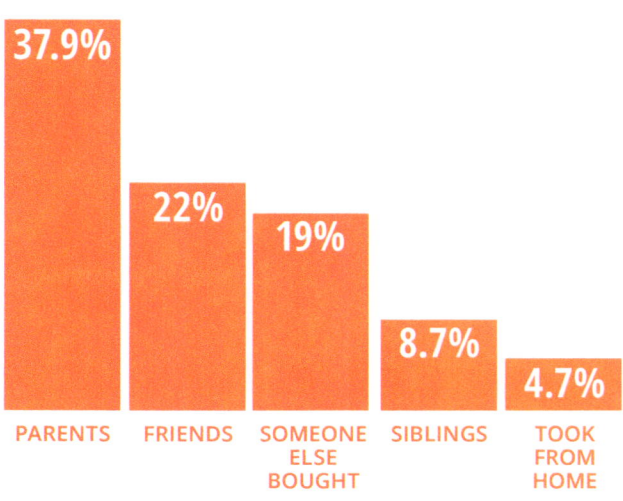

Australian secondary school students' use of tobacco, alcohol, and over-the-counter and illicit substances in 2014, Australian Government Department of Health Drug Strategy Branch.

// WARNING SIGNS A TEEN MAY BE MISUSING ALCOHOL

There are no definitive warning signs of alcohol misuse. But there are a range of signs and behaviours that, combined, may indicate excessive drinking. They include:
- Repeated health complaints.
- Changes in sleeping patterns.
- Changes in mood, especially irritability.
- Starting arguments, withdrawing from the family or breaking family rules.
- Dropping grades, frequent school absences or discipline problems at school.
- Changes in social activities and social groups.

WHO IS DRINKING ALCOHOL?

Almost seven in 10 (68 per cent) of children aged 12 to 17 have tried alcohol. The 2014 Australian secondary students' survey found 45.1 per cent of those surveyed had consumed alcohol in the past year. More than one in three 17-year-olds (36.6 per cent of girls and 34.8 per cent of boys) had drunk in the past week. All these figures were down on the 2011 findings.

AVERAGE NUMBER OF DRINKS STUDENTS WHO DRANK HAD IN THE PAST WEEK
(Current drinkers), by age group and sex, Australia, 2014

	12 to 15YO	16 to 17YO	12 to 17YO
MALES	5.5	8.6	7.3
FEMALES	3.9	5.4	4.8

Means are based on unweighted data. Respondents indicating they consumed more than 20 drinks on any one day excluded from calculations of means. *Australian secondary school students' use of tobacco, alcohol, and over-the-counter and illicit substances in 2014*, Australian Government Department of Health Drug Strategy Branch.

SHORT-TERM EFFECTS / LONG-TERM EFFECTS

RELAXED, HAPPIER, PASSING OUT, CONFUSED, SADDER, COMA, MEMORY LOSS, INCREASED CONFIDENCE, VOMITING, DEATH

SICK, MEMORY LOSS, CANCER, ERECTION DIFFICULTIES, HIGH BLOOD PRESSURE, BRAIN DAMAGE, DEPRESSION, LIVER DISEASE, HEART DISEASE

The following day they may have a hangover that may include a headache, diarrhoea and nausea, tiredness and trembling, increased heart rate and blood pressure, dry mouth, trouble concentrating, anxiety and restless sleep.

// ENERGY DRINKS

A typical 250mL energy drink contains about 50-80mg of caffeine, which is similar to the average cup of coffee. Larger 500mL drinks contain up to 160mg. Energy drinks are popular with teenagers who may not realise how much caffeine and other stimulants they contain. Energy drinks have varying amounts of caffeine, taurine, guarana, amino acids, vitamins and sugar. Short-term effects include feeling more alert and active, needing to urinate more frequently, increased body temperature and heart rate and stimulation of the brain and nervous system.

High doses can cause insomnia, nervousness, headaches, nausea, vomiting, rapid heart rate and heart palpitations. Several young people have died after consuming too much or mixing energy drinks with alcohol and other drugs. There is no reported evidence that energy drinks have any nutritional value. Research has found that children and young people who consume energy drinks may suffer from sleep problems, bed-wetting and anxiety.

Sales of energy drinks in Australia and New Zealand increased from 34.5 million litres in 2001 to 155.6 million litres in 2010 – a 23 per cent share of the total convenience beverages market.

Food Regulation Policy Options Paper: The Regulation of Caffeine in Foods. Produced for the Food Regulation Standing Committee (FRSC) by the FRSC Caffeine Working Group, August, 2013.

Profile // Yvonne Bonomo

THE PHYSICIAN

Yvonne Bonomo has worked with adolescents and specialised in addiction medicine for 20 years. She explains the harm-reduction approach to drug use.

"I started to see young people present with drug problems 20 years ago and initially my focus was alcohol and the trajectories individuals follow depending on the age they start drinking or using drugs.

"Alcohol is still the number-one problem, despite what we hear about ice. The escalation in drug problems we saw with heroin 20 years ago, we're seeing today with ice. There was a flood of heroin in the market then, and it's almost a replay of that, but with methamphetamine.

"I've also seen a change in attitude. Young people are becoming more prepared to consider drug use, so we need to keep education about the harms of drug use at the forefront.

"Harm reduction became prominent when HIV came on the scene in the 1980s. It refers to strategies aimed at reducing negative consequences of drug use and focuses on prevention of harm rather than prevention of drug use. It acknowledges that drug use is part of our world and we need to minimise its harmful effects, rather than ignoring or condemning people who use drugs.

"People have heard of needle and syringe programs (NSPs) where injecting drug users obtain clean equipment so they don't get infections like hepatitis C and HIV. Another example of harm reduction is injecting drug rooms (supervised injecting facilities or 'SIFs') where people go to a place supervised by health workers so their risk of overdose is reduced. At the same time, staff can provide other health care to these people.

"A new harm-reduction strategy will start this year for people who inject drugs. Naloxone is a medication that reverses the effects of an overdose so people start breathing again and it will be available without prescription. Another harm-reduction strategy is pill testing at dance parties.

"Some people worry that these strategies condone drug use. But it's important to understand that research shows they reduce deaths, infections and other health risks.

"But harm reduction for young people needs to be put into context. NSPs, SIFs and naloxone are for harder-end drug use. Harm-reduction strategies for young people also change as they mature. As young people develop their identity they may experience emotional turmoil, so understanding where they 'are at' is an important overlay to anything we do.

"Adolescence is usually when mental health problems emerge. Young people might turn to drugs, but in the long-term alcohol and drugs worsen mental health. Parents also should monitor risk and protective factors in their young person's life – is home stable and safe? Are they involved in education or employment and fulfilling activities?

"Most importantly, do they have a trusted adult in their life that they would turn to if they needed support? These things develop resilience and make alcohol, drugs or other risky behaviours less likely.

"Talk to your teenager, listen, talk again, listen again. Remember they are still developing maturity so their ability to see the bigger picture may not be immediate. Ask them if they have come across drugs. Many young people have been exposed to drug use in some way. Don't over-react if they say something that isn't in keeping with your opinion. Debate it and understand the different perspectives together.

"Acknowledge that we all want to make our own choices. Share why their experience might be different today and why, as a parent, you might worry. Talk through different scenarios to stay safe – alcohol, drugs and driving, drink spiking, aggression or violence, offers of pills etc.

"And don't forget to provide positive feedback about their strengths. Young people need to know they are cared for and that their parents want to make sure they're ready to manage potential harms in today's world."

> "Do they have a trusted adult in their life that they would turn to if they needed support?"

Photo by Fiona Hamilton

// Yvonne Bonomo is director of Addiction Medicine at St Vincent's Hospital.

LEAD BY EXAMPLE

Children look to their parents to set standards.

Parental attitudes to drinking have a big influence on their children. There is nothing wrong with having a drink, but parents need to be aware that their alcohol habits are observed by their children, who may take a lead from their behaviour.

PARENTS CAN MODEL RESPONSIBLE DRINKING BY FOLLOWING THESE TIPS *
- Limit your alcohol use, especially in front of your children.
- Do not get drunk, especially in front of your children.
- Sometimes decline the offer of alcohol.
- Provide food and non-alcoholic beverages if making alcohol available to guests.
- Never drink and drive.
- Do not let other adults drive after they have been drinking.
- Do not convey to your children the idea that alcohol is fun or glamorous through stories about your own or others' drinking.
- Use healthy ways to cope with stress without alcohol, such as exercise, listening to music, or talking things over.

MYTH BUSTER
Allowing under-18s to drink will "ease them into it"

FACT
Alcohol can be damaging to young, developing brains. Early drinking is also linked to increased alcohol consumption in adolescence and young adulthood and the possibility of damage to the developing brain and development of alcohol-related harms in adulthood.

SUPPLYING ALCOHOL TO MINORS
Under Victoria's Liquor Control Reform Act 1998, a person must not supply liquor to a minor aged under 18 and a minor must not receive, possess or consume liquor. It is an offence for adults to supply alcohol to a minor in a private home without parental consent. Adults must therefore have parental consent before supplying alcohol to their child's friends in their own home. An adult who breaks this law faces the same penalty as licensees who supply alcohol to minors in licensed venues – a maximum of more than $7000.

ALCOHOL TIPS FOR PARENTS *
- Talk about alcohol issues.
- Establish family rules.
- Have consequences when rules are broken.
- Monitor your child.
- Prepare for peer influence.
- Encourage positive friendships.
- Enlist the support of other parents.
- Prepare your child for a range of drinking scenarios such as being around drunk people.
- Discuss drink spiking and other dangers.
- Warn about drink driving.
- Never supply alcohol to your adolescent's friends.
- Give positive feedback if they act responsibly.
- Discuss any concerns you have.

* Parenting Strategies: preventing adolescent alcohol misuse.
www.parentingstrategies.net/alcohol

// GOOD NEWS, BAD NEWS

NATIONAL DRUG STRATEGY HOUSEHOLD SURVEY
It's good news and bad news for Australian drinkers. The proportion of people aged 14 and over who don't drink alcohol rose from 19.9 per cent in 2010 to 22 per cent in 2013. Of those aged 12 to 17, 72 per cent abstained, up from 64 per cent. But the National Drug Strategy Household Survey found almost four in 10 Australians aged 14 and over put themselves at risk of injury while drinking in the past year. One in four did so as often as monthly.

Binge drinking remains a problem. In 2013, about one in seven (15.6 per cent) people aged 12 or older had consumed 11 or more standard drinks on a single occasion in the past 12 months. One in 15 (7.3 per cent) had in the last month.
Find out more // www.aihw.gov.au

GLOBAL DRUG SURVEY
The online Global Drug Survey (GDS) is the world's biggest drug-use patterns survey. In 2016 the GDS predicted over 250,000 responses. Up 100% on previous years.
To take part visit // www.globaldrugsurvey.com

VERY HIGH RISK
Proportion of people exceeding the single occasion risk (had more than four standard drinks on one occasion) guidelines (at least monthly), people aged 12 or older, by age, 2013.

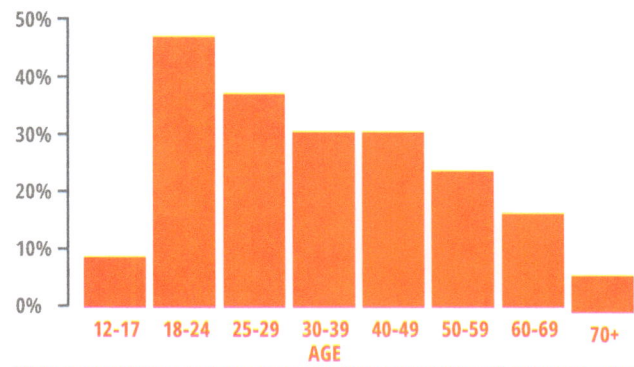

National Drug Strategy Household Survey detailed report 2013.
Australian Institute of Health and Welfare 2014.

CANNABIS

OTHER NAMES // MARIJUANA, GRASS, POT, DOPE, MARY JANE, HOOCH, WEED, HASH, JOINTS, BREW, REEFERS, CONES, SMOKE, MULL, BUDDHA, GANGA, HYDRO, YARNDI, HEADS, CHOOF

One in three adults and one in seven teenagers has tried cannabis.

Cannabis is Australia's most popular illicit drug and many of today's high-school parents have tried it. The 2013 National Drug Strategy Household Survey found that 35 per cent of Australians reported using cannabis at least once, with 10 per cent using it in the past year. A 2014 Australian high-school students' survey found cannabis was the most commonly used illicit substance by this age group, with 15.8 per cent of 12 to 17-year-olds reporting they had tried it.

Most people who use cannabis seek a sense of mild euphoria and relaxation, often referred to as a "high". Cannabis causes changes in the user's mood and also affects how they think and perceive the environment. Everyday activities such as watching television and listening to music can become altered and more intense.

Generally speaking, people who start smoking cannabis at a younger age and smoke heavily are more likely to experience problems. This may include mental health problems, and more general life problems, such as conflict at home or school/work, financial problems and memory problems. If a teenager has a genetic vulnerability, such as close family with depression, psychosis, bipolar disorder or anxiety, or if they have an existing mental health issue, cannabis should be avoided.

People with a family or personal history of mental health problems should avoid using cannabis

// WHAT IS CANNABIS?

Cannabis is derived from the cannabis plant (*Cannabis sativa*). The main active ingredient is delta-9-tetrahydrocannabinol, commonly known as THC. This is the part of the plant that gives the high. THC potency varies greatly between cannabis products.

SHORT-TERM EFFECTS

 FEELING OF WELL-BEING
 LOSS OF INHIBITIONS
 TALKATIVENESS
 ANXIETY & PARANOIA
 DROWSINESS
 BLOODSHOT EYES
 LOSS OF CO-ORDINATION
 INCREASED APPETITE
 DRY EYES, MOUTH & THROAT

LONG-TERM EFFECTS

 RESPIRATORY DISEASES
 CANCER
 DECREASED MEMORY
 DECREASED MOTIVATION
 MENTAL HEALTH PROBLEMS
 RISK OF DEPENDENCE

National Cannabis Prevention and Information Centre, **www.ncpic.org.au**

// HOW IT IS USED

Cannabis is usually smoked in hand-rolled cigarettes (known as joints) or in special waterpipes (bongs). These pipes or bongs can be bought or made from things such as orange-juice containers, soft-drink cans or even toilet rolls. Cannabis is used in three main forms:

MARIJUANA
Made from dried flowers and leaves of the cannabis plant. It is the least potent of all the cannabis products and is usually smoked.

HASHISH
Made from the resin (a secreted gum) of the cannabis plant. It is dried and pressed into small blocks and smoked. It can also be added to food and eaten.

HASH OIL
The most potent cannabis product, this is a thick oil obtained from hashish. It is also smoked.

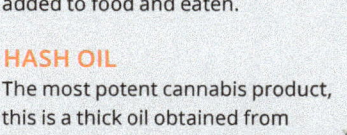

Q&A

Q. DOES CANNABIS LEAD TO HARD-DRUG USE?

A A direct link has not been established between cannabis use and the later use of "harder" drugs such as heroin and methamphetamine. Anecdotally, those working with disadvantaged young people see some who use cannabis and other drugs. Youth worker and Les Twentyman Foundation founder Les Twentyman has met hundreds of dependent hard-drug users and says most started with marijuana. He believes as they become more dependent on cannabis they need a stronger "kick". "So they go from one thing to the next," he says. Others disagree with this theory.

Q. DOES IT CAUSE MENTAL HEALTH PROBLEMS?

A Medical professionals and researchers have not found conclusive evidence that cannabis use causes mental health problems, but research does show a strong relationship between cannabis use and experiencing mental health problems. The causes of psychosis are not fully understood, but a relationship has been found between cannabis use and psychosis. It may cause symptoms similar to psychotic disorders, which can last several hours or, in rare cases, up to three days. In many cases the symptoms disappear when cannabis use is stopped.

Q. DOES CANNABIS CAUSE SCHIZOPHRENIA?

A Research has shown a relationship between cannabis use and mental health problems such as schizophrenia. However, despite major increases in cannabis use in Australia during the past 30 years, schizophrenia levels have not increased. There is evidence that regular cannabis use increases the likelihood of schizophrenia symptoms in people with certain risk factors, with the main one being a personal or family history of mental health problems. There is evidence that people with schizophrenia who use cannabis tend to have their first psychotic episode at a younger age than those who don't.

Q. DOES IT CAUSE DEPRESSION AND ANXIETY?

A Research has found a relationship between cannabis use and depression. The effects of cannabis may seem to help ease depression at the time, but is likely to worsen depression in the long term. Regular cannabis users are likely to have higher levels of depression than non-users. There is some evidence to indicate that cannabis use – heavy or frequent use in particular – can cause depression later in life. The relationship between cannabis use and anxiety is less clear, but anxiety and panic attacks are among the most-common negative effects reported by users.

// IF YOUR CHILD IS AFFECTED BY CANNABIS

LEARN ABOUT CANNABIS USE AND MENTAL HEALTH
The more you know, the better equipped you will be to help.

ENCOURAGE THEM TO GET HELP
Urge them to seek professional help – don't wait to see if they get better without treatment.

BE UNDERSTANDING
Tell them you're there for them, encourage them and help with their treatment.

BE PATIENT
Getting better takes time – even if they are committed to treatment. Be prepared for setbacks and challenges.

LOOK AFTER YOURSELF
Information and assistance is available for family, friends and people who use drugs. There is no need to deal with drug issues alone.

HOW MUCH DOES CANNABIS COST?

One gram of cannabis head	**$12 - $50**
An ounce of cannabis head	**$210 - $450**
A single mature cannabis plant	**$2000 - $5000**

The Australian prices for hydroponic cannabis. Australian Crime Commission *Illicit Drug Data Report* 2013-14.

// TOBACCO

While smoking rates have fallen dramatically, nicotine is still a serious health issue. Adult smoking rates have more than halved since 1980, when one in three Australians smoked.

Teenagers still experiment with smoking and some are taking it up. In 2014, 19.1 per cent of all Australian high-school students had tried smoking. By the age of 17, 39.1 per cent had tried it. Only 2.7 per cent per cent of all students had smoked more than 100 cigarettes in their lifetime, peaking at 7.9 per cent per cent of 17-year-olds.

Only 1.1 per cent of 12-year-olds were current smokers, having smoked in the past seven days, rising to 12.1 per cent of 17-year-olds. Boys were slightly more likely to smoke than girls aged 12, 16 and 17. Rates were similar at 13, while girls smoked slightly more at 14 and 15. Overall, slightly more boys (5.4 per cent) than girls (4.9 per cent) aged 12 to 17 were current smokers.

www.quit.org.au and *Australian secondary school students' use of tobacco in 2014*, prepared by Vicki White, Tahlia Williams, Centre for Behavioural Research in Cancer, Cancer Council Victoria, for Tobacco Control Taskforce Australian Government Department of Health, October 2015.

One in five Australian high-school students has tried smoking

// Profile

THE TEENAGER

Nick*, 17, began using drugs and drinking when he was 12. He has been to detox and rehab and is working with a counsellor at Odyssey House to overcome his addiction.

"I was about 12 when I began smoking a little bit of pot. I began drinking too and occasionally I tried speed. I never fitted into school and I found a pair of mates who were the same and we'd use with each other. It's hard to explain why I started but I suppose I relied on these things to make me feel better. When I got too many thoughts in my head – happy or sad – I'd try and wash them out with drugs.

"I started smoking pot more often in the week and doing crazy things on the weekend. By the time I was 13 or 14, I was using pot every day and drinking and popping pills and I was in and out of different schools.

"In early 2012 I got a job working with my family. I'd only smoke pot during the week but would go really crazy at the weekends – coke, amphetamines, methamphetamines … I got prescribed benzos as well. Whatever I could get, really.

"Mum was pretty strict and told me I was going to see a drugs counsellor. I knew she was right and that I needed to pull up. I've been seeing my counsellor since I was 16. I went into detox for a week and did all right for a few weeks afterwards – and then I realised I was a mess again. I've stayed with my counsellor and I've been in detox and spent three months in rehab. I had 100 days clean afterwards and then I got that 'I'm going to use tonight' feeling. I went to my mate's place and drank heaps and popped a goog – an ecstasy tablet.

"At the moment methamphetamines are my drug of choice – but I try and get a couple of days a week when I stay home and don't use. I had a pretty full-on one last night though – I'm not going to lie. I was coming down from a bender and seeing people running around outside my front yard. I was tripping out, which freaks me out a bit. When that happens I try and stay calm and remind myself it will stop.

"I had a solid group of mates but since I got out of rehab my friends have changed. Some mates got really full on and others stopped. They stopped robbing people to support their habit and robbing dealers to get some drugs in their system. I've been in some serious fights with my mates about drugs and money … it gets a mess. I don't know who to hang around with now because it's so easy to use when you're with mates.

"I see people being a bad influence on others. You'll see

"I had 100 days clean … and then I got that 'I'm going to use tonight' feeling."

Licensed material is being used for illustrative purposes only, any person depicted in the licensed material is a model.

innocent people hanging around and someone thinks it would be funny to see that person on drugs, so they give them something. I've told my mates not to give anyone their first drug.

"If I was a 12-year-old kid again I'd warn him to choose another life and not to go down this hectic path. Because you will always be in debt and you could go to jail. I used to think I was better than other drug users but I'm just the same – standing in Cash Converters hocking all my stuff.

"Mum has been pretty good and she's tried to get me the right help. I don't want to be a fully grown adult and still be using. I love drawing and I'd like to be a signwriter or a graphic artist one day. I've got to pull up before I get in big, big shit."

* Names have been changed to protect the person's identity.

// Profile

THE PARENT

Felicity* – Nick's* mum – has supported her son since realising he was using drugs. She believes parents need to better recognise the danger signs.

"Earlier in Nick's life we didn't realise he had dyslexia and other learning difficulties. He was in a supposedly top school in the state but they weren't interested in helping him. He was put in the 'too hard' basket and was ostracised. And Nick felt that. In hindsight, that's when all the trouble began …

"I didn't realise for quite a long time that when I dropped Nick at the school gate he'd walk out the back gate and spend the day smoking marijuana with his friends. Then he started arriving home from school a little later and a little later. Four o'clock became five o'clock and then 9 or 10pm. I'd drive around the streets looking for him.

"He was using drugs and drinking for three years before I realised what was going on – then our cleaner found marijuana in his room. Now I know the signs – your child gets into trouble at school, they drop out of sport and activities they used to enjoy, they change friends and don't spend as much time with the family. Nick has a soft spot for his grandparents and he even stopped listening to them. They don't respect anyone any more because the drug rules their life and in some ways they are not your child any more. You're dealing with a beast.

"I tackled the problem aggressively at first – you think if you are demanding and controlling you can put your child back into place. You try and ground them but they climb out windows. They have no boundaries.

"I took away his phone and one day I became so frustrated that I threw his computer out of a window. Nothing I was doing was helping him and I was so frustrated.

"I tried to get help through schools but ended up getting some recommendations from our church. I called Youth Support and Advocacy Service, who went through Headspace, and they called Odyssey House.

"I took Nick to psychologists but you need to find them a place that helps kids with an alcohol problem, or kids with a drug problem. They need to find a counsellor they relate to.

"And I now know that love and understanding works. It's the hardest thing to do to be kind when your kid is off his face and swearing at you. But it's like talking to a child of three or four who is having a tantrum – you have to stay calm and give them love.

"If you become aggressive, they run further away. If you make them feel guilty, they drink more or take more drugs. Drama makes it all worse. Kindness and support draws your child closer to you.

"There are always underlying problems. You'll be surprised what secrets you child hides, before it's too late. We live in a society where we respect a child's privacy – I think you need to snoop a little. You need to know what's going on – in their mobile phone, Facebook, diaries – and what they are hiding in their closets. That could save their future or their lives. If it wasn't for our cleaner finding Nick's drugs or alcohol, I would still be in the dark about it.

"Don't think this could never happen to your child and your family. It can. So education about drugs and alcohol and how it may affect your child is important. If it does happen, you need professional help as a parent too. There may be times when your child is off the rails and to cope you might start drinking or taking medication yourself, and that doesn't help.

"After rehab Nick was doing fantastic and although he has relapsed now, it isn't as bad as before he went to rehab. I can see positive signs and I will support him to get the help he needs."

"He was using drugs and drinking for three years before I realised what was going on."

* Names have been changed to protect the person's identity.

PARENT Q&A

Kirsten Cleland has worked in the mental-health field for more than 20 years and in youth mental health for the past eight years with headspace.

Q. ARE PARENTS INSTINCTS IMPORTANT IN RECOGNISING IF THEIR CHILD IS STRUGGLING WITH SOMETHING IN THEIR LIFE?

A "Parents know their children better than anyone else in the world. If you sense there is something going on for your child that is not usual, and it has happened consistently, see your GP. If you sense your GP is not taking you seriously then I strongly recommend you get a second opinion – maybe from a GP who specialises in young people or someone with an interest in mental health."

Q. HOW PREVALENT ARE MENTAL HEALTH DIFFICULTIES IN YOUNG PEOPLE?

A "One of the reasons headspace was set up was that 75 per cent of all mental health difficulties occur before the age of 25. By mental health difficulties I'm talking about social or family difficulties, bullying or stress at school and young people questioning their gender role or sexuality through to anxiety and depression. It's a time of massive change – puberty, the transition from primary to secondary school, young people making decisions about what they are going to do with their life and wanting to be more independent from parents ..."

Q. HOW DO YOU GET YOUR KIDS TO TALK ABOUT THESE ISSUES?

A "Kids can feel uncomfortable speaking with their parents about issues that are concerning them. So it is important for them to know who is in that young person's life that they can talk to? A footy coach, teacher, mum, dad, grandparents, godparents. Make yourself available. Kids always (often?) want to tell you the most important things as you're walking out the door, making dinner or on a business call. It won't always be at the most convenient time. It is important that you take this opportunity to engage with your young person, as this is the moment when they have come to you for help. If you're trying to start the conversation, evidence indicates statements help like 'I've noticed... it seems like... I'm wondering... you don't seem yourself, you seem really tired...' Be inquiring rather than accusatory. You shut off the opportunity for communication if young people see it as potentially adversarial or feel they're going to get in trouble."

Q. WOULD YOUR CHILD LIKE YOU TO FIX THE PROBLEM, OR DO THEY WANT YOU TO SIMPLY LISTEN?

A "I often say to my kids, 'would you like me to fix this or would you like me to listen?' By giving them an opportunity to decide what type of support is available you are allowing them to have a degree of control as well as letting them know you trust them to know what they need. Often, at first, they just want you to listen because listening is an opportunity to join around a shared concern. Then you can ask 'what can I do?', however you are enabling your child to have a degree of responsibility and you're demonstrating you have faith in their ability to make decisions. That's our job as parents – to help our kids made decisions. The decision might not be the one we would like, and it might blow up in their face, but as long as it's not going to do harm then it's a learning opportunity."

Q. HOW DO YOU KEEP COMMUNICATION OPEN WHEN YOUR CHILD DOES EVERYTHING TO AVOID TALKING?

A "Young people can feel they have nothing of value to offer or they believe that what they have to say is important, especially if they are feeling so awful in themselves. Check in with them regularly – tell them you're making a cup of tea and would they like something? If they say no, ask again in an hour. Make their favourite meal for dinner and If they don't leave their room, take a plate to them. Or sit with them and let them know you've noticed they are not themselves. Even if you're not getting much back, the young person sees that mum or dad are reliable and are there for them. Remember to be consistent in what you say and do, and to follow through as this will demonstrate your reliability to them as a support."

Photo: Supplied

// Kirsten Cleland is a manager with headspace Early Psychosis Services and a former centre manager – headspace Elsternwick & headspace Bentleigh.

INHALANTS

OTHER NAMES // GLUE, GAS, SNIFF, HUFF, CHROMING, POPPERS

Be careful what is left around the house.

Sniffing inhalants such as glue, petrol and aerosols is a cheap and dangerous way for young people to achieve a "high". The substances used are often affordable and easily obtained. About 15.9 per cent of Australia high-school students have used inhalants, making them more popular than individual illicit drugs such as heroin, cocaine and ice. These substances can seriously affect or even kill if an overdose occurs.

Essentially, inhalants are common household, industrial and medical products that produce vapours that can be inhaled to produce a "high". Common inhalants include aerosol sprays, spray paint and paint thinner, felt-tipped pens, correction fluid, gas from lighters or barbecues (butane), cleaning fluid, glue, petrol and nitrous oxide. The use of inhalants is more common in younger children than older children.

Inhalants are commonly sprayed into a plastic bag, poured into a bottle or soaked onto a cloth or sleeve before being inhaled. Sometimes they are inhaled directly from the container or are sprayed directly into the mouth or nose. This method can cause suffocation.

SHORT-TERM EFFECTS

- INITIAL RUSH/HIGH
- SPONTANEOUS LAUGHTER
- FEELING OF WELL-BEING
- LOSS OF CO-ORDINATION
- LOSS OF INHIBITIONS
- CONFUSED & DISORIENTED
- BAD BREATH
- RUNNY NOSE & NOSE BLEEDS
- BLURRED VISION & BLOODSHOT EYES
- AGITATION & AGGRESSION

LONG-TERM EFFECTS

- IRRITABILITY & DEPRESSION
- TROUBLE CONCENTRATING
- MEMORY LOSS
- PALE APPEARANCE & TREMORS
- TIREDNESS & WEIGHT LOSS
- EXCESSIVE THIRST
- LOSS OF SENSE SMELL & HEARING
- INDIGESTION & STOMACH ULCERS
- LIVER & KIDNEY DAMAGE
- RISK OF DEPENDENCE
- FINANCIAL/WORK PROBLEMS
- ANAEMIA, IRREGULAR HEARTBEAT & HEART MUSCLE DAMAGE

// COMMON SOURCES*

AEROSOLS	SOLVENTS	CLEANING AGENTS	GASES	FOOD PRODUCTS	ANAESTHETICS	ADHESIVES	NITRITES
Hairspray	Nail polish removers	Dry cleaners	Fuel gas	Whipped-cream aerosols	Gaseous	Airplane glue	Poppers
Deodorants	Paint remover/ thinners	Spot removers	Cigarette-lighter fuel		Liquid	Other glues	Fluids
Spray paint	Correction fluids and thinners	Degreasers	Refrigerant		Local		Room odorisers
Fabric-protector spray	Permanent marker pens	Video head cleaners					
Computer cleaners	Petrol						
Asthma sprays							

SOME OF THE CHEMICALS FOUND IN THESE PRODUCTS

Acetone, amyl nitrite, benzene, butane, butyl nitrite, chlorofluorocarbons, cyclohexyl nitrite, dimethyl ether, ethyl acetate, enflurane, ethyl chloride, freon, fluorocarbons, lead, halothane, methyl chloride, methyl ethyl ketone, methyl butyl ketone, methanol, nitrous oxide, n-hexane, propane, petroleum distillates, trichloroethylene, trichloroethane, tetrachloroethylene, xylene.

*National Inhalants Information Service

© Parenting Guides Ltd

AMPHETAMINES

OTHER NAMES // SPEED, FAST, UP, UPPERS, LOUEE, GOEY AND WHIZ, ICE, CRYSTAL METH, SHABU, CRYSTAL, GLASS, SHARD, P2

Highly addictive and extremely dangerous, problem amphetamines such as ice are becoming more common.

Ice is a highly addictive form of amphetamine known as methamphetamine. It is stronger than the powdered form of amphetamine, speed. Usage rates by Australian teenagers are generally low, but pockets of Melbourne and regional Victoria face growing ice-related problems, both physical and social. Drug overdose deaths and ambulance attendances involving ice have risen in metropolitan Melbourne and regional Victoria in the past two years.

While the use of amphetamines as a whole has not increased, more people are using it in the potent crystal methamphetamine form (ice), which produces strong highs very quickly and can be highly addictive. This is causing growing concern among police and medical professionals, as those using ice can become extremely violent and have been known to attack ambulance officers trying to help them. They may also commit violent crimes.

Youth worker and Les Twentyman Foundation founder Les Twentyman says in some areas of high youth unemployment up to 30 per cent of young people use or sell ice – or both. He says the drug is highly addictive and can cause users to become extremely violent. He has even heard of desperate parents buying it for their children.

"Once you start and you get an addiction you have to have more and more ... and that's when it becomes a problem," he says. "There's no easy fix for this."

Ice can be found in different colours such as fawn, brown, white and grey

// WHAT ARE AMPHETAMINES? *

Amphetamines are stimulants that come in powder form, tablets, capsules or crystals. They may be packaged in "foils" (aluminium foil), plastic bags or small balloons. Amphetamine powder has a strong smell and bitter taste. The capsules and tablets vary in colour and can be a mix of drugs, binding agents, caffeine and sugar. Some amphetamines are legally prescribed by doctors to treat conditions such as attention deficit hyperactivity disorder (ADHD) and narcolepsy (where a person has an uncontrollable urge to sleep).

SHORT-TERM EFFECTS

- HAPPINESS & CONFIDENCE
- TALKATIVENESS
- LARGE PUPILS & DRY MOUTH
- EXCESSIVE SWEATING
- INCREASED ENERGY
- REPEATED ITCHING & SCRATCHING
- TEETH GRINDING & DENTAL PROBLEMS
- FAST HEATBEAT & BREATHING

LONG-TERM EFFECTS

- EXTREME WEIGHT LOSS
- RESTLESS SLEEP
- MUSCLE STIFFNESS
- TROUBLE CONCENTRATING
- REGULAR COLDS & FLU
- ANXIETY & PARANOIA
- VIOLENT BEHAVIOUR
- DEPRESSION
- FINANCIAL/WORK PROBLEMS
- REDUCED APPITITE
- RISK OF STROKE
- HALLUCINATIONS
- HEART & KIDNEY PROBLEMS
- RISK OF DEPENDENCE & NEEDING MORE FOR THE SAME EFFECT

METHAMPHETAMINES

Ice, or crystal methamphetamine, is a potent amphetamine. The only difference between ice and speed is that ice is further refined to remove impurities. Ice is a stimulant and is generally stronger, more addictive and has more harmful side effects than speed. Ice usually comes as small chunky clear crystals that look like ice. It may also be a white or brownish crystal-like powder with a strong smell and bitter taste. Ice is generally smoked or injected. *Copyright © Australian Drug Foundation 2015*

WHO IS USING ICE?

While reported use of ice by high-school students is relatively low, those working at street level say it is much higher and growing fast, particularly in low socio-economic areas. Nationally, the 2014 secondary school students' survey found 2.4 per cent of 12 to 17-year-old high-school students have tried amphetamines.

> Ice users will often have a four to five-day bender, failing to sleep, eat or drink properly

// ICE-RELATED HARM

The number of Victorian fatal drug overdoses involving methamphetamines has risen by more than 250 per cent since 2010, putting it second behind heroin as an illicit drug contributing to overdose. The purity of ice also rose from 20 per cent in 2010-11 to 75 per cent in 2012-13.

Impacts of Methamphetamine in Victoria, Penington Institute report for the Victorian Department of Health, June, 2014.

After a massive increase the previous year, ambulance attendances involving ice continued to rise across regional Victoria between 2012-13 and 2013-14, up from 231 to 295. In metropolitan Melbourne they increased from 1116 to 1237. The local government areas with the highest attendance rate in regional Victoria were Greater Shepparton, Campaspe and La Trobe, and in the metropolitan area Melbourne, Frankston and Port Phillip.

Turning Point Ambo Project: Alcohol and Drug Related Ambulance Attendances: Trends in alcohol and drug-related ambulance attendances in Victoria 2013-14.

// EFFECTS OF ICE

Ice is much stronger than regular amphetamines. As well as constantly picking at their skin due to a feeling of bugs crawling underneath, users often become extremely paranoid and ultra-violent. One user threw a Molotov cocktail at youth worker Les Twentyman because she thought he was selling her daughter drugs. Twentyman says some people who use drugs also seem to gain superhuman strength, making it extremely dangerous for ambulance officers and doctors treating them. "They think everyone's after them and they cause havoc in the hospital system," he says.

Ice users will often have a four to five-day bender, failing "to sleep, eat or drink properly". They then tend to "crash" and sleep on and off for several days. This lifestyle puts enormous stress on their bodies. "It's far more potent than the other amphetamines," Twentyman says.

DEPENDENCE

Regular ice users can quickly become dependent and might need it to get through a normal day. Twentyman says dealers tell teenagers that ice will boost their energy and sex drive, when in reality it can lead to serious health and social problems. Twentyman says signs of dependence include a changed personality, unusual sleeping patterns, loss of appetite and theft. "Certain things start to go missing," he says. "You can't find your camera, you can't find your wedding rings."

MENTAL HEALTH PROBLEMS *

Some regular users may enjoy everyday activities less. They can get stressed easily and their moods can go up and down quite quickly. These changes can lead to longer-term problems with anxiety and depression. People may feel these effects for at least several weeks or months after they give up ice.

ICE PSYCHOSIS *

High doses of ice and frequent use may cause "ice psychosis", which is characterised by paranoid delusions, hallucinations and bizarre, aggressive or violent behaviour. These symptoms usually disappear a few days after the person stops using ice.

Copyright © Australian Drug Foundation 2015

Profile // Alan Eade

THE PARAMEDIC

A 20-year veteran of the ambulance service, paramedic Alan Eade attends incidents every week involving young people affected by drugs or alcohol.

"Around midnight last night we were called to help a 14 year-old boy on the city streets. He and some other teenagers did a snatch-and-run at a bottle shop. He consumed quite a bit of alcohol in a short space of time and became intoxicated. Police saw him and called an ambulance.

"He wasn't life-threateningly unwell and he hadn't run away from home either but he was taken to a children's hospital where he could safely sleep off the alcohol and be supervised while he recovered. Since I began this job alcohol has always been present but it was unusual in the under-14s. Now we see children in single-digit years drinking alcohol on a regular basis. Although, the age young people have their first alcoholic drink has increased over the past two years, which is a positive.

"More young people are getting exposed to illegal drugs at an earlier age and they want instant gratification. If under-18s used an illegal substance 20 years ago it was most likely marijuana. The current illegal drugs that young people use vary – there is no firm pattern and it is largely driven by local availability. Some drugs are reasonably easy to access because young people are incredibly tech savvy and many drugs are imported using the internet.

"The primary impact of this latest drug is disorientation and an acute confused state but they can result in kidney failure, liver failure and diffuse organ failure and it's not infrequent for people to end up having seizures.

"Most young people we see fall into a few categories – the isolated or disconnected group that roam the street, or young people provided alcohol by adults, often their parents. Then there are the house parties, celebrations, end-of-year break-ups and school formals where young people use whatever illegal drugs they've cobbled together through their networks. They dump it in a pile and help themselves.

"When something does go wrong, there's a reluctance to access emergency help for fear of cost, police prosecution, or other trouble from elders. Or they don't have credit and don't realise you can dial 000 even when you don't have credit. They're more likely to call a parent before they call 000.

"Our priority is to help the person who is sick, but one of the hardest things is getting young people to tell us the truth. It helps if we know what substances a person has used so we can work out the best way to keep them safe. Do they go home and sleep it off? Do they go to hospital? Or do we need to give them medicine to keep them safe while we take them to a hospital emergency department?

"Parents need to let their children know that they will always support them in making a safe decision, such as calling an ambulance to help themselves or a friend. Help them to make safe choices."

> "We see children in single-digit years drinking alcohol on a regular basis."

Photo by Fiona Hamilton

// Alan Eade is Victoria's Chief Paramedic Officer with Safer Care Victoria.

HEROIN

OTHER NAMES // SMACK, GEAR, HAMMER, THE DRAGON, H, DOPE, JUNK, HARRY, HORSE, WHITE DYNAMITE, HOMEBAKE, CHINA WHITE, CHINESE H, POISON

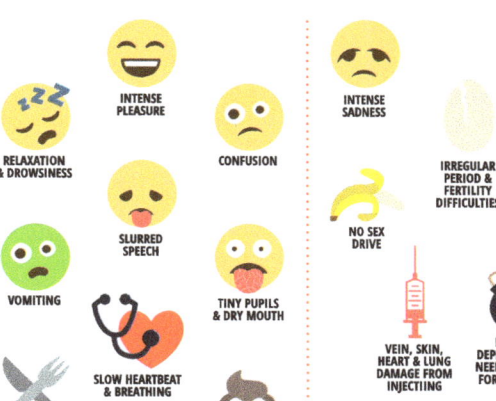

Methadone programs can be used to get people off heroin.

Heroin use is not common among Australian teenagers; latest figures reveal only 1.6 per cent of high-school students have used opiates or narcotics such as heroin or morphine other than for medical reasons.

Heroin is a depressant and belongs to a group of drugs known as "opioids" that are derived from the opium poppy. It comes in different forms, including fine white powder, coarse off-white granules and tiny pieces of light brown "rock". Heroin is usually injected into a vein, but it can also be smoked ("chasing the dragon") and added to cigarettes and cannabis. The effects are usually felt straight away. If snorted, it takes 10 to 15 minutes to take effect.

Unlike many other drugs, heroin addiction has a known treatment. Heroin users can be prescribed methadone, which is also an opiate but is much cheaper and less likely to result in an overdose. Used as a replacement drug, methadone can help stabilise heroin users as they withdraw. Methadone is also used as a pain reliever following heart attacks, trauma and surgery.

WHO IS USING HEROIN?
The 2014 Australian secondary students' survey found that 1.5 per cent reported using opiates or narcotics such as heroin or morphine other than for medical reasons. Only 1.1 per cent said they used opiates in the past year. Of those, 53 per cent had used them only once or twice.

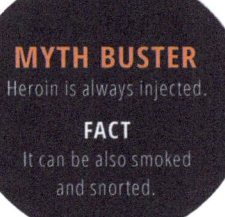

MYTH BUSTER
Heroin is always injected.
FACT
It can be also smoked and snorted.

// OTHER OPIATES

METHADONE
Methadone is often taken as part of treatment for heroin dependence, as it can help prevent physical withdrawal symptoms. It is also used to relieve pain following heart attacks, trauma and surgery.

MORPHINE
Morphine is widely used for pain relief in adults and children. It is highly effective but extended use can have side-effects such as constipation, low blood pressure, confusion and shallow breathing.

PETHIDINE
A synthetic version of morphine, pethidine is a pain reliever perhaps best known for its use during childbirth. It is generally used to treat moderate to severe pain.

SHORT-TERM EFFECTS

- INTENSE PLEASURE
- RELAXATION & DROWSINESS
- CONFUSION
- SLURRED SPEECH
- VOMITING
- TINY PUPILS & DRY MOUTH
- SLOW HEARTBEAT & BREATHING
- REDUCED APPITITE
- CONSTIPATION

LONG-TERM EFFECTS

- INTENSE SADNESS
- HEART, LUNG, LIVER & BRAIN DAMAGE
- IRREGULAR PERIOD & FERTILITY DIFFICULTIES
- NO SEX DRIVE
- FINANCIAL/WORK PROBLEMS
- VEIN, SKIN, HEART & LUNG DAMAGE FROM INJECTIING
- RISK OF DEPENDENCE & NEEDING MORE FOR THE SAME EFFECT

Injecting heroin and sharing needles may also transmit tetanus, hepatitis B, hepatitis C and HIV/AIDS.

OVERDOSE *
If too much or a strong batch of heroin is consumed, the user may experience trouble concentrating, falling asleep, wanting to urinate but finding it hard, itchiness, irregular heartbeat, cold, clammy skin, slow breathing, blue lips and fingertips, passing out, and even death.

Naloxone (also known as Narcan®) reverses the effects of heroin, particularly in the case of an overdose. It can be administered by authorised medical personnel such as ambulance officers. Family and friends can also administer naloxone if they join one of the trials taking place in Australia.

WITHDRAWAL*
Withdrawal symptoms usually start within six to 24 hours after the last dose and can last for about a week – days one to three will be the worst. Symptoms can include:
- Cravings for heroin.
- Restlessness and irritability.
- Depression and crying.
- Diarrhoea.
- Restless sleep and yawning.
- Stomach and leg cramps.
- Vomiting and no appetite.
- Goose bumps.
- Runny nose.
- Fast heartbeat.

*Copyright © Australian Drug Foundation 2015

Profile // Travis Barugh

THE ADDICT

Travis Barugh began drinking alcohol at the age of 12. Later he became addicted to speed, ecstasy and ice. Today, he believes abstinence is the most effective way to stay clean.

Photo: Supplied

Q. HOW DID YOU FIRST EXPERIMENT WITH ALCOHOL?

A "I grew up in a middle-class family. My father worked hard and my mother was a stay-at-home mother. They both drank every night. I wanted to be an Olympic high jumper – it's all I wanted – but I broke bones in my leg when I was 12. About two weeks later I was at a party and I didn't have an excuse not to drink any more. I'd go to parties and was given way too much free rein. From about the age of 15 mum would drive me to the bottle shop and buy me vodka. I could do whatever I wanted."

Q. WHAT DID ALCOHOL AND LATER DRUGS DO FOR YOU BACK THEN?

A "From the first time I tried alcohol, I loved it. It quietened that inner self-critic. Throughout my teenage years I was still a good kid, I still helped out the football club and played and coached basketball. I finished year 12 and did well but a few months after I finished school my parents separated. I had nobody to talk to and thought no one cared about me. A house of seven people turned into just me and my father. The broken family tore me apart. I find most drug addicts are really sensitive to everything in life and I guess from a young age I learnt that if you have a shit day and things get tough, you can get rid of it with alcohol or other drugs."

Q. HOW DID USING DRUGS HAVE AN IMPACT ON YOUR LIFE?

A "During the time I was using ice – from when I was 19 until 32 – I had what resembled a life. I had a partner, then had a wedding and a wife and we had a business. But I was using ice non-stop. When I was 25 my little brother committed suicide and I didn't feel I had any reason to live any more. The drugs totally exploded. I pushed myself to not feel. I was 78 kilos – now I weigh 105 kilos. My brain started shutting down. I would suddenly black out – that happened about 100 times in the last month before I stopped. I had five car accidents. My whole world fell down around me."

Q. WHAT DO YOU THINK WOULD HAVE HELPED YOU AVOID ALCOHOL AND DRUGS, OR REDUCED THE EXTENT OF THE PROBLEM?

A "The whole time I was using drugs, not once did someone say, 'What are you doing? You're a good bloke… you're going down the wrong path'. All I wanted as a child was some boundaries. I didn't get anything. I couldn't say as a child that I wanted boundaries and some love and that I wanted my parents to care. For boys, it's your father. I think it's a given that your mum's going to be good to you most of the time but having that strong fatherly figure and a good relationship with your father is important."

Q. HOW HAVE YOU GOT OFF DRUGS AND STAYED OFF THEM?

A "I had six months in rehab and going through all that, you learn to forgive. When I was growing up the parenting emphasis was more on, 'this is my way and this is how we're doing it'. Nowadays I think people discuss stuff more. Dad doesn't have too much to do with me although he's proud of the changes I've made. I get along well with mum. Through getting clean and abstaining from all drugs and alcohol, I've also learnt how to deal with the stuff that goes on in my head. It's been quite a journey in learning about myself."

"About two weeks later I was at a party and I didn't have an excuse not to drink any more."

// Travis Barugh is a construction manager for Delco Developments who in 2018 won the Master Builders Victoria Award of Excellence for best renovation/addition $500,000 to $750,000.

ECSTASY

OTHER NAMES // ECKIES, E, XTC, PILLS, PINGERS, BIKKIES AND FLIPPERS

Commonly supplied in pill form, ecstasy pills often have a symbol or picture printed on them.

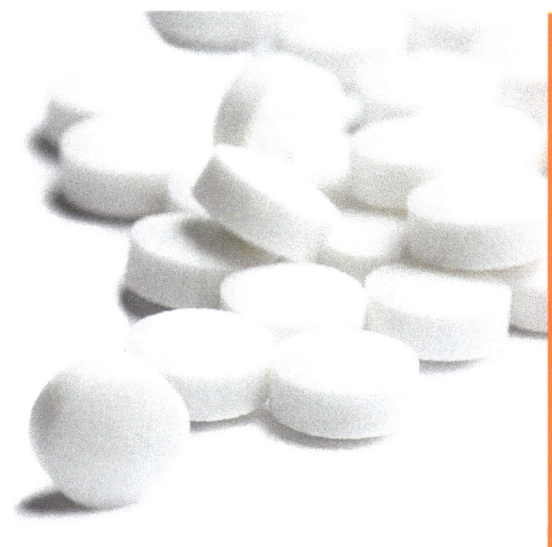

Ecstasy is relatively easily obtained on the street or at parties and raves; tablets can cost as little as $15 each. Unlike the 1970s and 1980s, when some of today's parents were teenagers and illicit drugs were deep underground, today's teens need only attend a music event or ask around to find ecstasy and other drugs. They can also use underground websites that sell illegal substances of all kinds.

Ecstasy is usually swallowed as a pill. The pills come in different colours and sizes and are often imprinted with a picture or symbol. Ecstasy is a stimulant containing the drug MDMA (methylenedioxymethamphetamine). However, many pills sold as ecstasy only have a small amount of MDMA or none at all. Other drugs and "fillers" such as household cleaning products, are often used instead. This makes it hard to know what reactions to expect or how bad the side-effects will be. Instead of MDMA, drugs sold as ecstasy may contain a mix of amphetamine, paramethoxyamphetamine (PMA), ketamine, NBOMe, methylone or other substances.

WHO IS USING ECSTASY?

About three per cent (3.1) of students aged 12 to 17 in the 2014 Australian secondary students' survey said they had tried ecstasy. Like most other substances, the proportion who said they had ever used it increased with age, from 0.9 per cent among 12-year-olds, to seven per cent among 17-year-olds.

Older boys were generally more likely to use ecstasy than girls, but girls aged 12 used it more than boys and use was similar at age 13. Of the 2.6 per cent of 12 to 17-year-olds who reported using ecstasy in the past year, 48 per cent had used it only once or twice.

Ecstasy use can cause cracked teeth due to clenching and grinding

// WHERE ARE KIDS GETTING IT?

Teenagers can source party drugs such as ecstasy easier than their parents could. They can ask around for a contact, search coded websites or find dealers at dance parties and rock concerts. In some cases, dealers are identified by markers such as a top or T-shirt with a particular number on it. Dealers might also ask "are you Jason?", a thinly disguised reference to "are you chasing?" Such methods change constantly to avoid police detection.

SHORT-TERM EFFECTS

- HAPPINESS & CONFIDENCE
- EXCESSIVE SWEATING
- MUSCLE ACHES & PAINS
- HEIGHTENED SENSES
- INCREASED ENERGY
- NAUSEA
- JAW CLENCHING & TEETH GRINDING
- FAST HEARTBEAT
- IRRATIONAL BEHAVIOUR
- REDUCED APPITITE
- LARGE PUPILS
- HEAT STROKE
- HALLUCINATIONS
- DEHYDRATION & EXCESSIVE WATER CONSUMPTION
- DEATH

LONG-TERM EFFECTS

- REGULAR COLDS & FLU
- DEPRESSION
- FINANCIAL/WORK PROBLEMS
- RISK OF DEPENDENCE & NEEDING MORE FOR THE SAME EFFECT

// GHB

GHB (gamma hydroxybutyrate) is often known as liquid ecstasy, but it is a different drug. It is also known as G, fantasy, grievous bodily harm (GBH), liquid ecstasy, liquid E, liquid X, Georgia Home Boy, soap, scoop, cherry meth and blue nitro. Some refer to it as "the date-rape drug" as it has been used to spike drinks before a sexual assault. It usually comes as a colourless, odourless, bitter or salty liquid, which is usually sold in small bottles or vials. It can also come as a bright-blue liquid known as "blue nitro".
Important note: It is easy to take too much GHB which could result in an overdose.

Profile // Paula Ross

THE PSYCHOLOGIST

Paula Ross helps clients and their families with issues related to substance use, addiction or 'substance-use disorder'.

"In the field of drug and alcohol treatment and intervention there are lots of different terms – addiction, problematic drug use, or substance dependence. Addiction as a word has gone a little out of favour and from a psychology perspective we tend to now use 'substance-use disorder', but the criteria for substance use disorder are mostly the factors people consider when talking about addiction.

"Some young people use substances experimentally, some recreationally and some become substance-use dependent, but they are the minority. Substance use and therefore dependency can be related to internal and external factors.

"External factors are things like peer-group behaviour and what might be going on in the young person's family and circumstances at the time. Internal factors include the fact that some kids are more naturally risk takers, and there is a group of young people who start taking drugs as self-medication for depression, anxiety and because they don't feel good about themselves. I think it's possible we'll discover that certain brain chemistry makes you more predisposed to addiction, too.

"There are a complex number of factors that are involved here and so it's not as simple as young people who develop substance-use disorders being from 'bad' families or from 'bad' parents. Parents and family members often feel they have failed or done something wrong and also need support.

"The things that start heading into substance-use disorder territory are when young people start spending increasing amounts of time using, obtaining, planning or sorting out their drug use or recovering from drug use.

"We are concerned if young people start not meeting their commitments in other areas of their life as a result of their drug use. So they don't get homework done, they can't get to school and they don't do their normal social and family activities. So things start to 'go'.

"It can be helpful if parents and family members don't jump to conclusions but instead start a conversation with their child about what might be happening – 'I notice this, this and this, what is going on?' Rather than 'I've noticed this, this and this – I think you're using drugs'.

"Stay calm and don't overwhelm your teenager. So don't sit down with your whole family and talk at them. Think about who is the best person to talk to the young person, who has the best communication with them, who is most likely to not get angry or emotional? And approach the conversation with warm curiosity – 'I'm interested in what is going on, how are you...'

"Parents need to have realistic expectations. You won't have one conversation and find that your young person says 'you're right, I'll stop'. Approach each conversation with an aim to start a dialogue and to keep communication channels open.

"If the conversation starts to go badly and you or your child gets angry or emotional, stop it. Don't pressure yourself to have the whole conversation in that one moment. Sometimes the first conversation is about flagging the issue and sending the message that your child can talk about anything with you and that they can come to you. It is an ongoing conversation.

"There is some debate around whether you disclose your own past (or present) drug use. Parents need to walk the line between disclosure with the aim of letting a child know that you understand versus how much of your disclosure will your child hear as permission giving. If you do disclose, don't turn it into a speech about every drug you've taken in your life – disclose a certain amount.

"Parents can talk to a professional to discuss what they are dealing with and to get advice on how they can support their child. Consistency in the family is important. Family members should talk among themselves about how they as a family are going to respond to this issue. So are you giving your child money or not? Are you letting them stay out all night or not? What do you tell your other children if they ask questions about what is happening?

"Above all, as a starting point, stay calm, get help and keep focusing on having conversations."

> "You won't have one conversation and find that your young person says 'you're right, I'll stop'."

Photo: Supplied

// Paula Ross is a psychologist in private practice at the Williams Road Family Therapy Centre in Caulfield.

COCAINE

OTHER NAMES // C, COKE, NOSE CANDY, SNOW, WHITE LADY, TOOT, CHARLIE, BLOW, WHITE DUST, STARDUST

Often portrayed as the jetset's drug of choice, cocaine is anything but glamorous.

Cocaine has a reputation as the drug of choice for celebrities, but its effects can be far from glamorous. Cocaine can be dangerous if taken in high doses or contaminated by other substances. Snorting cocaine regularly can cause a runny nose and nosebleeds, infection of the nasal membranes, perforation of the septum and long-term damage to the nasal cavity and sinuses.

Only 1.9 per cent of Australian high-school students surveyed in the 2014 Australian secondary students' survey had used cocaine, and only 0.8 per cent had used it in the past month. These levels have also fallen significantly since 2005, when almost three per cent of 12 to 17-year-olds had tried it. But any level of use in this age group is a concern because of its potential dangers.

> Extensive cocaine use can cause holes in the septum, which divides the left nasal passage from the right

// WHAT IS COCAINE AND HOW IS IT USED? *

Cocaine is a stimulant that speeds up the messages travelling between the brain and the rest of the body. It comes from the leaves of the coca bush (*Erythroxylum coca*), which is native to South America. The leaf extract is processed to produce three different forms of cocaine:

COCAINE HYDROCHLORIDE
A white crystalline powder with a bitter, numbing taste. Cocaine hydrochloride is often mixed, or "cut", with other substances such as lactose and glucose to dilute it before being sold.

FREEBASE
A white powder that is more pure than cocaine hydrochloride.

CRACK
Crystals ranging in colour from white or cream to transparent with a pink or yellow hue, it may contain impurities.

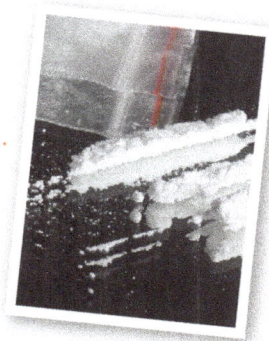

Cocaine is most commonly snorted. It can also be injected, rubbed into the gums, added to drinks or food. Freebase and crack cocaine are usually smoked.

*Copyright © Australian Drug Foundation 2015

SHORT-TERM EFFECTS

HAPPINESS & CONFIDENCE

TALKATIVENESS

QUIET CONTEMPLATION

REDUCED APPITITE

INCREASED ENERGY

FEELING STRONG & MENTALLY SHARP

HIGH BLOOD PRESSURE & FAST HEARTBEAT

LARGE PUPILS & DRY MOUTH

AGITATION & AGGRESSION

INCREASED SEX DRIVE

HIGHER BODY TEMPERATURE

LONG-TERM EFFECTS

INSOMNIA & EXHAUSTION

DEPRESSION

ANXIETY & PARANOIA

PSYCHOSIS

HEART DISEASE

SEXUAL DYSFUNCTION

HALLUCINATIONS

SENSITIVITY TO SOUND & LIGHT

EATING DISORDERS & WEIGHT LOSS

DEATH

COCAINE PSYCHOSIS *
High doses and frequent heavy use can also cause "cocaine psychosis", characterised by paranoid delusions, hallucinations and out-of-character aggressive behaviour. These symptoms usually disappear a few days after the person stops using cocaine.

Interview // By Sarah McVeigh from Triple J

NBOME* FREAKOUT

Georgie (21) describes being suddenly overwhelmed by a sense of doom, panicking, taking off her clothes, fleeing in her car, throwing away her phone, and shocking herself on electric fences.

"I'd just finished exams and we decided to go camping to one of my favourite waterfalls. It's just completely in the middle of nowhere. It's an hour and a half from any civilisation.

"We took [the tablets] in the morning so we could just really relax and enjoy the views and everything.

"I felt like I tasted something a little bit different to usual. Usually there's no taste at all. There was a little bit of bitterness but I didn't really think much of it.

"It took about half an hour, so it was pretty quick. I've had LSD before and sometimes it's taken an hour, an hour and a half, so it was pretty instant.

"After no time at all I had no concept of what the time was or how long it had been, or what day it was, or who I was.

"All of a sudden out of nowhere I was just convinced that we were going to die. I thought that everything was going to blow up. I had these petrol canisters in the back of my car that I had from another trip and I was just convinced they were going to blow up so I grabbed them both. I ran and threw them into the mountain. I was just convinced that everything was out to get us. I thought that my car was not safe there, we weren't safe there.

"All of a sudden it was this scary, dangerous place. I am a huge lover of nature. I have always felt safe in nature and all of a sudden I felt that my life was in danger. I was demanding the keys, I was just like 'we need to escape, we're not safe here, we need to leave'.

"We just got in the car and I drove. All of a sudden the car turned on me as well. I felt I wasn't safe in the car. I was in the middle of driving and I just opened the door and jumped out the window while the car was still moving. I grabbed my phone; I thought that was unsafe; I threw that into the river. I threw my watch into the river.

"I lost my mind. I was absolutely convinced I was going to die. I was screaming, I was crying. I took all of my clothes off. I jumped through this electric fence to try to run away and then I just stopped in the middle of this paddock and I was just completely naked and just screaming out any name of anyone I knew to try to get help.

"I was calling 000 out into the middle of nowhere, there was no one around. I was trying to talk to the ambulance. I was trying to talk to my mum.

"I was convinced that I had to sacrifice myself. There were two electric fences beside me and I just kept constantly jumping in and out of both of them – completely shocking myself and then rolling over, looking at the sky and just thinking, 'I cannot believe that I am 21 and I'm dying right now. I can't believe that I have got this far and my life has been so amazing and this is where it ends'.

"There were so many times where I was on the ground and I would roll over looking at the sky and just be like, 'take me, I'm ready. There have been 10 times where I have been so close to dying, please just take me now because I can't go through this any more'. I was terrified.

"I think [my friend] was trying to get to me but there were electric fences all around and I jumped through three to get to the area I was. He finally came to me and I didn't realise he was my friend, I thought he was a completely different person that I once knew and that he had come to save me because I had called out his name.

"[When we finally got back to the car] the door was still open, the keys were still in the car and a police car had pulled up to the car to try and figure out what was going on and I just saw them and was like 'wow, they must have heard me'.

"I was bleeding. I was bleeding all down my legs and all over my face and I was naked and they were just like 'what's happened, what are you doing?' and they drove me to the nearest hospital, which was about an hour drive.

"I remember calling my mum in the police car and saying 'Mum, I've been in a car accident, there's blood everywhere. The car is a write-off, I'm going to the hospital now, can you please come and pick me up'.

"I didn't tell her the whole story right away, I just said 'Mum we took LSD and I drove the car' and she just looked at me with complete shock and disgust and I just lost it because I was still affected at that point, I was still under the influence, but I knew that was my mum and I had hurt her.

"I was reading about that young footballer that passed away from NBOMe*. I just kept reading this one part saying that the main causes of death (when taking the drug) are cardiac arrest and bizarre behaviour such as jumping off balconies and running into oncoming traffic and I was just like 'yeah, that's exactly the types of stuff I was doing'. I was insane, I was completely in another world and I didn't have any care for my safety. I just thought I was going to die. My experiences seem to link to what this young man had.

"My friends are saying every day it will get easier but that was such a massive thing to happen. At the moment I don't know how I can move on from it. I don't know how I can ever move on from something like that, it's traumatic, it is.

"I'm anxious even driving, I'm anxious all the time. It's not worth it, it's not. All of a sudden I hate myself, I can't believe that I would put myself and my family in this position. What if I got in the car and kept driving, what if I got to a main road and what if I killed someone, what if I killed us? I am just so lucky to be alive and I am so lucky that I can turn this around and change my life and hopefully try and educate other people because it's not worth it. It's not worth it."

> "I was in the middle of driving and I just opened the door and jumped out the window while the car was still moving."

// * Editor's note: The tablets mentioned in this story have not been tested to prove it was an NBOMe. ** Names have been changed. Republished with permission from Hack on Triple J // www.druginfo.adf.org.au/contact-numbers/help-and-support

HALLUCINOGENS

OTHER NAMES // LSD, ACID, TRIPS, TABS, MICRODOTS, DOTS, MAGIC MUSHROOMS, SHROOMS, MUSHIES, BLUE MEANIES, GOLDEN TOPS, LIBERTY, MESCALINE, CACTUS, CACTUS BUTTONS, CACTUS JOINT, MESC, MESCAL

A bad trip on hallucinogens can be a nightmare.

Hallucinogens, such as LSD, were popular with young people during the 1960s and 1970s "flower power" era. While many more drugs have been developed since, LSD is still available in Australia. Hallucinogen use among young people is relatively uncommon; about three per cent of Australian high-school students report having tried them.

Also known as "psychedelics", hallucinogens can make you see, hear, smell, feel or taste things that aren't really there or are different from reality, hence the word hallucinate. LSD (Lysergic acid diethylamide) is made in a laboratory and in its pure state is a white odourless powder. It usually comes in squares of gelatine or blotting paper that have been dipped or soaked in LSD and is sometimes sold as a liquid, in a tablet or capsules. LSD is usually swallowed, but it can also be sniffed, injected or smoked. Some plants, such as magic mushrooms, can cause similar hallucinations to chemically produced hallucinogens.

Flashbacks of hallucinations can occur weeks, months or even years after the drug was last taken.

WHO USES HALLUCINOGENS?

The 2014 Australian secondary students' survey found 2.8 per cent had used hallucinogens such as LSD. The proportion increased with age, from 0.7 per cent of 12-year-old students to six per cent of 17-year-olds. Only 2.2 per cent of all students reported having used hallucinogens in the past year and only 0.9 per cent had used them in the previous month. Boys were generally more likely than girls to use them, particularly at ages 16 and 17. Most of the 2.2 per cent of students who reported using hallucinogens in the previous year did so infrequently.

SHORT-TERM EFFECTS

 HAPPINESS

DIZZINESS & BLURRED VISION
 TROUBLE CONCENTRATING
 IRREGULAR OR FAST HEARTBEAT & QUICK BREATHING
 SWEATING & CHILLS
 VOMITING
LOSS OF CO-ORDINATION
 NUMBNESS
HALLUCINATIONS

LONG-TERM EFFECTS

 RISK OF DEPENDENCE
 FINANCIAL/WORK PROBLEMS
 FLASHBACKS (HALLUCINATIONS THAT OCCUR WEEKS, MONTHS OR YEARS AFTER THE DRUG WAS LAST TAKEN)

// FOUND IN NATURE

MAGIC MUSHROOMS

There are many different types of magic mushrooms. In Australia, the most common are called golden tops, blue meanies and liberty caps. Magic mushrooms look similar to poisonous mushrooms that can cause sickness and possible death. They are usually collected and then sold as dried mushrooms, a powder or as capsules. The mushrooms can be eaten fresh, cooked or brewed into a tea. They are sometimes mixed with tobacco or cannabis, and smoked.

MESCALINE (PEYOTE CACTUS)

Mescaline is the active ingredient of the peyote cactus plant. It contains "buttons" that can be cut from the root and dried before eating or smoking. It can also be produced synthetically. In its pure form, mescaline sulphate is a white crystal-like powder. Synthetic mescaline comes in different colours.

ARE MAGIC MUSHROOMS LESS DANGEROUS THAN LSD?

Magic mushrooms have similar effects to LSD. They contain psilocybin, which belongs to the same chemical family as LSD. It is dangerous to pick and eat wild mushrooms because they are difficult to distinguish from edible mushrooms. Poisonous mushrooms can cause stomach pains, vomiting and diarrhoea; some can cause permanent liver damage, respiratory failure, unconsciousness and even death. Symptoms can take up to 40 hours to develop.

A BAD TRIP

In some cases, hallucinogen users experience a "bad trip" involving a disturbing hallucination. This can lead to panic and risky behaviour, like running across a road or attempting suicide. If a large amount or a strong batch is taken, the negative effects of hallucinogens are more likely.

Profile // Hanna Cheng

THE PSYCHIATRIST

The Austin Hospital's child and adolescent psychiatrist Dr Hanna Cheng has specialised in this field for five years.

"CAMHS at the Austin looks after children from zero to 18 years of age. We have a multidisciplinary team with clinical psychologists, nurses, occupational therapists, speech therapists, social workers, training registrars and psychiatrists.

"A range of people refer children to us – parents, general practitioners, paediatricians, private psychiatrists and psychologists, schools and the Department of Human Services.

"Initially we do an assessment to establish the presenting difficulties and one of our team takes on a care co-ordination role and looks at any psychological interventions received up to this point, social skills, drug and alcohol use, and family relationships. They meet with the school to work out a curriculum and to identify any special needs in that area.

"Depending on the clinical needs identified, CAMHS offers a variety of psychological and therapeutic interventions, for example cognitive behavioural therapy, social skills training, supportive psychotherapy, and parent and family therapy.

"I do think kids are starting to experiment with alcohol and illicit substances at a younger age. That is a significant concern because we now know parts of the brain don't mature until the mid-20s and that maturation occurs from the back to the front of the brain. The part that matures last – the pre-frontal cortex – is responsible for high-level reasoning, decision making and impulse control.

Photo: Supplied

"Their brain cells are less sensitive to intoxication ... they drink and drink and drink and crash."

"Adolescence is a complex and confusing time for young people and their families. It's a constantly shifting landscape and can be sunny one minute and hailing the next. Adolescents are easily overwhelmed by high emotions, risk taking and unpredictability. They're impulsive and often overestimate short-term payoffs and underestimate long-term consequences.

"Adolescents are vulnerable to alcohol not only because of peer pressure or experimentation. Studies show alcohol is more effective in reducing social discomfort in a child's brain. So for children who are shy and introverted, it gives them a sense of ease and confidence in their interaction with others. Their brain cells are less sensitive to intoxication, too, and that's risky because they drink and drink and drink and crash – it's like stepping on an accelerator downhill without proper brakes.

"Alcohol aside, marijuana is probably the most regularly used illicit substance in adolescence. It's relatively affordable and accessible and is somewhat more socially accepted in peer groups in this age range. It's not perceived as dangerous as ecstasy or speed but is equally harmful. Ongoing marijuana use results in amotivation, low mood, poorer academic functioning and, in the long term, it increases the risk of acute and chronic psychotic and mood disorders.

"The permissiveness around marijuana is worrying. Parents might think 'my kid is not using speed, he smokes a cone or two every now and then with his mates...'. There is a downplay of how significant marijuana impacts on kids.

"Studies show the most significant protective factor against alcohol and substance abuse is a good parent-child relationship – an open, confiding parent-child relationship where different opinions, strong emotions and difficult situations can be talked about; where parents acknowledge and accept that experimentation and making mistakes is very much part of the process of growing up.

"It's not difficult for parents to feel desperate and angry. At times it's hard to understand why their child is not listening to them like they did when they were younger – why are they using drugs when they've been provided with all they need in their lives? Fears and worries can get in the way of parents being able to talk to, and hear, young people properly.

"Don't get into a dynamic where parents control and discipline and the young person withholds and deceives. Listen and acknowledge that adolescence is different these days. Talk about emotions, general health and wellbeing – and not just when there is a problem. Have clear rules and expectations about when your children must be home and where they are going. Being a parent is a bit like being a helicopter – hover close and, as they get older, hover a little further away. Pick the moments where your child can afford to figure out their own mistakes – and which moments you need to hover closer and rescue."

// Dr Hanna Cheng is a child and adolescent psychiatrist and acting clinical director for Austin Child and Adolescent Mental Health Service (CAMHS).

STEROIDS

OTHER NAMES // ROIDS, GEAR, JUICE, HYPE, GYM CANDY, ARNOLDS, STACKERS, PUMPERS

Use of steroids has spread from athletes to the general public.

Steroids and other performance and image-enhancing drugs (PIEDs) have long been associated with elite sportspeople desperate for an edge. PIEDs are used by people of all skill levels and ages, whether they want to boost their sporting performance or simply build muscle mass. Among the most notorious cases was champion cyclist Lance Armstrong, who was stripped of seven Tour de France wins after admitting he took EPO (erythropoietin), which regulates red blood cell production.

PIED use is not common and in some cases steroids are used legitimately to treat medical conditions such as osteoporosis. But if used privately and without professional supervision they can have health implications. Steroids may be injected intramuscularly, taken orally or rubbed on the skin as a cream. Only 2.3 per cent of Australian high-school students aged 12 to 17 say they have used steroids without a doctor's prescription, with boys (2.7 per cent) slightly more likely than girls (1.9 per cent) to have tried them. Among the 1.8 per cent of students who tried steroids in the year before the 2014 survey, use was infrequent.

MYTH BUSTER
Do steroids shrink your private parts?
FACT
They can. Shrinking testicles and prostate problems are among the many possible side-effects.

WHAT ARE STEROIDS?
Performance and image-enhancing drugs (PIEDs) claim to improve the effects of physical training and a person's physical appearance. There are two broad types. One includes drugs that enhance muscle growth or reduce body fat, such as steroids, peptides, diuretics and stimulants. The other includes hormones and hormone-stimulating drugs such as human growth hormone. PIEDs were traditionally used by body-builders and athletes but are increasingly used more widely. Those who use them without medical supervision often exceed the recommended dosage and expose themselves to side-effects. Some black-market drugs, such as synthetic hormones, haven't been approved for human use.

ARE STEROIDS LEGAL?
Commercially produced steroids fall into three groups – human consumption, veterinary use and illegal. The possession, use and supply of steroids, other than by prescription from a medical practitioner, dentist or veterinarian, is illegal in Australia, as is unauthorised importation. The use of steroids by competitors in most sports is banned.

// TYPES OF STEROIDS

ANABOLIC STEROIDS *
Anabolic-androgenic steroids are derived from testosterone and can be taken as an injection or tablet. Their anabolic effects help with the growth and repair of muscle tissue.

PEPTIDES *
Peptides stimulate the release of human growth hormone, which has an important role in muscle and bone growth. Peptides have become increasingly popular among professional and amateur athletes as they are hard to detect due to speedy absorption.

HORMONES *
Hormones are chemicals released by the body. There are many artificial hormones and hormone-stimulating drugs, including growth hormones such as AOD-9604, which has fat-burning properties and is used to increase power-to-weight ratios.

SIDE-EFFECTS

 HAIR LOSS
 HIGH BLOOD PRESSURE
DEPRESSION
 HEART & LIVER PROBLEMS
ACNE
FLUID RETENTION
SHRINKING TESTICLES & PROSTATE
 AGITATION & AGGRESSION
 BREAST TISSUE GROWTH

The long-term effects of PIED misuse in young people are still unknown, but it's especially risky to take any substance while the body and brain are still developing.

* Copyright © Australian Drug Foundation 2015

SOME PIEDS *
Clenbuterol: classed as a "beta-2 agonist", short-term effects are similar to stimulant drugs such as amphetamine or ephedrine.
Creatine monohydrate: a naturally occurring compound synthesised from amino acids by the kidneys and liver.
Erythropoietin (EPO): a naturally occurring hormone produced by cells in the kidneys that regulate the production of red blood cells in bone marrow.
Human chorionic gonadotrophin (hCG): when taken by males, hCG can stimulate the testes to produce testosterone rapidly.
Insulin-like growth factor (IGF-1): a naturally occurring growth factor that stimulates many processes in the body.

Profile // George Braitberg

THE PROFESSOR

Professor George Braitberg has witnessed first-hand the impact of drugs and alcohol on teenagers.

Photo by Fiona Hamilton

"I've looked after a patient of 14 or 15 who had one of the highest blood alcohol levels I've seen – he was 0.5 – 10 times the legal limit for driving. When he arrived at hospital he was unconscious and needed a couple of days in ICU attached to a ventilator.

"I think the age at which young people begin experimenting with drugs has dropped, and that started with the advent of pills, such as ecstasy, when kids were looking to supplement the pleasurable experience at rave parties. Young people don't want to take anything that involves a needle, so the proliferation of pills has made drugs more accessible for them. But these pills are not safe. They're not made by pharmacists and usually have contaminants – other drugs and bulking agents such as starch that may create a reaction.

"Synthetic cannabinoids that are around now can raise the heart rate, raise blood pressure and they're associated with bleeding in the brain. If young people are also drinking alcohol and aren't drinking a lot of water, then dehydration compounds the effect.

"You can never control what the likely effects of drugs are going to be. It's a major downfall of children experimenting with drugs. They hear from friends that if you take this tablet you will have this experience, but they can actually experience something quite different, something dangerous.

"Add a child's sense of invulnerability – 'nothing can happen to me' – and this is a dangerous combination.

"We've seen people in emergency with very disturbing presentations. Their pulse rate and blood pressure rise and they can become quite paranoid and confused. Parents might notice a child is hallucinating and if they've taken a significant amount of drugs they can go from agitated to a comatose state.

"We can see more aggression and agitation and we have a code-grey team that is activated when a patient is at risk of harming themselves or others. Most of our code greys are drug-related issues and we have around 50 code greys a day.

"A young person's lungs, heart and kidneys are better able to tolerate drugs than an older person who has heart disease. And if the child doesn't have an addictive tendency and has a single experimentation with drugs, we'd hopefully see a good outcome.

"But there is the problem of recurrent use. There is data that shows you're more likely to go on to take hard drugs if you start with soft drugs, and chronic drug use brings concerns about long-term brain development and mental health issues.

"I don't think children can use drugs responsibly and I don't think there is a safe level of drug-taking behaviour."

"I used to teach schoolchildren about harm minimisation and my message was if you are going to use drugs, use them responsibly. But I've changed that message. I don't think children can use drugs responsibly and I don't think there is a safe level of drug-taking behaviour. There is no benefit at all in taking recreational drugs – they won't make your child's life any better, but they do bring lots of potential problems."

// Professor George Braitberg is emergency medicine specialist at the Royal Melbourne Hospital and former ED Director.

ANALGESICS

OTHER NAMES // ASPRIN, PARACETAMOL, IBUPROFEN, CODEINE, DOXYLAMINE

Often seen as harmless, analgesics and tranquillisers can have a dark side

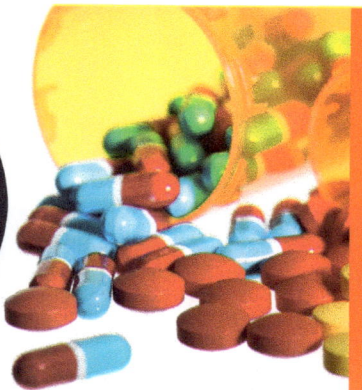

Nearly all Australian high-school students (95.2 per cent) have used pain-killing analgesics such as Panadol at least once. Almost seven in ten (69 per cent) told the 2014 national secondary school students' drug survey that they had used pain killers in the past month; four in ten (40.5 per cent) had in the past week. Girls were more likely than boys to have used analgesics in the past week (47.6 per cent v 33.7 per cent).

The most common reason girls and boys used pain killers was to help ease headache/migraine pain, followed by easing cold and flu symptoms. More boys than girls reported using them to help relieve sports injury pain. One in four (25.8 per cent) girls used them for menstrual pain. Nine in ten (90.4 per cent) students who had used analgesics in the past year obtained them from their parents. About four per cent (3.8) took them from home and 3.1 per cent bought them.

THE PRICE OF FIGHTING PAIN**

100 tablets a day are swallowed by over-the-counter codeine addicts.
1.3 million packets of "pharmacy only" codeine-based products are bought each month in Australia.
1078 Australians were treated for codeine dependency in 2012-13.
Three-day use only. Can cause addiction.
This is the small warning label that now adorns many pharmacy-only codeine products.

** The Sunday Age, April 26, 2015.

PERCENTAGE OF STUDENTS WHO HAVE CONSUMED ANALGESICS IN THE PAST SEVEN DAYS

	12 YO	13 YO	14 YO	15 YO	16 YO	17 YO
MALES	31.3%	30.7%	34.9%	34.6%	35.4%	35.6%
FEMALES	39.7%	42.6%	46.4%	51.2%	54.5%	51.9%

Australian secondary school students' use of tobacco, alcohol, and over-the-counter and illicit substances in 2014, Australian Government Department of Health Drug Strategy Branch.

// OXYCODONE

Also known as hillbilly heroin, oxy, OC and O, common brand names include Oxynorm®, OxyContin®, Endone®, Proladone®, Targin®. It comes in capsules, tablets, liquid and suppositories.

Oxycodone is one of Australia's most abused prescription drugs and caused 806 deaths from 2001-2011. A Monash University study found oxycodone-related deaths rose from 21 in 2001 to 139 in 2011. Six in 10 of those who died were males and most of those who died were trying to relieve pain.

The Monash report, *An update on oxycodone: lessons for death investigators in Australia*, looked at National Coronial Information System data and found that 39 per cent of cases involved a legitimate prescription, mostly for chronic pain. It called for more care in prescribing oxycodone and better information for preventive strategies.

TRANQUILLISERS

OTHER NAMES // BENZOS, TRANX, SLEEPERS, DOWNERS, PILLS, XANNIES, SERRAS, MOGGIES, NORMIES

In 2014, 18.3 per cent of high school students had used tranquillisers, such as Xanax and Valium, for non-medical reasons. Use in the past month was low, peaking at 5.7 per cent for 15-year-olds. Of the 12 per cent who had used them in the past year, 19 per cent of boys and 22 per cent of girls had used them 3-5 times.

Young people can buy prescription-only drugs such as Xanax for about $20 each on the black market

WHAT ARE BENZODIAZEPINES?

Benzodiazepines, also known as minor tranquillisers, are most commonly prescribed by doctors to relieve stress and anxiety and to help people sleep. Some people use them illegally to become intoxicated or to help with the "come down" effects of stimulants such as amphetamines or cocaine. They are usually swallowed, but some people inject them. Short-acting benzodiazepines have stronger withdrawal or "come down" effects and can be more addictive than long-acting ones.

STUDENTS WHO HAVE EVER USED TRANQUILLISERS*

	12 YO	13 YO	14 YO	15 YO	16 YO	17 YO
MALES	14.5%	16.8%	16.8%	17.3%	19.4%	19.7%
FEMALES	14.3%	17.6%	20.6%	21.7%	21.5%	20.8%

* Percentage of student from the survey who have ever used tranquillisers. Australian secondary school students' use of tobacco, alcohol, and over-the-counter and illicit substances in 2014, Australian Government Department of Health Drug Strategy Branch.

Profile // Shane Cashman

THE POLICE

Acting Detective Senior Sergeant Shane Cashman says parents need to be more proactive in warning their children about the devastating impact of drugs.

"Parents need to put themselves in the driver's seat in terms of drug education and awareness for their children. They need to learn about the types of drugs prevalent in the community and the harm associated with each drug – in relation to the health of their child, community harm resulting from drug use and the law.

"A drug dealer doesn't have a look or a certain style of dress. A drug dealer doesn't drive a certain vehicle or live in a certain suburb or come from a certain social background – they have a mobile phone, an ability to access drugs and a willingness to sell them. Our children have the potential to access drugs via mobile phones and social media. Parents must be on top of their children's usage of those forums.

"Because some parents have come through past alcohol or drug issues in their own lives they think their children will be similarly OK. Alternatively, if parents didn't have any of those challenges, they can assume their children won't have any issues.

"There has been such a change in drug culture in the last 20 years. Some drugs can devastate lives in a short period. The health of a child can be so affected that he or she may never reach their potential.

"Ice is the worst drug I've seen. In the past there was a propensity for some people to start with alcohol use and progressively scale up to the heavier drugs. Now we see young people go from alcohol to ice use, and the ramifications for that child, their family and the community are devastating. A large percentage of people who try ice become addicted. Young people who should be entering university or the workforce don't even begin to take the steps to reach their potential in life. That's tragic.

"Young people commit crimes such as theft of motor car and theft from motor car to get money to buy ice. They then commit crimes when they are on the drug because it takes away their inhibitions and makes them violent. We've seen drug use as a driver in people killed and injured on our roads and in family violence where young people have offended against their own parents and siblngs.

"But let's not forget alcohol too. Parents underestimate how much their children are drinking and they underestimate the harms. Just because a child drinks alcohol in the home, the harm isn't removed. The earlier a child drinks alcohol, the greater the chance of them using other drugs.

"Parents must never administer alcohol to a friend of a child who is under 18. If you have a party and some children are under-18, there should be no alcohol available. This should be on the invitation and made clear. Endeavour to employ security and monitor children closely as they arrive – and if they're already affected by alcohol, don't let them in. It's your party, your rules. If teenagers try and drink alcohol or bring alcohol in, ask them to leave. If the party becomes unruly, contact the police for early intervention.

"It's not a parent's role to be a friend to their child or to be cool or popular. It's your role to keep children safe and to keep their friends safe. Some teenagers can be difficult. Parents must persevere and be consistent in their messaging. Link in with the child's school or employer. I believe children want to know what their boundaries are – and they will test them to see if that boundary is going to be reinforced. It's your responsibility to reinforce endlessly to your child why they should not use drugs and their devastating effects."

> "Just because a child drinks alcohol in the home, the harm isn't removed. The earlier a child drinks alcohol, the greater the chance of them using other drugs."

Photo: Supplied

// Acting Detective Senior Sergeant Shane Cashman is based at Kingston crime investigation unit and has had experience working in drug investigation for more than 20 years. Shane runs drug information sessions at schools, sporting clubs and employee groups and can be contacted to assist in organising these events. Kingston crime investigation unit is at 1011-1013 Nepean Highway, Moorabbin. Email: shane.cashman@police.vic.gov.au

INGREDIENTS IN ILLICIT DRUGS

Pill testing may not discover these additives.

DRAIN CLEANER
Used in the production process of methamphetamine drugs (stimulant) including **ice** and **speed**. Furthermore traces of drain cleaner are regularly found in **ecstasy** tablets.

Drain cleaner reacts with other chemicals to create the methamphetamine substance. The human body is not designed to deal with such chemicals, like drain cleaner, and therefore has both an immediate and long-term effect on the body, which has to work extra hard (increased heart rate, brain activity, organ function, sweating) to remove the chemical once taken.

Drain cleaner is also found in substances such as **GHB** or **GBH** (depressant). Drain cleaner is mixed with paint thinner and cooked down to create a liquid substance known as **GHB/GBH** (Juice, Zonk). This illicit substance puts the body into a sedated state as the body decides that the best way to fight the chemicals is to shut down. **GBH/GHB** is commonly used in drink spiking and as a "date rape" drug.

BATTERIES/CAR BATTERY
The acid is used in drugs such as **acid/LSD** as it has a significant effect on brain activity and functioning. **Acid** is extremely dangerous to the human body and can cause severe long-term complications.

Battery acid is also used in the manufacture of **ecstasy**. There can be an increase in heart rate, brain activity and sweating caused by the central nervous system which is all associated with taking a "stimulant" drug. The user is unable to know what exactly is in an **ecstasy** tablet so overdose or death is always a possibility.

PANADOL/NUROFEN/PARACETAMOL
Used as a cutter or filler in drugs such as **speed**, **cocaine**, **ecstasy** and **heroin** as it bulks up the drug and also thins the blood, allowing the chemicals to get into the blood stream faster. Some drug dealers coat paracetamol with household chemicals and pass it off as **ecstasy**. In the '80s throughout Europe and the UK, **ecstasy** was making its mark in the club scene as the "dance drug". It contained about 15-18 per cent **MDMA** (the active ingredient for **ecstasy**), as well as caffeine and sugar supplements. Today's **ecstasy** would be lucky to contain one per cent, if that, of **MDMA**.

CRUSHED UP GLASS FROM LIGHT GLOBES
Found regularly in **ecstasy** tablets. When the user swallows the tablet, the glass will cut them either on the way down in their oesophagus or in the stomach lining. This therefore releases the chemicals into the blood stream quicker, however, increasing the chance of scarring, infection, overdose and death.

BABY POWDER
Used as a filler to bulk up illicit substances such as **speed**, **cocaine** and sometimes **heroin**. The issue with baby powder (or talcum powder) is that some users are now using needles to inject these illicit substances, including **speed** and **cocaine**. Baby powder clots the blood if it is injected into the vein/s and the user increases the risk of causing serious damage or losing limbs.

Illustration by Anita Layzell

URINAL CAKES
Contain a corrosive acid which causes internal bleeding. Urinal cakes are commonly used in **ecstasy** as it increases the functioning of the central nervous system (heart rate, brain activity etc.) as the body fights to remove the chemical. This is another chemical used to replace and mimic **MDMA**.

WEED KILLER
Used at base point in the manufacture of methamphetamine substances such as Ice, **speed** and **ecstasy**. The weed killer contains a substance called glyphosate – a herbicide. By the end of the manufacturing process the glyphosate becomes a powdery substance that sticks to the methamphetamine.

// Ashley Gurney, managing director & founder, Alcohol & Drug Education Specialists // www.adesaustralia.com

Profile // Michael Carr-Gregg

THE PSYCHOLOGIST

Dr Michael Carr-Gregg is a child and adolescent psychologist. He's also the author of *Strictly Parenting: Everything you need to know about raising school-aged kids.*

// "There are risk factors that dramatically increase the chances of your children using illicit drugs – the more risk factors there are in their life, the greater the risk. One of these is your child hanging out with friends who use. Using drugs can be associated with genetics, too – so if someone in the family has a drug problem, that can increase the likelihood your kid uses drugs too.

"But we also know there are protective factors, like your child having a close relationship with an adult where they feel safe, valued and listened to. Having open communication and feeling that they belong in a friendship group, or having a real connection to school are also protective. If your children hang out with kids who do arts, drama, music or sport and who are not using alcohol or drugs – that's another protective factor.

"So my advice to parents is to be a good role model, to show you are proud of your child when they do the right thing – because they get discouraged if you only notice when they do something wrong! Set clear rules about alcohol and other drug use – it makes it easier for young people to do the right thing. And get to know your teenager's friends and their parents, so drive them everywhere you can and invite their friends over to your place.

"It's also important to be informed about drugs because there's a mixture of ignorance, fear and anxiety out there. At the moment you could easily think there's an ice pandemic and that our schools are flooded with drug dealers, but by far and away the biggest drug problem is alcohol.

"So don't be shy about having a conversation about drugs and alcohol. Teens have an inability to predict the consequences of their actions because their brain connections are not fully wired up yet. They are susceptible to peer influence and they have a profound deficit in being able to put brakes on their behaviour. Use teachable moments that illustrate the dangers of drugs – so if you read about someone who played a drinking game, drank a shot of vodka every minute for 100 minutes and died, it's not about scaring your child but saying 'what do you think about that?'.

"Stay calm and clearly articulate what you think is acceptable and unacceptable behaviour around alcohol and other drugs, and learn everything you can to give your child the right information. There's a tendency for parents to outsource responsibilities for this to schools, but that's a major failing. Parents need to step up to the plate and lead the battle on this."

> "There are protective factors, like your child having a close relationship with an adult where they feel safe, valued and listened to."

Photo: Penguin Books Australia

// BOOKS

Strictly Parenting: Everything you need to know about raising school-aged kids
Available from Penguin Books Australia.
www.penguin.com.au
Hardcopy // **$29.99**   e-book // **$16.99**

OTHER BOOKS BY MICHAEL CARR-GREGG

Beyond Cyberbullying: An Essential Guide for parenting in the digital age

Princess Bitchface Syndrome

Real Wired Child

Surviving Adolescents: The Must-Have Manual for All Parents

Surviving Step-Families

When to Really Worry: Mental health problems in teenagers and what to do about them

Surviving Year 12

// Dr Michael Carr-Gregg is managing director of The Young and Well Cooperative Research Centre.

HISTORY

Drugs are by no means a modern problem.

1788
Sir Joseph Banks sent cannabis plants to Australia with the First Fleet to produce products such as rope.

For many years, alcohol and tobacco were the drugs of choice in the colony.

1857
Australia's first drug law imposed an import duty on opium, introduced by Chinese immigrants during the gold rush.

1890s
Before 1900, drugs were generally legal and Australia was among the world's biggest consumer of opiates, due largely to medicines containing alcohol or morphine.

Laudanum, a mixture of opium and alcohol, was taken regularly by upper-class matrons and given to children to calm them.

1900s
By 1905, laws prohibited the import and use of smoking-grade opium.

1920s
Cannabis was sold as cigarettes called "Cigares de Joy".

Federal legislation outlawed cannabis importation in 1926.

An international approach overseen by the League of Nations saw more drugs banned.

1950s
Until it was banned in 1953, heroin was available on prescription as a painkiller and in cough mixtures. Australia had the world's highest per capita usage rates.

When it was banned in Australia, heroin was not a major social issue.

1960s
A new drug culture emerged as young people used the likes of cannabis, heroin, LSD and other psychoactive drugs recreationally.

1970s
By 1970, all the states had enacted laws making drug supply a separate offence to drug use or possession.

Anti-drug campaigns focused on abstinence and the dangers of drugs.

Illegal drugs such as heroin and cannabis became major social issues.

1980s
Cocaine became popular among some professionals and in the entertainment industry.

In 1985, the federal and state governments adopted a National Drug Strategy focusing on harm minimisation that aimed to minimise drug demand and supply. It does not advocate drug use but accepts that some use will occur and addresses the harm caused.

Needle-exchange programs helped minimise the spread of diseases such as HIV/AIDS.

1990s
The ACT government considered trialling a heroin prescription program, but the federal government refused to allow heroin importation.

High-quality, cheap heroin flooded in from south-east Asia, causing an epidemic.

2000s
After trialling a Kings Cross Medically Supervised Injecting Centre from 2001-2010, NSW Parliament passed legislation in 2010 making it Australia's first permanent facility.

Raves became synonymous with party drugs.

The potent methamphetamine, ice, emerged as a health and social issue.

2017
The increased use of ice is causing addiction and violence among some users.

Teenage use of alcohol and some illicit drugs is down slightly, but remains a social issue.

New South Wales Government State Library. www.druginfo.sl.nsw.gov.au/drugs/legal/legal_history.html

---

// IMMEDIATE SUPPORT

Anyone who needs help with a drug or alcohol problem or knows someone who does should call the state government's DirectLine:

1800 888 236

DirectLine provides 24/7 counselling, information and referral with professional counsellors experienced in alcohol and drug-related matters. The service is free, anonymous, confidential and available to people using drugs, relatives and friends of those using drugs, and health and welfare professionals. For more information, visit:
health.vic.gov.au/aod/directline

GET THE EFFECTS
The Australian Drug Foundation's *Get the effects by txt!* SMS service allows parents to text the name of a drug to **0439 TELL ME (0439 835 563)**, then receive an SMS about the effects of the drug and links to more information and help. The reply lists a number of the drug's effects and links to find further information on the ADF's DrugInfo website.
www.druginfo.adf.org.au

There is no safe level of drug use as drugs affect everyone differently, based on a person's size, weight and health, whether they are used to taking it, the amount taken and the strength, which varies from batch to batch.

The Australian Drug Foundation

ASSISTANCE

Alcohol and drug issues can be daunting for families. Below are some useful contacts for parents who feel that they need more information.

THE STATE GOVERNMENT'S DIRECTLINE
Those seeking help for drug or alcohol-related problems should call the state government's DirectLine, which will advise of the closest and most appropriate service.
Driectline // **1800 888 236**
www.directline.org.au

FAMILY DRUG SUPPORT
Family Drug Support was formed in 1997 after its founder Tony Trimingham lost his son to a heroin overdose. FDS is a caring, non-religious and non-judgmental organisation primarily made up of volunteers who have had family members with drug dependency and run courses and hold support meetings.
National support line // **1300 368 186**
www.fds.org.au

AUSTRALIAN DRUG FOUNDATION
The Australian Drug Foundation works with parents to help them talk with their children about alcohol and other drugs. It also runs community programs such as Good Sports, which promotes responsible drinking in local sporting clubs.
1300 858 584
Parents website // theothertalk.org.au
Drug facts // druginfo.adf.org.au
Blog // grogwatch.adf.org.au

LES TWENTYMAN FOUNDATION
Born out of a Christmas party for 10 young homeless people in Sunshine in 1984, Les Twentyman's 20th Man Youth Fund provides resources and programs for Melbourne's homeless, disadvantaged and disconnected youth.
ltfoundation.com.au

// MORE ALCOHOL AND DRUG RESOURCES

Ambulance, fire and police.
000

Anglicare drug and alcohol support services.
anglicarevic.org.au/alcohol-drug-support

Al Anon and AlaTeen.
Al Anon Assists families and friends of alcoholics recover from the effects of living with someone whose drinking is a problem.
Alateen is a fellowship of young Al-Anon members, usually teenagers, whose lives have been affected by someone else's drinking.
al-anon.org/australia

Alcoholics Anonymous.
9429 1833
aavictoria.org.au

beyondblue.
1300 22 4636
beyondblue.org.au

Cannabis Information and Helpline.
1800 30 40 50
Drug information in other languages.
1800 123 234

Family Drug Help. Advice and support for families affected by drugs.
1300 660 068
sharc.org.au/program/family-drug-help

The First Step Program.
9537 3177
firststep.org.au

Headspace.
Advice and help for 12 to 15-year-olds with mental health issues.
headspace.org.au

Hepatitis Council of Victoria.
1800 703 003
hepvic.org.au

Kids Help Line.
1800 551 800

Lifeline.
13 11 14

Narcotics Anonymous.
9525 2833

Odyssey House.
odyssey.org.au

Parentline.
13 22 89

Parenting Strategies: preventing adolescent alcohol misuse.
parentingstrategies.net

Raymond Hader Clinic.
rayhaderclinic.com.au

SANE Australia mental health helpline.
1800 187 263

Say When: online support for monitoring alcohol intake.
betterhealth.vic.gov.au/saywhen

Smoking Quitline.
13 78 48

The Other Talk.
theothertalk.org.au

Turning Point drug and alcohol treatment, research and education.
www.turningpoint.org.au
Turning Point offers online counselling at www.counsellingonline.org.au

Youth Support and Advocacy Service.
24 hour free YoDAA (Youth Drug and Alcohol Advice) line:
1800 458 685

// FREE ALCOHOL AND DRUG APPS

QUIT NOW: MY QUITBUDDY APP
Australian National Preventive Health Agency quit smoking app.

BETTER HEALTH CHANNEL APP
Health information and a Victorian-based health services search directory.

TEEN DRINKING LAW APP
This VicHealth app is aimed at parents and explains drinking laws relating to young people.

ON TRACK WITH THE RIGHT MIX APP
Federal government alcohol consumption app.

WADA PROHIBITED LIST 2014 APP
The World Anti-Doping Agency's latest banned list.

ICE. YOUR BODY BELONGS TO YOU APP
Australian Lions Drug Awareness Foundation video about the effects of ice.

DRINKSMART APP
Drinking diary that sends reminders and tips to regulate consumption.

ALCOHOL AND YOUR BRAIN APP
For those aged 17+
Australian Lions Drug Awareness Foundation and DrinkWise App that shows the effects of alcohol on the brain.

NATIONAL HEALTH SERVICES DIRECTORY APP
Federal government health services directory.

NATIONAL DRUGS CAMPAIGN APP
Federal government site with good advice for parents on teen drug use.

// USEFUL VIEWING

AUSTRALIAN DRUG FOUNDATION YOUTUBE CHANNEL
youtube.com/user/AustDrugFoundation

FAMILY DRUG SUPPORT YOUTUBE CHANNEL
Go to youtube.com and search Family Drug Support

VICTORIAN STATE GOVERNMENT'S WHAT ARE YOU DOING ON ICE? CAMPAIGN VIDEO
ice.vic.gov.au/#videos

AL JAZEERA 2014 ICE DOCUMENTARY 101 EAST – THE ICE AGE
Go to youtube.com and search Al Jazeera the ice age

ABC FOUR CORNERS 2014 DOCUMENTARY: ICE RUSH
youtube.com/watch?v=qQ-JO6bWD5Y

ABC FOUR CORNERS 2012 DOCUMENTARY: THE ICE AGE
youtube.com/watch?v=yxKst8BaPbc

POPULAR QUITLINE VIDEOS
Go to youtube.com and search Australian Quitline videos

UNDER CONSTRUCTION: ALCOHOL AND THE TEENAGE BRAIN
A practical TurningPointTraining animation that looks at how the teenage brain develops and its vulnerabilities to alcohol
youtube.com/watch?v=g2gVzVIBc_g

THE GREATER GEELONG COLLECTIVE COMMUNITY EFFORT ON SUBSTANCE ABUSE ICE CAMPAIGN: OUR TOWN'S ICE FIGHT; THERE'S NO PLACE FOR ICE.
icefight.com.au

Emoji icons provided free by EmojiOne // emojione.com

Photos used throughout this publication, unless otherwise credited, are supplied by Thinkstock.

++ The first-person interviews in this booklet are not necessarily the views that all agencies agree upon.

© Parenting Guides Ltd

SEX 101

What you and your children need to know.

SEXUAL ACTIVITY

How sexually active are our teenagers? Most year 10 to 12 students surveyed nationally have engaged in some form of sexual activity, from deep kissing to sexual intercourse.

The sixth National Survey of Australian Secondary Students and Sexual Health 2018 (Australian Research Centre in Sex, Health and Society, La Trobe University) is Australia's bible of teenage sexual activity.

Led by Dr Christopher Fisher, Dr Andrea Waling, Lucille Kerr, Rosalind Bellamy, Pauline Ezer, Dr Gosia Mikolajczak, Dr Graham Brown, Marina Carman and Professor Jayne Lucke, the latest survey in 2018 involved 6,327 year 10, 11, and 12 students from government, Catholic and independent schools nationally.

"Most sexually active students discussed sexual health before sex."

// WHAT THE SURVEY FOUND*

CONTRACEPTION
- The most common form of contraception for sexually active students having vaginal sex was the condom (53.5 per cent) and/or the contraceptive pill (41 per cent).
- 7.6 per cent of sexually active students reported using no contraception the last time they had sex; 19.6 per cent used withdrawal.
- Almost seven in 10 students (68.2 per cent) believe that their peers use a condom, while 62.2 reported doing so.
- Most (56.9 per cent) sexually active students reported using a condom the last time they had sex.
- Most sexually active students discussed sexual health before sex, including 'having sex' (81.2 per cent), using a condom (76.9), avoiding pregnancy (61.8), sexual pleasure (48.2), STIs (36.2) and HIV (30.1).

SEXUALLY TRANSMISSIBLE INFECTIONS
- HIV knowledge is relatively high.
- Students' correct general knowledge about STIs averaged 63 per cent.
- Knowledge of possible STI symptoms was generally good, averaging 71 per cent correct across all questions.
- Few students knew that genital warts can spread without intercourse (56.3 per cent), chlamydia can leave women infertile (53.8), the herpes virus stays with you for life (40.9) and the virus that causes genital warts also can cause cold sores (7.7).
- Gender differences in HIV knowledge was small, but young women generally had better knowledge than young men about STIs.

View the full 6th National Survey of Australian Secondary Students and Sexual Health 2018: Australian Research Centre in Sex, Health and Society, La Trobe University // teenhealth.org.au

// STUDENTS WHO HAVE EVER HAD SEXUAL INTERCOURSE
(VAGINAL OR ANAL) BY YEAR LEVEL*

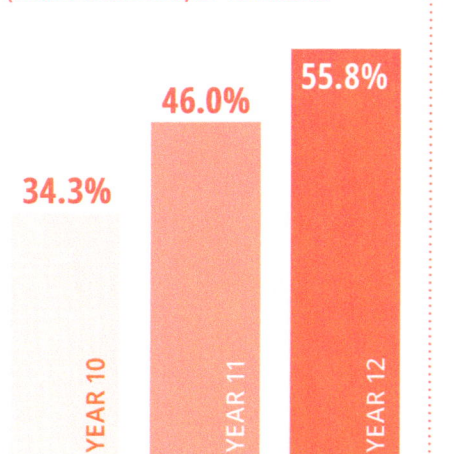

- YEAR 10: 34.3%
- YEAR 11: 46.0%
- YEAR 12: 55.8%
- TOTAL STUDENTS WHO HAVE NOT HAD SEXUAL INTERCOURSE (VAGINAL OR ANAL) %: 53.4%

// STUDENTS' SEXUAL EXPERIENCES USING NEW TECHNOLOGIES*

// SENT A SEXUALLY EXPLICIT WRITTEN TEXT MESSAGE

	Male %	Female %	TGD %
Yes	43.3	37.7	40.4
No	56.7	62.3	59.6

// RECEIVED A SEXUALLY EXPLICIT WRITTEN TEXT MESSAGE

	Male %	Female %	TGD %
Yes	49.8	51.3	50.7
No	50.2	48.7	49.3

// SENT A SEXUALLY EXPLICIT NUDE OR NEARLY NUDE PHOTO OR VIDEO OF YOURSELF

	Male %	Female %	TGD %
Yes	31.3	32.6	32
No	68.7	67.4	68

* Source: 6th National Survey of Australian Secondary Students and Sexual Health 2018: Australian Research Centre in Sex, Health and Society, La Trobe University.
+ In the past two months
NOTE: Trans and gender diverse (TGD)

DEEP KISSING
74.4%

RECEIVING ORAL SEX
51.4%

GIVING ORAL SEX
52.1%

VAGINAL SEX
44.4%

ANAL SEX
12.6%

*Students' reported sexual activities * (Combined year 10, 11 and 12 totals %)*

"YOUNG PEOPLE ARE CONFIDENT" *

Most sexually active students report positive feelings after having sex.
- Almost two in 10 sexually active students (19 per cent) had sex with three or more people in the past year.
- About 20 per cent of non-sexually active students (20.4) reported feeling "fantastic" and 17.2 per cent felt proud about not having had sex yet.
- About half of non-sexually active students did not feel ready to have sex; they were proud to say no and mean it, and that they thought it important to be in love the first time they had sex.

The authors were generally positive about young people's sexual knowledge and decision-making.

"Young people should be applauded for their largely healthy and responsible sexual relationships; Australian communities should continue to support young people in their efforts to enact healthy sexual relationships," they said.

THE ROLE ALCOHOL PLAYS

There were some concerns, including some young people feeling pressured into unwanted sex and the role alcohol played in this. Of those who had had unwanted sex, 34.2 per cent said it was because they were too drunk and 13.7 per cent were too high.

"My partner thought I should" [was] the most common reason (52 per cent) [for unwanted sex]," the report found. "There was some consistency across genders; however, male students were significantly more likely to indicate perceived peer pressure than female students."

THE USE OF SOCIAL MEDIA

The survey indicates that young people's increasing use of the internet as a source of sexual-health information needs to be seen as a strength which can, with the development of skills improving critical inquiry, give them access to reliable and confidential information in areas where questions may be too hard to ask. The use of social media plays a large role in the negotiation and development of sexual relationships. This includes the sending of explicit messages and images, most of which appear to occur within relationships.

"In the two months prior ... the vast majority of students had used Facebook (99.3 per cent), YouTube (96.7 per cent), SnapChat (92.6 per cent) and Instagram (92.5 per cent)," the report found. "The most frequently used platform was SnapChat, with 65.7 per cent of students using it five or more times a day. Dating apps, such as Tinder, were used the least (7.7 per cent) of all the platforms asked about."

// SENT A SEXUALLY EXPLICIT NUDE OR NEARLY NUDE PHOTO OR VIDEO OF SOMEONE ELSE+

	Male %	Female %	TGD %
Yes	31.3	32.6	32.1
No	68.7	67.4	67.9

// RECEIVED A SEXUALLY EXPLICIT NUDE OR NEARLY NUDE PHOTO OR VIDEO OF SOMEONE ELSE+

	Male %	Female %	TGD %
Yes	44.1	44.2	42
No	55.9	55.8	58

// USED A SOCIAL MEDIA SITE FOR SEXUAL REASONS+

	Male %	Female %	TGD %
Yes	38.8	23.2	41.8
No	61.2	76.8	58.2

PARENT Q&A

Our panel of sex and education experts tackles some common questions ...

CAN WE TELL OUR CHILDREN TOO MUCH ABOUT SEX?

"Absolutely not. Kids take in what is relevant to them. If you are armed with information you can make reasoned decisions. It's a concern of parents that knowing what sex is will ruin their kids' innocence but that makes sex shameful, rather than it being seen as an everyday thing that happens when you get older. Kids may then access pornography and then see things like double penetration, for example, as a form of sex. That is worse than parents providing kids with information so they can make reasoned decisions. US research shows that providing information about sex actually delays the onset of a child's first sexual experience, and if kids are already sexually active it promotes safer sex practices."

Dr Debbie Ollis, senior lecturer in education at Deakin Uni

HOW CAN I SUPPORT MY CHILD WHEN IT COMES TO SEX AND THE ONLINE WORLD?

"I've got these four Ps for social media. Never post anything online that you wouldn't want your Parents, the Police, a Principal or a Predator to see. It's as easy as that. Pornography is now the leading sex educator in Australian schools by far. It's much more violent than it used to be, too. Please don't for one second think there's anything you can do to stop them from seeing it because – newsflash – there isn't. What's sad about this though is the research shows the impact that violent pornography has toward changing our kids' attitudes about sexual harassment. It suggests that it's OK to hold a girl down for sex; it's OK to be callous; it's OK to be abusive. My greatest fear is that we're socialising boys and some girls into a very brutalised version of masculinity. If ever there was a website that you need to dive into on the subject of online pornography, it's 'It's time we talked' (www.itstimewetalked.com.au). It's a genius website to equip parents with the skills, knowledge, and the strategies to deal with this issue. It's not a matter of if, it's when they see it, and you need to be ready. Do I wish it were different? Of course I do, but this is our reality."

Dr Michael Carr-Gregg, child and adolescent psychologist

HOW DO I KEEP MY KIDS SAFE?

"Give them information. Have condoms in the bathroom where teenagers can get them if they need them. You don't have to give them to your child yourself, but it lets them know that safe sex is important. And make it clear that, if something goes wrong, there is nothing so awful that your child can't tell you. Let them know that we all make mistakes and that's OK and I am the parent who can help. Don't use fear, shame and danger. Kids tell us the messages they often get is that sex is dangerous, shameful and negative. Tell them that sex is a wonderful thing when you are with someone you love. The aim of sex education is not about preventing sex but making sure it is respectful and enjoyable." **DB**

MY KIDS DON'T WANT TO TALK ABOUT SEX TO ME DO THEY?

"It depends on the parent. In every focus group of five or six teenagers that I did recently, one kid would go 'but why wouldn't you talk to your parents? I can talk to my parents'. So it's the way the conversational tone is set. If parents approach this topic along the lines of talking about the birds and the bees and the biological facts, that makes things awkward. If there is a broader conversation about relationships, human communication and gender, how you ask for what you want, how you know what someone else wants, that can open up conversations where you don't have to focus solely on sexual intercourse."

Professor Catharine Lumby, educational author

WHAT DO I DO IF MY KIDS TALK ABOUT SEX AND I DON'T KNOW THE ANSWER OR I'M NOT COMFORTABLE ANSWERING A QUESTION?

"Children ask questions around sex because they are just curious and it's best to deal with their questions in a matter-of-fact way. Often when kids ask questions about sex we go to the worst-case scenario and worry about why they are asking this and that. If you don't know the answer or you need a bit of time to work out how to respond, say 'that's a good question, let me think about it and come back to you'. You don't have to have the answers there and then but show your child that you have heard them. Or show them respect by inventing a related scenario, bouncing it off them and asking their advice and what they think about it." **CL**

WHAT CAN I DO NOW?

"Understand the issue from both your own and your child's perspective. Discuss your family values, beliefs and hopes early. Acknowledge that children are developing intimate and sexual citizens with rights and responsibilities to care for themselves and others. Take a non-judgmental approach to your child's desire for sexual knowledge and understanding about intimate relationships. Model health and respectful relationships in your home and highlight the value of communication in all relationships. Actively discuss the need for open conversations around choice, negotiation and consent for all types of intimate relationships, whether they are sexual or not. Open up discussions that explore the range of feelings and emotions that occur around intimate and sexual relationships. When talking with children and young people about intimate relationships, we need to teach them that intimacy and sexuality is about sharing love, pleasure and ourselves!"

Linette Etheredge, designs and delivers interactive presentations to students, parents and teaching staff at schools across Melbourne

> Kids tell us the messages they often get is that sex is dangerous, shameful and negative.

Profile // Jenny Walsh

POSITIVE BYSTANDER

Jenny Walsh says we need to help our children develop empathy.

"As parents we need to help our kids step up when they see hurtful or hateful behaviour. We need to help them critique their assumptions about what kinds of behaviour everyone else thinks is OK. In adolescence, children place high value on what friends think, and they use that to guide their behaviour because they want to belong.

"When you talk about these assumptions, children may find that actually their mates don't want to be that kind of mate or that kind of boyfriend. Instead, they want to be a good friend, and our children need to think about what that means in terms of their behaviour towards other people.

"One of the most powerful things we can do as parents is hold up a light and show not everyone thinks it is OK. This gives children courage to speak up. So it's important that schools and families highlight when something is unacceptable, such as sexual harassment or the harassment of girls about their bodies.

"We've seen lots of examples quite recently of girls being ranked and rated online based on their looks.

"In those situations, we need to ask 'how do you think it would feel to be one of the many young women put up on that website having people making comments about their appearance?'. We need to help our children develop empathy. Without that conversation it's easy for young people to get carried away.

"Take advantage of a story in the media or a storyline on TV and say 'what would your friends do if that happened at school?' or 'how do you think the girls there would feel?'. Ask them how they would feel if this happened to their sister. What do they think the repercussions are for girls whose images are put up on a website?

"And remind them what it takes to do the right thing. It takes courage to not just be a bystander and to step up. Firstly, children need to be able to recognise that something is wrong. We need to identify scenarios and say that was wrong and this is why it was wrong and then assist them to think about its impact on the individual.

"Secondly, our children need to be able to suss out if that other person can take care of themselves, or does your child need to say something? And they have to know how to do that safely. Give them strategies, such as starting a conversation with the person who is being harassed or calling them to come and see something. Or it might be a case of saying to whoever is doing the inappropriate behaviour that what they are doing is not on and letting kids know that other people think what is happening is wrong.

Photo: iStock

"Remind them what it takes to do the right thing. It takes courage to not just be a bystander and to step up."

"A key thing about bystander action is that it has been shown to make a big difference. Education programs that teach kids how to step up show it can limit the harm of a particular situation. And it helps change a culture because other boys and girls see that not everyone thinks a certain behaviour is OK. That has an enormous impact.

"So have that conversation with children about the impact of bystander action on others. And keep talking to children about their definition of a good man or a good boyfriend or girlfriend. What does that mean to them? Help them set up an aspiration of the type of person they want to be.

"Finally, what if your kids see that a situation is potentially very damaging and hurtful to someone and they aren't able to safely step up? Ask them which adults they could talk to, to take action. It's great to encourage kids to act, but it's just as important to know when to seek help."

// Jenny Walsh has written a range of publications about relationship and sexuality education. She is a former senior member of the Australian Research Centre in Sex, Health and Society at La Trobe University. www.jennywalsh.com.au
Jenny also wrote/co-wrote *Talk Soon Talk Often; a parent's guide for talking to your kids about sex*, *Catching On Early: Sexuality education for Victorian primary schools* and *The Practical Guide to Love, Sex and Relationships* for years 7-10.

YOUNG PEOPLE HAVE THEIR SAY ON SEXTING

GIRL // AGE 17 // YEAR 11

"I think sending nudes is totally fine. A body is a body and nothing should be taboo about that.

"If sending those kinds of photos is something that makes you feel good about yourself and you're doing it for your own reasons and the person you're sending them to wants to see them, then I don't see how that can be seen as shameful.

"I sure have sent photos to my platonic friends and partners. It can be super fun. Because I looked good and felt comfortable and confident in myself.

"My friends do not see the human body as something to be shameful of, we embrace diverse bodies and lift up each others' self-confidence.

"I've never had any experience of people leaking my nudes.

"The people I've sent them to are trustworthy and respectful enough to keep that private. But if someone I trusted ever did show anybody else, I'd feel pretty betrayed.

"It's a breach of my privacy as I shared those photos with specific people, not for everyone's eyes. It's just like consent with sex; you consent to having sex with specific people and it's not up to anyone else to choose those people for you.

"I have felt pressured, it was more people begging for me to send photos. But I never did anything I was uncomfortable with, and they respected that.

"Adults have been telling us from a young age that you shouldn't send nudes and if you do all the consequences and backlash that may occur is your own fault. I completely disagree.

"My friends and I have informative, in-depth educated discussions free of embarrassment and judgment. We learn from each other and draw our own opinions from the media.

"I've also learnt a lot from my mum, who speaks out against victim blaming and slut shaming.

"I have been sent many unsolicited d--k pics from random men I don't know online, many as old as 30. I personally find it disgusting that men think we want to see their genitals. It's not attractive. If you're sending it to someone who you have a mutual trust and you know them it's completely different, but girls don't owe you anything and don't want to see your d--k."

BOY // AGED 15 // YEAR 9

"Personally, I don't think people should do it unless they are in a relationship and feel comfortable with sending them.

"Unfortunately I have done it. I sent one to a girl who is in the year above me. I wasn't really thinking at the time. I sent it because she asked me for them after she sent me some.

"I have never directly asked for nudes and I don't think I ever will. I think it might be because of people thinking I'm needy.

"I have only kept one, which was consented by the person sending it.

"Never in a million years would I show anyone pictures of people that trusted me to see them naked.

"If I did show anyone and she found out, I think it would make her feel violated and vulnerable. I would feel ashamed."

GIRL // AGED 14 // YEAR 9

"A year or so ago I sent a 'nude' to a close guy friend of mine and he sent it around soon after. It didn't bother me too much that people had seen it – more that he broke my trust.

"I felt really betrayed when he showed others. At the time I didn't do very much about it as I was fairly scared and anxious about what others would say.

"I've sent quite a few, honestly. I've sent them to my boyfriend, and ex-boyfriend. They didn't show anyone. I only send them to people I really trust or love.

"Guys message me continuously, asking and begging me for a nude. Some say 'don't you want to make me happy?' and 'I'm so sad and I really need this'. They tell me that my boyfriend will never know or find out.

"I hate when they say that. I stop talking to anyone who constantly asks me or tries to pressure me into it.

"A few guys send me random d--k pictures, without me asking or us even talking beforehand.

"It makes me feel uncomfortable. Sometimes they say I have to send a photo back because they sent me something. Of course I don't and I often try to tell them how wrong it is.

"I believe it's your choice if you decide to send them, as long as it's consensual, you trust the person and you're both being respectful.

"Guys who send random d--k photos to girls who don't ask for them need to learn that we really don't like it. We find it disrespectful and gross."

Photo: iStock
Illustrative purposes only: the person pictured is a model.

// Copyright Elissa Doherty, education reporter, *Herald Sun*, September 9, 2016. Read the full version online at goo.gl/QAE818

Profile // Katie Acheson

THE NEW STANDARD

Katie Acheson believes sexting between consenting teenagers has become a routine way of young people expressing and exploring their sexual development.

"Some studies say two out of three young people between the ages of 16 and 18 have sexted. Whatever the precise figures, sexting is very prevalent at an important time in a young person's development when they are expressing their sexuality – and they are utilising technology to do that.

"Sexting is part of being a young person. We are in the iPhone era. A young person has an iPhone or smartphone with them much of the time and it has become part of how they are developing their sexual identity. We've done it through generations with art, the press and by writing risqué things. Every time we have a new technology coming in to the sexual space we get worried.

"I think parents are scared about sexting because the internet feels permanent. But young people are aware of the internet and its ramifications. They've grown up with it and they know how images are stored. A parent sees that a young person's picture could be taken from a phone and put somewhere else, but young people understand there are billions of images flooding the internet, and that makes their image only one of billions.

"But we need to make a clear distinction between sexting – two consenting people expressing themselves to each other in a sexual manner – and revenge porn, where someone takes an image or video they've received and passes it on or posts it without a person's consent. That is very, very different.

"State and federal laws are struggling to keep up with technology in this area. While some jurisdictions have moved to ensure teenagers who consent to send or receive explicit photos of themselves are not committing a crime, in others it may still be depending on the situation and the ages of those involved.

"If sexting with consent it shouldn't come under a criminal act. It is very important to have laws to protect children but we don't want to see young people with a criminal history for expressing themselves while working out their sexual identity.

"Have a conversation about sexting in the same way you'd have a conversation about sex. Talk about what they feel comfortable with around sexting. Has anybody asked you to send images? Did you send them? Where did that picture go and to whom? How did it make you feel? Did you feel pressured? If someone is asking you for an intimate picture you need to make an informed decision about whether to send it or not. Do you trust that person? And talk about how things can change. Someone may say they love you and that picture is just for us – but if you send a picture, you don't really know what will happen to it.

Photo: Jay La Photography

"For many teenagers, sexting is part of being a young person ... Every time we have a new technology coming in to the sexual space we get worried."

"Ignoring the fact that many young people are sexting won't make the issue go away. If they are going to do it, they can manage the negative effects of someone passing it on by having no identifying elements. So don't put your face in the image or don't show a birthmark that is obviously you and then your child can deny it is them if their picture is passed on.

"If you talk about sexting and start from a place of 'I can't believe you've done this' ... your child won't tell you how deep this has gone. It's part of their healthy sexual development but they may make a mistake and not know how to handle it. As a parent, you can help them through that."

// Katie Acheson is CEO of Youth Action, a peak organisation representing young people and youth services. www.youthaction.org.au

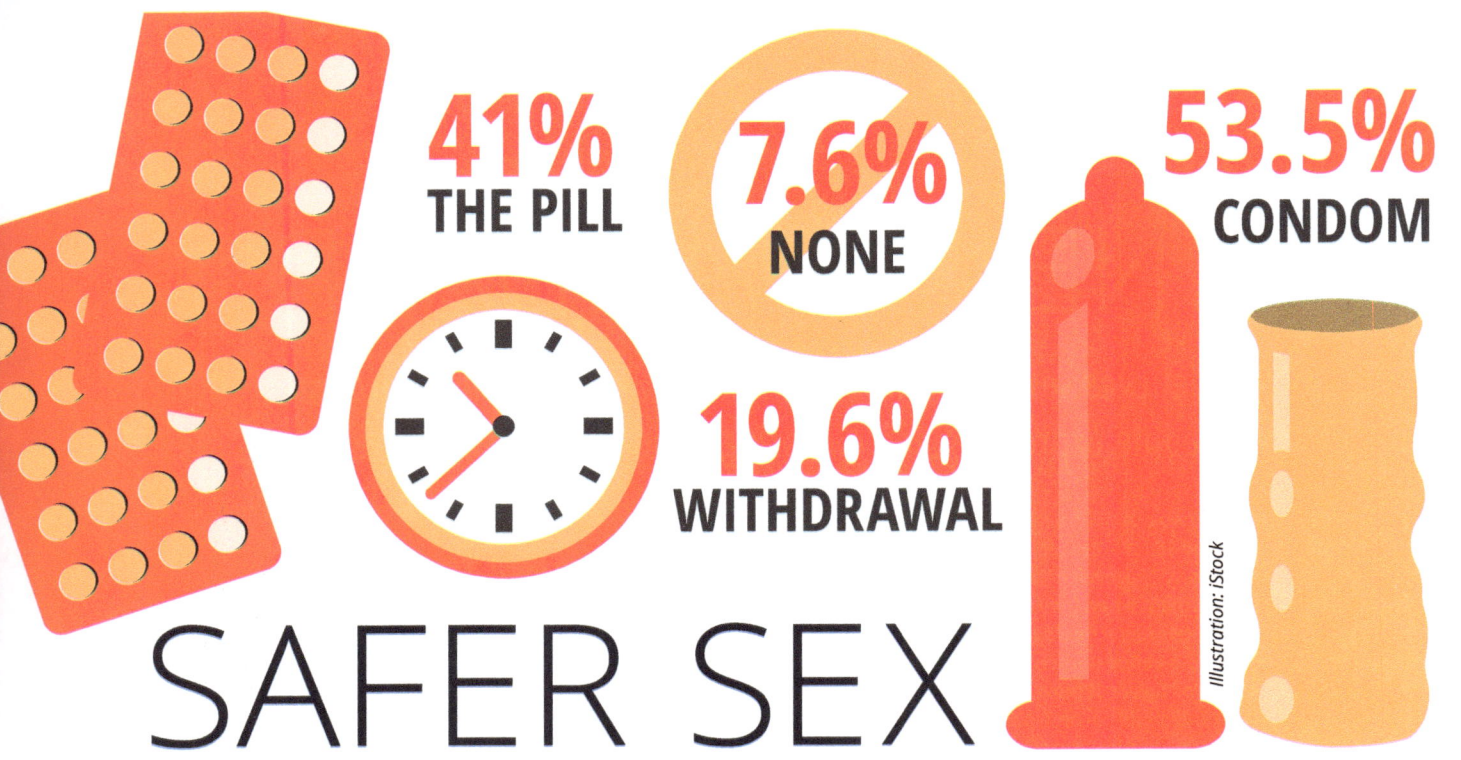

SAFER SEX

Sexually active teenagers are generally responsible, but some don't use contraception and a small percentage have sex that results in a pregnancy.

The sixth National Survey of Australian Secondary Students and Sexual Health 2018 (Australian Research Centre in Sex, Health and Society, La Trobe University) found 53.5 per cent of sexually active secondary students used a condom and 41 per cent used the contraceptive pill the last time they had vaginal sex. Almost two in 10 (19.6 per cent) used the withdrawal method.

Almost four in 10 (38.4 per cent) always used condoms during sex over the previous year, 34.3 per cent did sometimes/often and 12.8 per cent never did. Most sexually active students (69.8 per cent) said a condom was available at their last sexual event, while 56.9 per cent used it. Those who didn't use a condom last time they had sex said they knew their partner's sexual history (37.7 per cent), trusted their partner (36.9 per cent), "it just happened" (33.5 per cent), or they (28.5 per cent) or their partner (28.5 per cent) didn't like condoms. Almost two in 10 (18.3 per cent) had both been tested for STIs.

// THE SURVEY SAYS ...

QUESTION // "THE LAST TIME YOU HAD VAGINAL SEX WHICH, IF ANY, FORMS OF CONTRACEPTION DID YOU OR THE PERSON YOU HAD SEX WITH USE? PLEASE TICK / CLICK AS MANY AS YOU THINK APPLY "*

	Male %	Female %	TGD %
Condom	54.5	53.1	30.4
The pill	37.7	43.5	30.4
IUD	1.6	1.4	0
Diaphragm	0.3	0.1	0
Emergency contraception	3	4.6	8.7
Withdrawal	17.4	21.2	13
Rhythm method	1.4	1.1	4.3
Injection	0.7	0.7	0
Contraceptive implant	6.7	9.6	26.1
None	7.2	7.8	13
Other	0.7	0.7	8.7

Base: Sexually active students. Note: Multiple responses.

QUESTION // "IF A CONDOM WAS NOT USED, WHY?" *

	Male %	Female %	TGD %
I don't like them	29.9	28	16.7
My partner does not like them	26	31.7	25
I trust my partner	35.9	37.6	25
It just happened	38.1	31	41.7
We both have been tested for HIV / STIs	12.4	21.6	8.3
Too embarrassed	3.9	1.7	16.7
I know my partner's sexual history	36.9	38	50
It is not my responsibility	1.2	0.6	8.3
Other	31.1	39	50

Base: Sexually active students who reported not using a condom the last time they had sex. Note: Multiple responses.

* Source: 6th National Survey of Australian Secondary Students and Sexual Health 2018: Australian Research Centre in Sex, Health and Society, La Trobe University.
NOTE: Trans and gender diverse (TGD)

CONTRACEPTION

SEXUAL ABSTINENCE // 100% EFFECTIVE

VASECTOMY // 99.85% EFFECTIVE (PERMANENT)
A vasectomy involves cutting the tubes that carry sperm, to stop sperm moving from the testes to the penis.

FEMALE STERILISATION // 99.5% EFFECTIVE (PERMANENT)
Female sterilisation blocks the fallopian tubes, stopping eggs from moving down the tube and being fertilised. The most common methods are tubal ligation, ("having your tubes tied"), where a clip is put on each tube under general anaesthetic, and tubal occlusion, where a small coil (Essure) is put in each tube under local anaesthetic.

CONTRACEPTIVE IMPLANT // >99.95% EFFECTIVE
The matchstick sized implant sits under the skin of the arm and lasts up to three years. Inserted by a qualified heath professional, it slowly releases a small amount of hormone.

COPPER INTRAUTERINE DEVICE (Cu-IUD) // >99.5% EFFECTIVE
This device is inserted into the uterus and lasts up to 10 years. It contains no hormones.

HORMONAL INTRAUTERINE DEVICE (IUD) // >99.5% EFFECTIVE
This device is inserted into the uterus and lasts up to five years. It slowly releases very small amounts of hormone into the uterus.

INJECTIONS // >99.95% EFFECTIVE
Depo-Provera and Depo-Ralovera are hormonal injections containing a progesterone-like hormone given every 12 to 14 weeks.

COMBINED PILL // 93% EFFECTIVE
The combined pill contains synthetic forms of the hormones oestrogen and progesterone. It stops ovulation and makes the fluid at the opening to the uterus thicker, stopping sperm from getting through.

MINI PILL // 93% EFFECTIVE
The mini pill contains a synthetic form of progesterone. It usually suits women who either have side effects when they take oestrogen or cannot take oestrogen for health reasons.

VAGINAL RING // 93% EFFECTIVE
The vaginal ring has similar hormones to the combined pill and works in the same way. A "one size fits all" ring is inserted into the vagina and stays there for three weeks, slowly releasing hormones that move from the vagina into the bloodstream.

MALE CONDOM // 88% EFFECTIVE

FEMALE CONDOM // 79% EFFECTIVE

DIAPHRAGM // 82% EFFECTIVE
This soft, shallow silicone dome fits in the vagina and covers the opening to the uterus, stopping sperm from getting through. It needs to stay in place for at least six hours after sex. If it is used, fitted and positioned correctly, a diaphragm is 94 per cent effective. They need to be fitted by a trained doctor or nurse and may not protect from STIs.

EMERGENCY CONTRACEPTION
The morning-after pill is a hormonal method of contraception that may stop ovulation. It can be taken to avoid getting pregnant in an emergency situation, such as after having unprotected sex, if a condom slips off or breaks during sex or if the contraceptive pill is missed. It prevents 85 per cent of pregnancies.

It is best to take emergency contraception as soon as possible, ideally within 24 hours of having sex.

NATURAL METHODS
Known as natural family planning, these methods monitor body changes during the menstrual cycle to identify when a women is most fertile.

> Students who didn't use a condom most commonly said they were not prepared.

Edited text // Better Health Channel material is copyright © 2016. State of Victoria. Reproduced from the Better Health Channel (www.betterhealth.vic.gov.au) at no cost. The information published here was accurate at the time of publication and is not intended to take the place of medical advice. www.betterhealth.vic.gov.au/health/healthyliving/contraception-choices
Efficiency of contraception methods // Family Planning Alliance Australia. www.fpv.org.au/about/f-p-a-a

// ABORTION

In Victoria, abortion is legal up to 24 weeks without a doctor's referral. After 24 weeks you can have an abortion if at least two doctors agree. The doctors must consider all relevant medical circumstances and your current and future physical, psychological and social circumstances.

Family Planning Victoria says you are not legally required to have counselling but can do so through your doctor, who can also refer you to a specially trained psychologist or nurse. FPV offers one-hour pregnancy choices information sessions with a nurse, which provide factual information about all the options available.

GROWING UP

Parents and carers should be open, honest and supportive during puberty.

Puberty can be a challenging time for children and their parents and carers, who may find it difficult to answer questions about sexuality and relationships.

There are no perfect answers but support and honesty are important as children enter puberty, which can start as young as eight in girls and nine in boys.

Parents, carers and families are the most important source of sexuality and relationship information. They should also admit when they don't have an answer and offer to find it together.

The internet provides a wealth of starting points. Programs such as WA Health's *Talk Soon. Talk Often* offer tips for parents and carers who are unsure about what to do or say.

As the program says, talking a little and often makes a positive difference to a child's sexual health.

The key is to make yourself available, continue to show affection, listen, answer questions honestly and simply, don't assume heterosexuality and don't always wait to be asked a question.

For more information visit // healthywa.wa.gov.au/Articles/S_T/Talk-soon-Talk-often

// MASTURBATION

We've come a long way since the days when parents used to tell their kids they would go blind if they masturbated. Most parents now realise it is safe and even healthy – as long as it's done in private.

But masturbation can be a tricky topic to raise with teenagers. How do you start a conversation about something so personal and what do you tell them?

First and foremost, kids need to know there is nothing shameful about masturbation and it won't affect them physically or mentally. In fact, it is good for their health and allows them to explore their burgeoning sexuality in private.

If you feel embarrassed about discussing masturbation, buy your child a book that covers it and other sexuality issues well – and speaks to them in their language. Don't forget to tell them you are happy to discuss it with them at any time.

// A TIME OF CHANGE**

PHYSICAL CHANGES FOR GIRLS

- Breast growth – the first stage is called "budding". Sometimes, the breasts are different sizes. This is normal, but girls can speak with a doctor if they are worried.
- Hair growth – hair will start to grow around the pubic area and under the arms, and hair on the legs and arms will darken.
- Vaginal discharge – they may start to get a clear or whitish discharge from the vagina. This is normal.
- Periods – menstrual periods will start. Periods are part of a monthly cycle where the lining of the uterus (womb) thickens as the body gets ready for pregnancy. Once a month, the lining is shed over a few days if a pregnancy has not happened.
- Period pain – they may start to have pain or cramps just before or at the start of their period.

PHYSICAL CHANGES FOR BOYS

- Genital growth – their testicles and penis will get bigger. It is normal for one testicle to be bigger than the other. Some boys worry about their penis size, but sexual function, including the ability to have sex and father children, does not depend on penis size.
- Hair growth – body hair starts to grow around the pubic area, legs, under the arms and on the face. It starts off fine and then gets thicker and darker. Some young men keep growing and getting more body hair into their 20s.
- Voice changes – their voice gets deeper.
- Muscle growth.
- Wet dreams – they may have wet dreams, where they ejaculate in their sleep. This is a normal part of growing up.
- Erections – sometimes erections happen when they get nervous or excited, or for no reason at all, which can make them feel embarrassed. Other people will not usually notice them and they will go away after a few minutes.
- Breast changes – they may get some breast growth and tenderness. This is a normal response to the changing hormones in their body and will eventually go away.

EMOTIONAL CHANGES FOR GIRLS AND BOYS

- Coping with a changing body – young people have to deal with a lot of physical changes that happen around the same time. They now have a new body shape and may start to feel self-conscious about how they look.
- Mood swings.
- Physical growth and other changes can make a young person feel full of energy one moment and tired the next.
- The way young people think changes around puberty as they develop their own identity as an individual and as part of a family. They are starting to figure out their own standards and ideals, form their own ideas, morals and values and rely less on their parents.

** Better Health Channel material is copyright © 2016. State of Victoria. Reproduced from the Better Health Channel (www.betterhealth.vic.gov.au) at no cost. The information published here was accurate at the time of publication and is not intended to take the place of medical advice. www.betterhealth.vic.gov.au/health/healthyliving/contraception-choices

Profile // Isabel Fox

UNDERSTANDING ENTHUSIASTIC CONSENT

Isabel Fox leads a consent education and sexual assault prevention program, Playing Right. A key message of which is, 'it's not a yes unless it's a hell yes'.

"Playing Right was developed in response to the Australian Human Rights Commission's *Change the Course: National Report on Sexual Assault and Sexual Harassment at Australian Universities*. Published in 2017, it found that in 2015-16, one in five students were sexually harassed and 6.9 per cent of students were sexually assaulted on campus or at university events.

"The program is tailored to school leavers and people in their late teens. Research suggests they are given a lot of information about the biology of sexual relationships – about disease prevention and pregnancy and birth control – but they are often not educated about the emotional and social issues of sexual relationships.

"One of our key messages is 'it's not a yes unless it's a hell yes' – based on the idea of enthusiastic consent. Quite often young people who haven't found their voice yet aren't sure how to communicate consent, or to understand if consent has been given.

"We emphasise that unless a person you are engaging in a sexual encounter with is enthusiastically wanting to be there, assume they don't want to be there. Because young people can be scared to say no, or they may feel pressured into doing things they may not want to do. It's important to teach students what consent is and what it looks or sounds like. It's more enjoyable for everyone if they understand the rules of the game and play the game with someone else who wants to be there.

"We teach students basic things like checking in – and that can be repeating the question 'is this ok?' If you keep asking that question during a sexual encounter, and the person you are with keeps saying 'yes', then you can be sure they want to be there. There is no 'grey' area in consent. There's an enthusiastic 'yes' and everything else is a no. We also show students a video about consent – a simple way for parents to start the conversation about consent, too. And we emphasise that someone can't give a 'yes' if they are under 16, if they are under 18 and with someone in a position of power, or if they are intoxicated or under the influence of drugs or medication. The absence of a no doesn't mean a yes, either.

"Enthusiastic consent is if you are asking your partner 'do you want me to do this and they say yes. Do you like this? Yes'. It's about mutual enjoyment and engagement. It's about checking in and getting confirmation. Everyone will have a much better time if you are with someone who's enthusiastic about what you are enthusiastic about doing. If something didn't feel OK, it probably wasn't. If someone pressured you to do something, even if they're your boyfriend or girlfriend, that's not OK.

"The program empowers bystanders to be active, too, and it encourages mates of a perpetrator to step in and say, 'I don't think he or she is in a good state to do that'. Once we've had discussions around consent, people are more likely to say or do something because they understand it's not all right.

"If young people want to engage in sexual relationships, we want them to be enjoyable and nourishing. The more we talk about these concepts like consent and empower them to understand and play by the rules, the more we can help that happen."

Watch video about consent //
www.youtube.com/watch?v=h3nhM9UlJjc)

> If something didn't feel OK, it probably wasn't. If someone pressured you to do something, even if they're your boyfriend or girlfriend, that's not OK.

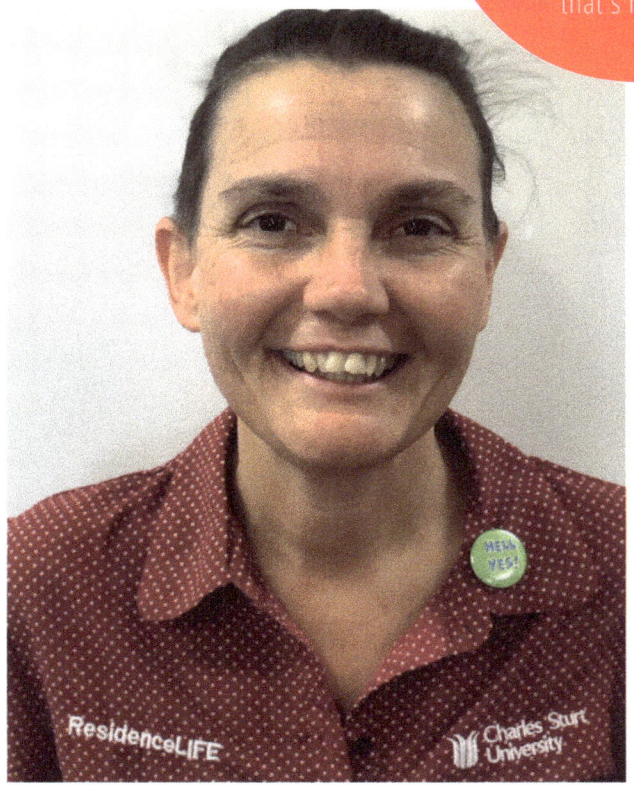

// Isabel Fox is Student Initiatives Coordinator at Charles Sturt University and leads the Playing Right program. She also recently presented the program to universities in the US.

SEX EDUCATION

With many children physically developing sooner than in the past, sexuality and relationships education is important from a young age.

Most young Australians receive sex education, many in primary school. Experts say they should learn about body parts and respectful relationships from a young age, both at home and at school.

The sixth National Survey of Australian Secondary Students and Sexual Health 2018* found 83.6 per cent of Australian teenagers had received sex education at school. More than one in 10 (13.2 per cent) hadn't and 3.1 per cent didn't know.

Students' most recent sexuality and relationship education was primarily taught by teachers (82.1 per cent), people outside the school (9.8 per cent), or the school nurse (5.6 per cent). School counsellors (1.5 per cent) or chaplains (0.7 per cent) were less likely to be used.

While most schools teach it, the quality of sex education varies. Many have excellent programs but some offer the bare minimum.

It doesn't hurt to ask your school what it is doing. If an outside group is providing the service, you may also want to check to ensure its values align with yours.

WHAT THE EXPERTS SAY

Good sex education starts at home from a very young age and continues at school with a comprehensive program covering all aspects of adolescence, relationships and diversity issues.

Sex Education Australia's Jenny Ackland says a child's early sexuality education has nothing to do with sex, but should involve using the correct names for body parts and understanding the concepts of public and private and appropriate and inappropriate touching.

She says children can ask questions from a very young age and parents and carers should answer them in an age-appropriate way. It's also important for very young children to understand "same" and "different", basic ideas about gender, correct names for basic reproductive body parts and thinking about respectful friendships.

As children get older, Ackland says they should learn about reproduction, how babies are made and born, including the different ways they can join families such as adoption, IVF, surrogate, donor sperm and/or eggs and so on. "Being inclusive is important," she says.

In late primary school, Ackland says sex education should cover the physical, mental and social changes of puberty and how to manage them. This can include key messages on sexting and sexually explicit material online. "Friendships, managing social media, greater freedom and responsibility are all important topics," she says.

Ackland says most children in years 5 and 6 know or have heard about sex. Some even younger students may have too. "In sex education in school it's good for them to have a simple, clear explanation to inform and clarify if what they might have heard before is untrue," she says.

While it is important for primary and secondary schools to have comprehensive sex education programs, Ackland says as their children's primary carers, parents know them better than anyone else.

"Ideally sexuality education should also be covered at home," she says. "Home is where individual values, beliefs and expectations can be shared, and it's important that parents are available to answer questions and provide support."

Some parents feel uncomfortable discussing sex with their kids. Ackland says this is OK, but if that's the case you need to let them know this and show you are available to offer support.

"Reliable age-appropriate books are good to have in the house so young people can read these in private as well as referring them to quality websites," she says.

> Good sex education starts at home from a very young age.

*Source: 6th National Survey of Australian Secondary Students and Sexual Health 2018: Australian Research Centre in Sex, Health and Society, La Trobe University.

// PRIMARY RESOURCES

WEBSITES FOR PRIMARY STUDENTS
www.ubykotex.com.au/puberty
www.cyh.com (click on kids health)
www.kidshealth.org

BOOKS FOR LOWER/MIDDLE PRIMARY
Mummy laid an egg by Babette Cole
Hair in funny places by Babette Cole
The baby tree by Sophie Blackall
So that's where I came from by Gina Dawson
The amazing true story of how babies are made by Fiona Katauskas

BOOKS FOR UPPER PRIMARY
Secret girls' business by Fay Angelo
More secret girls' business by Fay Angelo
Secret boys' business by Fay Angelo
The puberty book by Wendy Darvill & Kelsey Powell
Poppy Pretzel – passage into puberty by Debi Slinger
100+ questions kids have about puberty by Interrelate

PARENT RESOURCES
ONLINE // Talk soon. Talk often: a guide for parents for talking to their kids about sex healthywa.wa.gov.au/Articles/S_T/Talk-soon-Talk-often

READ // *The New Puberty* by Amanda Dunn tackles the topic of how we should talk to our kids and teens about sex. Puberty is changing. We need to change with it.

Note: Parents should check websites and books first, to make sure they are OK with them.

// WHAT DOES A GOOD SEX EDUCATION PROGRAM COVER?

A good school sex education program is nonjudgmental, with no hidden agenda. Information is accurate and up-to-date, inclusive and respectful of sexual diversity and different values and beliefs.

Diversity is crucial. LGBTIQ+ students should not feel invisible or that their needs are not being met or considered unimportant. Being inclusive can help reduce the feeling of isolation that some same-sex-attracted young people feel in schools. They experience higher rates of verbal and physical abuse than heterosexual peers and are at higher risk of depression, self-harm and suicide.

Sex Education Australia's Jenny Ackland says a good school sex education program covers:
- The domains of sexuality, including sexual diversity, sexual stereotypes, same-sex attraction, respectful and healthy relationships, male and female sexual response, sexual decision-making, safer sex;
- STIs and contraception;
- Consent;
- Sex and the law;
- Sex and technology, including a detailed discussion about pornography and sexting;
- Where to go for help; and
- Explanation of doctor and patient confidentiality and the cost of medical visits.

SEX EDUCATION IN VICTORIA

In Victoria, it is compulsory for government schools to provide sexuality education within health and physical education, including assessment and reporting against the Australian curriculum.

The Education Department says the goal of sexuality education in Victorian schools is to build on knowledge, skills, and behaviours, enabling young people to make responsible and safe choices.

"Good sexuality education focuses on love, safer sex, abstinence, respect for others and oneself, diversity, personal rights and responsibilities, relationships and friendships, effective communication, decision-making and risk behaviours," its website says.

The most effective sexuality education programs also take a whole-school learning approach. Good school-based sexuality education is:
- Driven by the school leader;
- Comprehensive;
- Inclusive;
- Supported by the latest research;
- Ongoing and integrated into a student's cross-curriculum learning;
- Assessed and reported against student achievement in the Victorian Essential Learning Standards; and
- Part of a student's whole-school learning experience.

Catholic and independent schools are welcome to use the department's policies, training and resources.

SEX EDUCATION

Parents and schools each have a role to play.

Most schools teach sexuality education, but parents and carers cannot assume that their child is learning enough to stay safe. More than one in 10 teenagers receives no sex education at school.*

Half (53 per cent) confide in their mother/female guardian and 25.9 per cent approach their father/male guardian about their sexual health. Some talk to friends, doctors and teachers. Almost eight in 10 (78.7 per cent) use the internet.*

While a parent's role is important, they should also ensure their child's school has a comprehensive sexuality education program.

SEX EDUCATION*
- Most students (83.6 per cent) have received sex education at school; about four per cent were uncertain. More than one in 10 students (13.2 per cent) reported having no sex education.
- Most students are taught sexuality and relationship education in health and physical education classes (70.6), while 14.6 per cent had it as a separate class, 5.3 per cent in science and biology classes and 4.4 per cent as part of a religious instruction program.
- Sexuality and relationship education was mainly taught between years 7 and 10 with 75.9 per cent taught in years 7-8 and 80.8 per cent in years 9-10.

WHERE YOUNG PEOPLE GO*
- Students most commonly consulted websites (78.7 per cent), a female friend (74.7 per cent), their mother/female guardian (53 per cent), or the school sexual health program (53.7 per cent) for sexual health advice.
- Doctors (32.6 per cent) and teachers (30.8) were also a common source of advice.
- More young women than men gained sexual health advice from their doctor (40.6 per cent vs 22 per cent), websites (82.2 per cent vs 74.1 per cent), an older brother or sister (23 per cent vs 18 per cent), their mother/female guardian (62.4 per cent vs 41.1 per cent), and a female friend (51 per cent vs 27 per cent).
- Young men were more likely to use their father/male guardian (36.6 per cent vs 17.8 per cent), or a male friend (64 per cent vs 53.7 per cent).

Students most commonly consulted a website or a female friend ... for sexual health advice.

SURVEY RESULTS // SEXUALITY & RELATIONSHIP EDUCATION*

QUESTION // "SEXUALITY / RELATIONSHIP EDUCATION WAS PRIMARILY TAUGHT BY ...?"

	Male %	Female %	TGD %
A teacher	82.5	82	76.5
A school nurse	5	5.8	9.8
A chaplain	0.7	0.6	2.9
School counsellor	1.5	1.5	1
Someone from outside school	10	9.8	8.8
Someone else	0.3	0.3	1

QUESTION // "HAVE YOU EVER HAD SEXUALITY / RELATIONSHIP EDUCATION AT SCHOOL?"

	Male %	Female %	TGD %
Yes	86.5	81.7	76.1
No	11.1	14.6	20.1
Don't know	2.4	3.7	3.7

QUESTION // "HOW RELEVANT DID YOU / DO YOU FIND SEXUALITY / RELATIONSHIP CLASSES?"

	Male %	Female %	TGD %
Not relevant at all	7.3	6.9	10.8
A little relevant	18	20.5	23.5
Somewhat relevant	39.1	33	27.5
Very relevant	26	26	27.4
Extremely relevant	9.7	13.7	10.8

*Source: 6th National Survey of Australian Secondary Students and Sexual Health 2018: Australian Research Centre in Sex, Health and Society, La Trobe University.
NOTE: Trans and gender diverse (TGD)

Profile // Professor Catharine Lumby

TALKING SEX

Human sexuality is a source of pleasure and we need to be careful about attaching shame to it, explains Professor Catharine Lumby.

"I recently interviewed over 100 students aged 13 to 17 from diverse high schools about sexuality, social media and relationships. They continually told me that sex education is always about plumbing and the negatives – how to not get a disease, how not to get pregnant.

"What they don't know a lot about, and what they desired to get more information about and to ask questions about, were relationships and communication. So how do you ask what someone wants? How do you know what you want? How, in a heterosexual relationship, does the other gender think? What's it like to be a boy or a girl? How does it feel different?

"The big problem in Anglo culture is the shame around bodies and sexuality and our deeply gendered ideas. There is an assumption that boys at a certain age just want to have fun and that girls need to protect themselves from that. With girls there are a lot of messages around feminine comportment and how they display their body. On one hand there is a pressure on girls to be attractive but on the other hand is the idea of not flaunting it.

"As parents we need to have open and honest conversations that don't treat boys and girls differently. But in my recent research only one in five of the young people I spoke to would ever discuss sexuality or relationships with their parents – so these conversations are not happening.

"A lot of parents are uncomfortable discussing bodies and sexuality with their children, but it's all on the internet. You can unplug every computer in your house but your teenager will still access material online. And if you're not having those conversations about values and attitudes towards sexuality and gender, your kids will form their views through their peer group instead.

"A La Trobe University study found up to 90 per cent of older teenagers send each other sexy images, either explicit or flirty images. That's the real world and that toothpaste is not going back in the tube.

"So how is that stuff managed? Too much of what cyber-safety experts teach in schools tells young women, 'Never send an image like that'. But in a world where this is a new form of flirting, this will happen in the heat of teenage romance so we need to help our children manage this.

"A lot of parents are uncomfortable discussing bodies and sexuality with their children, but it's all on the internet."

"There is huge pressure on girls – parents talk about how they struggle with their daughters' desire to be thinner, prettier … and we have bright young girls who become obsessed with appearance. But as soon as that young woman explores her sexuality, we shut that down and tell her to lower her hem and never send an image like that.

"We spend a lot of time policing girls and I think they are dangerous messages to send to young women. That horrible word 'slut' is still in use and we don't spend enough time asking young men what they are doing to young women when they share images they don't have permission to share. We don't ask the guys why they shame and blame young women when they encouraged those young women to send images in the first place, or when they sent similar images of themselves?

"Parents who want to raise ethical young men and confident young women need to open up the conversation about gender. Boys are trying to work out what it means to be a man in the world. A lot of boys are insecure. Some boys I interviewed said 'I watch porn online but I'm too scared to talk to the girl at the bus stop'.

"From a young age, we need to talk to our children about their body and that they have to give permission for someone to touch their body. 'No means no' is an important message but it's too simplistic and can translate into 'nice girls always say no'. What matters is young people knowing whether they are ready for something, knowing what they want and ensuring it is safe and consensual. Human sexuality is a source of pleasure and we need to be careful about attaching shame to it."

Photo: Supplied

// Professor Catharine Lumby is the author of books and numerous journal articles and regularly presents on topics including young people and media, social media, gender equality and media content regulation.   www.catharinelumby.com

TEEN Q&A

Sex Education Australia answers real questions from anonymous year 9 and 10 students collected in a range of classrooms across Melbourne.

WHAT IS THE AVERAGE AGE TO HAVE SEX?
Sometimes statistics and constant talk about sex from peers make people feel they "should" be doing sexual things at certain ages, but it should be the right time for you with the right person. For some people, having sex for the first time is a big deal, for others, not so much.

IF A GUY'S PENIS IS BIG DOES THAT MAKE SEX BETTER?
The penis can be a source of anxiety for a lot of men, straight and gay. We often get the impression that to have pleasurable sex the male's penis needs to be a certain size, and the bigger the better. But sex is about a lot of other things than penis size.

SHOULD I WAX, SHAVE OR GO NATURAL BEFORE SEXUAL ACTIVITIES? WHAT DO BOYS EXPECT?
This is very much a personal choice but remember pubic hair is natural and normal. Waxing/shaving increases the risks for some STIs, such as genital warts and herpes, so it's important to know that it can be problematic.

DOES SEX HURT THE FIRST TIME?
It might, but it mightn't. It shouldn't. If you are feeling relaxed and comfortable it will help. Using additional lubrication is very important. "Wet" sex is good sex, more pleasurable. Not rushing, being ready.

CAN PEOPLE HAVE STIs WITHOUT KNOWING. IF SO, HOW DO YOU FIND OUT?
Yes. Many STIs (for example, chlamydia) may not show symptoms. The only way a person knows is by getting tested.
For more info visit // www.sti.health.gov.au/internet/sti/publishing.nsf and www.betterhealth.vic.gov.au/health/conditionsandtreatments/sexually-transmissible-infections-stis

CAN YOU GET AN STI FROM GETTING FINGERED OR GIVING A HAND JOB?
It's not likely that you can get an STI from this type of sexual activity but there is always a risk when it comes to skin-to-skin contact and STIs. Some of the infections that you may have a low risk of contracting are HPV, genital warts, chlamydia, herpes and/or syphilis.

I'VE HAD SEX A FEW TIMES AND IT DOESN'T FEEL GOOD. WHAT'S WRONG?
Take your time – it's important not to rush any kind of sexual activity, and essential to make sure both people are ready, happy about the contact (consenting), able to consent (not drunk or asleep), that protection against STIs and pregnancy is being used, and that you and your partner are of legal age.

IS PORNOGRAPHY OK TO WATCH AT 16?
Pornography isn't for children. It can give people an unrealistic idea of what sex is, or what "good" sex is. There are lots of things missing from porn, particularly condom use and authentic conversations about consent and pleasure. Some porn is illegal.
To explore this topic more visit // www.itstimewetalked.com.au/young-people

IS MASTURBATION HEALTHY?
Yes, masturbation is a normal and healthy way for people to explore their own bodies. It's OK to do it, OK not to.

DOES TAKING THE PILL MAKE YOU FAT?
Doctors tell us this isn't true, however some pills may cause fluid retention. Most girls go on the pill for the first time when they are studying more, have more stress, might be eating more and exercising less, which could explain weight gain.

DOES ORAL SEX COUNT AS LOSING YOUR VIRGINITY?
Everybody defines "sex" differently. Traditionally, virginity was considered "penetration of the vagina with the penis" but this doesn't cover all the types of sex that people can have, or sexual activity with a same-sex partner.

IF YOU WERE BISEXUAL AND IT WAS EASY TO TELL YOUR FRIENDS, WOULD IT BE EASY TO TELL YOUR PARENTS?
Sometimes talking about your sexuality with parents can be difficult. It's important to talk with someone about how to bring up the subject and rehearse what you will say. Start by talking to a supportive friend, trusted adult or a school counsellor.
Go to // minus18.org.au or au.reachout.com

HOW DO YOU PREVENT SOMEONE FROM PRESSURING YOU INTO SOMETHING SEXUAL YOU DON'T WANT TO DO?
Everybody has the right to say "no" to something sexual. If someone is doing this they are not showing respect, and if it's a sexual behaviour it is also illegal (in the form of harassment or assault). Talking to a trusted adult or friend may help.
Find out more // lovegoodbadugly.com

// www.sexeducationaustralia.com.au

LGBTIQ+

Family support for same-sex attracted and gender diverse young people is important.

It is important for parents to support their children regardless of their sexuality or gender identity. The LGBTIQ+ (lesbian, gay, bisexual, transgender, intersex and questioning) community is diverse. Data presented in the Safe Schools Coalition's *All of Us* teaching resource reveals that Australian and international research had found that about 10 per cent of people are same-sex attracted, about four per cent are gender diverse or transgender, and about 1.7 per cent are intersex.

Three in four same-sex attracted young people experience some form of homophobic abuse or bullying and gender diverse and transgender young people face discrimination that results in negative health and well-being.

Eighty per cent of this abuse and bullying occurs at school. Research has also found that the homophobia experienced by same-sex attracted young people has a direct impact on their academic engagement and achievement, including missing classes or days at school and dropping out altogether.

At schools with active policies against homophobic abuse, students were less likely to have poor mental health and significantly less likely to experience homophobic violence and well-being risks such as self-harm and suicide.

For parents, educating young people about sexuality and gender identity in a non-judgemental way can help them feel more comfortable with who they are. It is also helpful to role model inclusive language and behaviours.

It is also helpful to role model inclusive language and behaviours.

// THE SEXUAL ATTRACTION QUESTION FOR STUDENTS

QUESTION // PEOPLE ARE DIFFERENT IN THEIR SEXUAL ATTRACTION TO OTHER PEOPLE. WHICH BEST DESCRIBES YOUR FEELINGS?

	Male %	Female %	TGD %
Only attracted to females	67	1.5	6.5
Mostly attracted to females	17.5	3.4	22.6
Equally attracted to females and males	3.3	8.7	30.6
Mostly attracted to males	5.3	29	29
Only attracted to males	6.1	55.6	6.5
Not sure	0.8	1.9	4.8

* Source: 6th National Survey of Australian Secondary Students and Sexual Health 2018: Australian Research Centre in Sex, Health and Society, La Trobe University. NOTE: Trans and gender diverse (TGD)

// UNDERSTANDING THE TERMS

GENDER DIVERSE // People whose gender expression or identity differs from the gender identity associated with the sex assigned them at birth or society's expectations …

GENDER IDENTITY // Gender identity refers to a person's sense of being masculine or feminine, or both or neither …

HETEROSEXISM // Views or behaviours that assume everyone is, or should be, heterosexual and that other types of sexuality or gender identity are unnatural or not as good as being heterosexual …

INTERSEX // People who are born with natural variations in genital, chromosomal or other physical characteristics that differ from stereotypical ideas about what it means to be female or male. Intersex refers to biology rather than sexual orientation or gender identity …

SAME-SEX ATTRACTED // People who experience feelings of sexual and/or emotional attraction to others of the same sex …

SISTERGIRLS AND BROTHERBOYS // Aboriginal, Torres Strait Islander and South Sea Islander communities use various terminology to describe or identify a person assigned female or male at birth and identifying or living partly or fully as another gender …

TRANSGENDER // An umbrella term used to describe people whose gender identity is different from the sex assigned to them at birth. An example is a child who is assigned a male sex at birth but actually feels more comfortable living as a girl and identifies as female …

For more information visit // studentwellbeinghub.edu.au

LIVE YOUR WAY

It takes all kinds of people to make a world.

LIAM // 17 // STRAIGHT

HOW DO YOU IDENTIFY IN TERMS OF GENDER AND SEXUALITY?
I identify as a straight male.

HAVE YOU EVER FELT CONFUSED OR UNSURE ABOUT YOUR SEXUALITY?
When I was about 14 I thought it was possible that I might be bisexual, but those feelings were gone within about a year.

HOW DID THIS MAKE YOU FEEL?
I was extremely worried because I wanted to live a normal life with a woman and have a normal family.

IT FELT AS IF YOU WERE SOMEHOW 'LESS' OF A MAN IF YOU WERE BISEXUAL?
Yeah. There's a pressure for blokes to be tough and manly, and for someone to be gay or bisexual would erase that whole ego.

DID YOU TALK TO FRIENDS OR FAMILY ABOUT THIS?
I spoke to my mum and she gave me total support and either way I chose was fine. I told my best friend at the time, she was very supportive also; told me she wouldn't care either way.

WERE YOU ABLE TO DISCUSS THESE FEELINGS WITH ANY MALE FRIENDS?
Yeah, after awhile I told a couple of close mates, people I really trusted, and they were completely cool. It was a relief.

WOULD YOU HAVE CONSIDERED TALKING TO YOUR DAD ABOUT IT?
No, I don't reckon he would have coped at all.

TORI // 19 // LESBIAN

WHEN DID YOU FIRST BEGIN TO IDENTIFY AS LESBIAN?
When I was in prep I tried to look like a boy to make the girls like me. In grade 5, I had a crush on a girl in my class. In year 7, I discovered the names for different sexual orientations and that's when I realised that I mightn't be straight.

WAS IT CONFRONTING TO REALISE YOU WEREN'T HETEROSEXUAL?
I found it very difficult to accept. The first person I told was my best friend at the time. After I told her she said she didn't feel comfortable with me staying over [at her house] any more. So I told her I was joking. I thought that if that's how my best friend reacted there was no way anybody else would accept it. I denied being a lesbian for the next four years. I kissed boys to fit in; but I knew I wasn't sexually attracted to males.

DID YOU GET SUPPORT DURING THIS TIME?
The best support was my dad being OK with it. Then I felt as though I was free, I suppose, to work it all out myself.

HOW DID YOUR MUM REACT?
We were already arguing and I... said it knowing it [would] upset her. She threatened to call the police and have them throw me out. Mum took my belongings to my dad's and left them out in the rain.

HAVE THINGS IMPROVED AT ALL?
My girlfriend and I have been together for 15 months. She's been coming to family events on my mum's side for a couple of months now, which is progress!

KAIDEN // 16 // QUEER

YOU IDENTIFY AS PANSEXUAL AND GENDER QUEER. HOW DOES YOUR SCHOOL SUPPORT YOUR CHOICES?
My school is quite supportive. I'm able to wear the uniform I feel comfortable in. There's a unisex toilet and plans for more.

WHO HAVE YOU DISCUSSED YOUR GENDER AND SEXUALITY WITH?
So far I've only told my mum. At first she didn't believe me. She said it was a phase, or that I'd grow out of it, which hurt a lot, but she has now come around and is very supportive.
My friends have also been understanding and very supportive.

HAVE YOU RECEIVED SUPPORT FROM ANY ORGANISATIONS?
I got help at Headspace, and I met a lot of people going through similar things as me at Minus 18. Both places provide safe places to hang out and resources, so mum and I can learn more.

WHEN DID YOU FIRST EXPERIENCE CONFUSION ABOUT YOUR SEXUALITY AND GENDER?
I first started questioning my sexuality about four years ago, and my gender a little under two years ago.

DO PEOPLE FIND YOUR GENDER IDENTITY CONFUSING AT TIMES?
Sometimes, but when I explain it most people get it. It doesn't bother me too much when people get confused, except when they refuse to accept that being pansexual is a real thing.

PEARL // 16 // BISEXUAL

ARE YOU COMFORTABLE BEING OPEN ABOUT YOUR SEXUALITY?
I'm pretty shy when it comes to being out as a bisexual woman, but I'm open about it with my close friends. People are aware of it but I prefer to keep most of it to myself.

WHAT SORT OF RESPONSES HAVE YOU HAD WHEN YOU'VE SHARED YOUR ORIENTATION?
People reacted really well when I told them, most of my friends were just interested in it and had a lot of questions. My mum listened to me and told me it changed nothing, and we haven't really talked much about it since.

HAVE YOU FACED ANY NEGATIVITY?
Some slight bullying, but most of it was minor and I was able to ignore it and realise how much happier I was [being honest].

WHAT WAS YOUR OWN REACTION WHEN YOU FIRST BECAME AWARE OF YOUR SEXUAL PREFERENCE?
When I was 15 I realised that I felt a lot more than friendship for my best friend, which was strange because I never thought that I would be any different from the straight girls that I grew up with.

HOW DOES IT AFFECT YOU NOW?
Being bisexual has no impact on my life at the moment. To me it's no different than anyone else's orientation. I've had more relationships with males, because I didn't realise I felt the same about girls as boys until recently, but I've had relationships with females too.

ARE YOU MORE ATTRACTED TO OTHER BISEXUALS?
No one's orientation has any effect on how I see them. Everyone is different and we like who we like.

KATE // 18 // QUEER

CAN YOU EXPLAIN YOUR SEXUAL AND GENDER IDENTITIES?
Pansexual is my sexuality, whereas gender queer is my gender identity. With pansexuality, I'm attracted to people, not gender. Of course I have my preference for partners (male and transgender male) but I fall for whomever I fall for. I identify as both genders depending on how I feel. It's very fluid.

WHEN DID YOU FIRST NOTICE THIS FLUIDITY?
I realised when I was about five that I didn't want to be entirely female, but I didn't know what it really was at that age. I started identifying as gender queer when I was 13 or 14. There have been stages in my life where I have thought I was transgender and wanted to go on hormones and transition to male.

WHAT STOPPED YOU GOING AHEAD WITH THAT?
I realised I didn't want to live my life fully as a male. I still love makeup, dresses and girly things, as well as dressing male.

HAS YOUR SEARCH FOR SEXUAL IDENTITY HAD ANY EFFECT ON YOUR WELL-BEING?
I did go through four years of very bad mental health, including self-harm and suicide attempts. I went through two years of wanting to transition to male.

DID YOU HAVE SUPPORT FROM YOUR FAMILY AND FRIENDS?
I was very scared to come out to my mum because she's always been quite conservative, but after I told her it was all support. My dad has definitely been the most supportive and I came out to him first. My friends have always given me support and help.

MARCUS // 19 // GAY

HOW WOULD YOU DESCRIBE YOUR EXPERIENCE OF COMING OUT?
Such an anticlimax! After expecting the world to cave in, it was actually no big deal, and I was super thankful for that. I told my best mate at the time, and he was fine.

WHEN DID YOU FIRST BEGIN TO RECOGNISE THAT YOU MIGHT BE HOMOSEXUAL?
At puberty, when I was about 12 or 13. I totally freaked out. It was really hard to accept that things were going to be different for me. I thought I would get married and have kids.

WAS YOUR MENTAL HEALTH AFFECTED?
Absolutely. I became more and more depressed and desperately tried to think of ways that I could possibly change my orientation. I was self-harming at this stage.

WHAT HELPED YOU GET THROUGH IT?
I think I'm lucky to have been born at a time when people can live openly. Seeing older gay men leading successful lives really helped. I also went to super lame gay dance parties at Minus 18 and just loved it.

WAS IT DIFFICULT TELLING YOUR FAMILY?
I was so worried that I would disappoint them. Family is the most important thing to me and to lose that would be devastating. When I did tell them, when I was 13, it was such a relief that I could be myself around them.

HOW DID THEY REACT?
Initially they had their doubts that it might have been a phase, and I can understand where they were coming from. But soon they were like: "When are you going to bring a boy around?".

STIs

Most secondary-school students' knowledge of STIs is relatively poor.

The instance of chlamydia, a potentially serious infection that can cause infertility, has doubled in the past 10 years. The 6th National Survey of Australian Secondary Students and Sexual Health 2018* found only 1.6 per cent of young men and 2.7 per cent of young women had been diagnosed with an STI (Sexually Transmissible Infection). This rose to 9.1 per cent for those who identified as trans and gender diverse.

Most (94.8 per cent) knew they could have an STI without displaying obvious symptoms. But fewer knew that genital warts could be spread without intercourse (56.3 per cent), chlamydia can make women sterile (53.8 per cent), and once a person has genital herpes, they will always have the virus (40.9 per cent).

Almost three in four (74.8 per cent) correctly identified the risk of hepatitis C posed by injecting drug use, and most knew it could be transmitted by tattooing and body piercing (56.1 per cent).

Asked about STI symptoms, most students correctly identified pain or discomfort when urinating (95.7 per cent), a rash in the genital area (91.5 per cent), lumps and bumps in the genital area (91.9 per cent), discoloured skin in the genital area (80.1 per cent), and "discharge from the penis or vagina" (73.8 per cent). Fewer knew that "muscular soreness in the thighs" (39.4 per cent) and "severe headache" (29.8 per cent) could be STI-related.

Knowledge of human papillomavirus, or HPV, was not great. Six in 10 students (62.5 per cent) had heard of HPV, with girls more likely to have than boys. About half (54.6 per cent) knew condoms did not provide complete protection against it.

Less than half said they had been vaccinated against HPV – 44.9 per cent of females, 30.8 per cent of males and 37.5 of trans and gender diverse young people. Almost 40 per cent (38.8) were unsure.

// WHAT ARE STIs AND BBVs?

Sexually transmissible infections (STIs) and blood borne viruses (BBVs) can be passed on by sexual contact. This includes vaginal, oral and anal sex, as well as genital touching and skin-to-skin contact. Some STIs and BBVs can be passed from a mother to her child during pregnancy or childbirth.

It's impossible to tell if a potential partner is infected just by looking at them as most people with an STI or BBV have no obvious symptoms. The best protection is safer sex, which means always using condoms or dams during anal, vaginal or oral sex. Regular sexual health checks are also important.

PROTECTING YOURSELF FROM STIs AND BBVs

- Always use condoms or dams when you have vaginal, anal or oral sex and if you need more lubrication, make sure it's water based.
- Make sure semen, blood and vaginal and anal fluid are not passed between partners.
- Talk about sex with your partner/s (i.e. what you want and don't want to do).
- Always use clean needles and never share drug-injecting equipment.
- If you see sores, lumps or ulcers around the mouth or genital area or any unusual discharge, avoid vaginal, anal and oral sex and any activity involving skin-to-skin contact with the affected area.

Where to go for help // **www.mshc.org.au**

★ Source: 6th National Survey of Australian Secondary Students and Sexual Health 2018: Australian Research Centre in Sex, Health and Society, La Trobe University.

// CHLAMYDIA

Chlamydia is Australia's most frequently reported STI, and the number of new diagnoses has more than doubled in the past 10 years. It is often symptomless and can cause infertility if left untreated. The infection is caused by a bacteria and affects men and women. Family Planning Victoria urges those under 30, who have had sex, to be checked annually.

In women, it might cause an increase in vaginal discharge, unusual bleeding, pain during sex, a burning feeling when urinating or pain in the lower abdomen. In men, it might cause a discharge from the penis or a burning feeling when urinating.

If women aren't treated, chlamydia can cause pelvic inflammatory disease (PID), which can lower the ability to have a baby (fertility). It's easily diagnosed with a urine test and treated with antibiotics. Sexual partner/s also need to be treated as soon as possible.

The *HIV, viral hepatitis and sexually transmissible infections in Australia. Annual Surveillance Report 2015* (University of NSW/Kirby Institute) found the number of new chlamydia diagnoses more than doubled nationally from 2005-2014 from 40,601 to 86,136.

Female cases jumped from 24,062 to 49,307 and male from 16,457 to 36,790. The over-40 age group had the biggest increase, from 2381 to 6421. In Victoria, the number increased from 8877 to 19,922.

In 2014, there were 86,136 chlamydia notifications nationally. Of those, 57 per cent were in females, 78 per cent were in people aged 15-29 and 68 per cent lived in major cities. In the 15-19 age group the female-to-male sex ratio was 3:1, but it fell to 1:1 at 25-29.

If untreated, chlamydia can cause infertility in both sexes.

For more information visit // **www.fpv.org.au** or **www.fpv.org.au/assets/Chlamydia.pdf**
Further reading // **pursuit.unimelb.edu.au/articles/we-need-to-talk-about-chlamydia**

// WHO'S AT YOUR NEXT PARTY?

GENITAL HERPES
Genital herpes is caused by the herpes virus and spreads through vaginal, anal and oral sex or by genital skin-to-skin contact. It can be symptom free or can emerge at any time, including some time after infection. Herpes usually appears as small, painful genital blisters which turn into shallow ulcers that scab over and heal up. It can also appear on the buttocks or thighs.

Herpes is diagnosed by a swab test and, while it can't be cured, symptoms can be treated with antiviral tablets, but the virus stays in the body for life. Infection risk is greatest when sores are present, but you can transmit it while symptom free. Symptoms can return after treatment.

GONORRHOEA
Gonorrhoea is caused by a type of bacteria. In women, it can cause an increase in vaginal discharge, unusual bleeding, pain during sex, a burning feeling when urinating or pain in the lower abdomen. In men, it can cause a discharge from the penis or a burning feeling when urinating. It can be symptomless. It is diagnosed by a urine or swab test and is treated with antibiotics. If untreated, women can develop pelvic inflammatory disease (PID), which can lower the ability to have a baby (fertility).

VAGINAL DISCHARGE, INCLUDING CANDIDA (THRUSH)
Most women have a whitish or clear vaginal discharge during their cycle, which is normal. Discharge changes may mean an infection with signs such as an odour, yellowish or grey discharge, thickened appearance, itching or pain.

HEPATITIS A
A viral infection that can affect the liver, hepatitis A is spread by small amounts of faeces from an infected person entering the mouth (e.g. licking the anal area or another part of the body which has had contact with the anal area, such as fingers). It can also be spread by contaminated food and water and is diagnosed by a blood test. There is no treatment; the body naturally clears itself of the virus. Vaccination is available.

HEPATITIS B
Hepatitis B is a viral infection that can affect the liver. It's spread by the exchange of body fluids (e.g. blood, semen, vaginal discharge, anal mucus) during unprotected sex and sharing needles. Diagnosed by blood test, most newly infected adults will clear the infection naturally. Treatments are available. A small percentage of carriers risk serious liver damage. Vaccination is available.

HEPATITIS C
Hepatitis C is a viral infection that affects the liver and can cause serious damage. It's not easily spread by sexual contact but by blood through activities such as sharing needles or being tattooed with used needles. Hepatitis C is diagnosed by a blood test. Some people will clear it from their body naturally, but treatment is available if that doesn't happen. No vaccination is available.

GENITAL WARTS (HPV)
HPV (human papillomavirus) is spread by genital skin-to-skin contact and may not cause obvious symptoms. HPV can appear as lumps around the vulva or in the vagina, on the penis or around or inside the anus. Genital warts can take months to appear. The warts can be removed by freezing or applying a special paint or cream. They can return, but the body eventually clears itself of the virus. Vaccination is available and free for school-aged women. Young men can access it from their doctor.

SYPHILIS
Syphilis is caused by a bacteria and is more common in men who have sex with men. The first infection might cause a sore (ulcer) on the genitals. If untreated, syphilis, which is diagnosed by a blood test, can cause other symptoms such as a skin rash, patchy loss of hair and generally feeling unwell. It is treated with antibiotics, and this should start as soon as possible, as it can cause serious health problems. Sexual partners should also be treated as soon as possible.

Source : Family Planning Victoria www.fpv.org.au

HIV/AIDS

Generally, young people have good knowledge about HIV. But we need to ensure that they don't become complacent due to modern treatments.

Various treatments can now keep those living with HIV relatively healthy, which is an enormous step forward but still not a cure.

The HIV, viral hepatitis and sexually transmissible infections in Australia: Annual surveillance report 2018[1] found HIV notifications fell by 7 per cent in Australia in the five years to 2017 due to fewer notifications among men reporting male-to-male sex.

High treatment coverage was achieved in 2017. The proportion of people on treatment with a suppressed viral load increased, effectively eliminating the risk of transmission.

Notifications in people who acquired HIV from heterosexual sex increased in 2017, and the HIV notification rate increased by 41 per cent in the Aboriginal and Torres Strait Islander population from 2013-2016, compared with a 12 per cent decline in Australian-born non-Indigenous people.

"Overall, these data highlight the need to maintain and strengthen strategies of health promotion, testing, treatment and risk reduction, but also to expand and promote PrEP and other forms of prevention to people who could benefit from these strategies and to increase prevention initiatives in people born overseas and Aboriginal and Torres Strait Islander people," the report said.

Students generally have good knowledge of HIV. The sixth National Survey of Secondary Students and Sexual Health 2018* found that most knew it could be transmitted by sharing needles (92.8 per cent), that a woman could get HIV from having sex with a man (93.9 per cent) and that a man could get it from having sex with a woman (90.7 per cent).

They know that hugging a HIV positive person could not transmit the virus (94.3 per cent), that men could get HIV from having sex with men (91.7 per cent), the contraceptive pill offers no protection against HIV for women (91.6 per cent) and that a pregnant woman with HIV could pass on the infection to her baby (65 per cent).

Most students knew that using condoms during sex offered some protection from HIV (88.8 per cent), that someone who looked very healthy could still pass on HIV infection (81.5 per cent) and that coughing or sneezing could not transmit HIV (66.7 per cent).

The poorest knowledge related to mosquitoes – 75.2 per cent did not know that mosquitoes could not transmit the virus. Only 6.7 per cent felt that they were "likely" or "very likely" to become infected with HIV.

Harm reduction among people who inject drugs had been highly successful.

// HIV IN AUSTRALIA[1]

- An estimated 0.14 per cent of Australians was living with HIV in 2017, which is low compared with other relevant high-income and Asia-Pacific countries.
- Australia had 963 HIV notifications in 2017, the lowest since 2010.
- The overall decrease was due to an 11 per cent decline in notifications reporting male-to-male sex as likely exposure over the past five years, and a 15 per cent decline from 2016-2017.
- Of 238 HIV notifications in 2017 attributed to heterosexual sex, 61 per cent were in males, and 45 per cent were in people born in Australia. A further 15 per cent were in people born in Sub-Saharan Africa, and 13 per cent in people born in Asia.
- There were 31 notifications among Aboriginal and Torres Strait Islander people. The age-standardised rate of HIV notification increased by 41 per cent in the Aboriginal and Torres Strait Islander population between 2013 and 2016, compared with a 12 per cent decline in Australian-born non-Indigenous people.

Of all HIV diagnoses made in Australia in 2017:
- 63 per cent occurred among men who have sex with men.
- 25 per cent were attributed to heterosexual sex.
- 5 per cent were attributed to male-to-male sex and injecting drug use.
- 3 per cent were attributed to injecting drug use.

HIV notification rates[1]:
Between 2008 and 2017, Australia's HIV notification rate per 100,000 population has hovered between 4.0 in 2017 and 4.7 in 2012 and 2014.

WHAT IS PrEP?
PrEP is an anti-HIV medicine taken by a person who does not have HIV to lower their risk of infection.

It should not be confused with PEP, which is a short course of anti-HIV medicines taken by someone who might have been exposed to HIV, with the aim of preventing infection.
For more information visit // www.healthdirect.gov.au/Pre-exposure-prophylaxis-PrEP

---

[1] HIV, viral hepatitis and sexually transmissible infections in Australia Annual surveillance report 2018, The Kirby Institute
*Source: 6th National Survey of Australian Secondary Students and Sexual Health 2018: Australian Research Centre in Sex, Health and Society, La Trobe University.

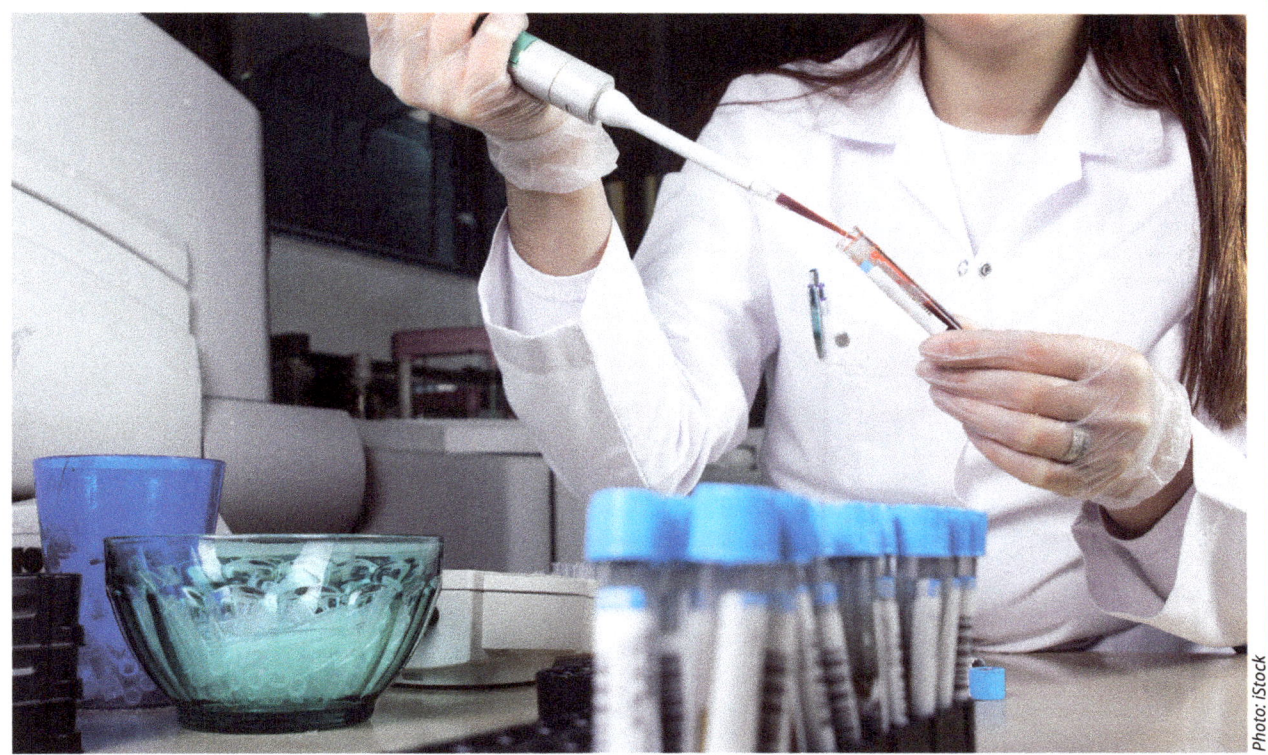

// WHAT IS HIV?

HIV (Human Immunodeficiency Virus) is a virus that weakens the immune system. It attacks and takes over immune cells, using them to reproduce itself. Infected cells can be found in many parts of the body and in body fluids such as blood, semen, vaginal fluid, breast milk and anal mucous.

AIDS (Acquired Immune Deficiency Syndrome) is a serious weakening of the body's immune system caused by HIV. When a HIV-positive person's immune cells (CD4 cells) drop below a certain level, they can be vulnerable to opportunistic infections that their body would normally fight off. AIDS can also be defined as having HIV and an opportunistic infection regardless of your CD4 count.

HIV, not AIDS, is transmitted between people. HIV is spread by unprotected sex and sharing needles and syringes. It is not passed on by kissing, hugging, saliva, sweat, tears, urine, sharing utensils or insect bites. There is no cure, but effective treatments can keep people with HIV healthier.

HIV TREATMENT

In the mid-1990s, effective treatment for HIV infection became available in Australia. HIV is now a manageable infection, with treatment that not only controls the virus in the person but also reduces their infectiousness (though not completely).

Treatment means that HIV is no longer a gradual progression to AIDS and then death. However, many people living with HIV still deal with a range of problems and health issues because of their HIV status.

HIV PREVENTION

Victoria has contained mother-to-child transmission and infection rates among injecting drug users, sex workers and those who receive blood transfusions. Sexual transmission is still the main cause of HIV infection. However, transmission through vaginal sex is slowly increasing, though this is often due to being from, or having sex with, someone from a country with a high HIV prevalence.

The most reliable way to prevent the sexual transmission of HIV is to use a condom, in conjunction with a water-based lubricant (petroleum-based lubricants can make condoms break). If injecting drugs, always use a clean syringe, and never share syringes.

Victorian AIDS Council // www.vac.org.au/hiv-aids

SEX & THE LAW

If you are the victim of sexual assault tell someone in a position of authority.

Victoria's sexual assault laws cover a range of offences that parents of teenagers should be familiar with. Essentially, forcing someone of any age to take part in any sexual act is an offence. Having sex with someone who is underage is also an offence, but there are some defences available in exceptional circumstances.

Teenagers should know about laws relating to sexual assault and harassment, and that they can talk to their parents and carers if they feel an offence has been committed against them or a friend.

It is important to tell police or employers as soon as possible if you become aware of an offence.

Parents and carers should also ensure that young people know they are never at fault if someone assaults them sexually or sexually harasses them, and that help is available.

RAPE
A person rapes you if:
- they sexually penetrate you without your consent and do not reasonably believe that you are consenting;
- during sexual penetration, you withdraw consent to sex, but they continue to penetrate you; or
- they make you sexually penetrate (or not stop penetrating) them or another person. It does not matter if the person being penetrated consents to the act.

Sexual penetration means putting any part of the penis into the vagina, anus or mouth. It also means putting any part of an object or another part of the body, for example, finger or tongue, into the vagina or anus of another person. The penetration can be just the tip of the finger or penis and can happen for even a very short time. It does not matter if semen comes out or not.

Consent means free agreement of your own free will.

Under the law you are not consenting if penetration happens:
- because you were physically forced to do it or you feared someone else would be forced;
- because you were scared of what might happen to you or someone else; or
- because you were unlawfully detained (held), for example, locked in a house or car.

Under the law you also cannot consent if you:
- are asleep, unconscious or so affected by alcohol or drugs that you cannot freely agree;
- are not able to understand the sexual nature of the act; or
- mistake the sexual nature of the act or think the person is someone else.

If you do not consent to sex, it is rape whatever the relationship between you and the other person. A man can be guilty of raping his wife or girlfriend.

INDECENT ASSAULT
Indecent assault covers sexual acts other than sexual penetration, such as touching your breasts or bottom without your agreement.

INCEST
Incest happens when an act of sexual penetration is done with a close relative, for example, a father, stepfather, grandfather or brother.

SEXUAL OFFENCES AGAINST CHILDREN
These are offences that are committed against young people under 18. They include:
- sexual penetration of a child under the age of 16;
- indecent act with a child under the age of 16;
- persistent sexual abuse of a child under the age of 16;
- sexual penetration or an indecent act with a child aged 16 or 17 by an adult who cares for, supervises or has authority over the child. This may include a teacher, employer, foster parent, sports coach and other roles;
- procuring a child under 16 for sexual penetration or an indecent act by an adult;
- procuring a child aged 16 or 17 for sexual penetration or an indecent act by an adult who cares for, supervises or has authority over that child;
- grooming a child for sexual conduct; or
- producing child pornography or procuring a child to be involved in child pornography.

A person may not have broken the law if the child consented and:
- they had reasonable grounds (reasons) for believing the child was older than 16 (or 18 where the offence involves a child aged 16 or 17);
- the accused was no more than two years older than the child; or
- the accused had reasonable grounds to believe they were married to the child.

Assistance and helplines // see page 172

AGE OF CONSENT LAWS // SUMMARY TABLE

	ACT/VIC	NSW	QLD	SA/TAS	NT	WA
Homosexual	16	16	16	17	16	16
Heterosexual	**16**	**16**	**16**	**17**	**16**	**16**

NOTE: There is often a defence if the gap between the parties is no more than two, three or even five years (ACT, Tasmania, Vic).
Special provisions can apply to persons under guardianship or a student.

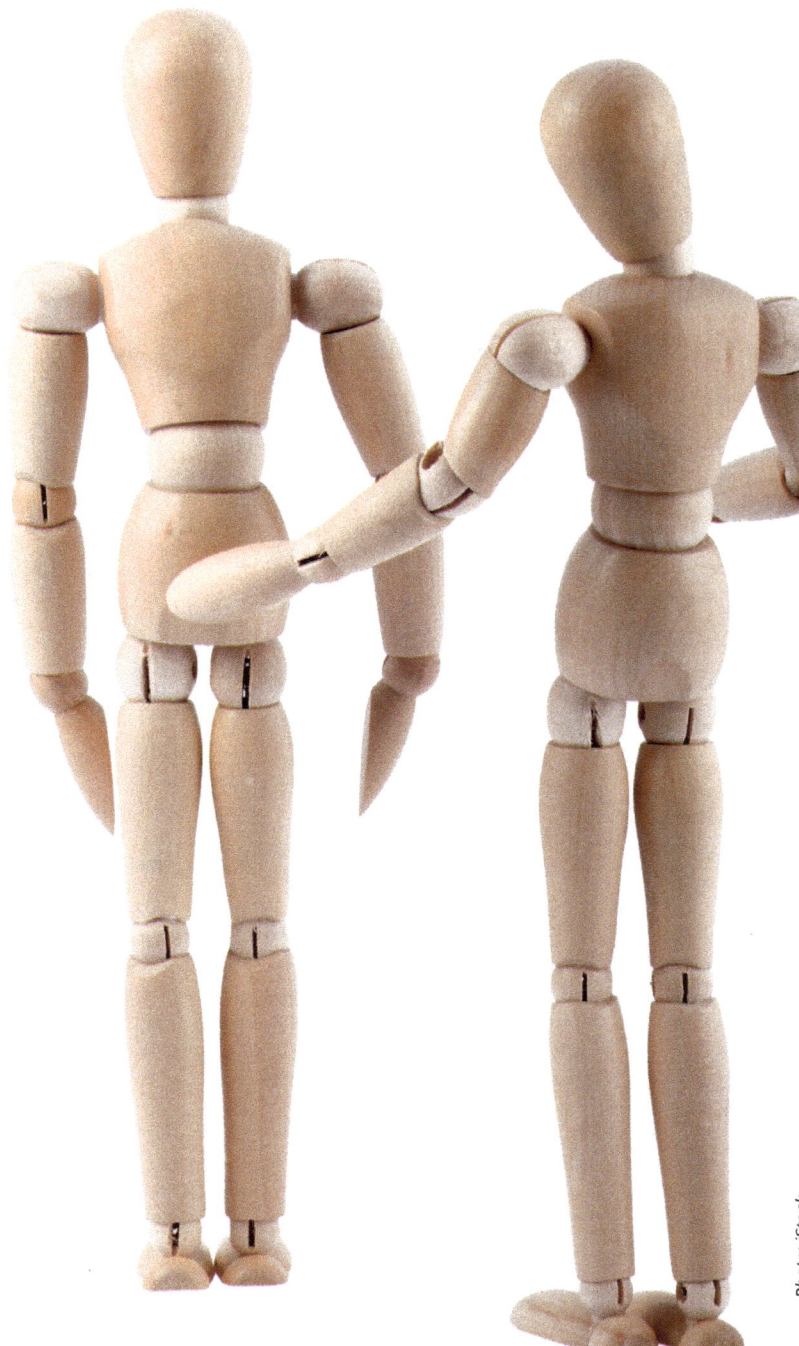

Photo: iStock

// WHAT IS SEXUAL HARASSMENT?

Sexual harassment is when someone behaves in a sexual way that offends, humiliates or intimidates you. It can include things like:
- telling dirty jokes;
- staring and leering;
- someone making comments about another person's sexual behaviour;
- offensive pictures, emails or text messages;
- someone touching, pinching or brushing up against another person unnecessarily; or
- someone kissing or hugging another person when they didn't say yes to it.

It's also sexual harassment if you agree to someone behaving sexually towards you because you were scared or pushed into it. Sexual harassment is against the law, and if the person's behaviour is serious then the police could charge that person with a criminal offence.

// UNWANTED SEX *

Almost three in 10 sexually active teenagers reported having had unwanted sex. Young women were more likely to have had unwanted sex than young men (36.8 per cent vs 15.9 per cent).

Teenagers should know about laws relating to sexual assault and harassment.

SEXUALLY ACTIVE STUDENTS WHO HAVE EVER HAD UNWANTED SEX

	Male %	Female %	TGD%
Total	15.9	36.8	50

SOME REASONS WHY PEOPLE HAVE UNWANTED SEX. CHECK ALL THAT APPLY TO YOU

	Male %	Female %	TGD %
Too drunk	34.6	34.3	20
Too high	13.7	13.6	20
My partner thought I should	53.8	51.5	50
My friends thought I should	17	6.6	10
I was frightened	27.5	32.3	50

Base: Sexually active students who have had unwanted sex.
Note: Multiple response questions.

* Source: 6th National Survey of Australian Secondary Students and Sexual Health 2018: Australian Research Centre in Sex, Health and Society, La Trobe University.
NOTE: Trans and gender diverse (TGD)

© Parenting Guides Ltd

KNOW THE LAW

Being familiar with the law is an important part of keeping young people safe sexually. Parents and their teenagers should know how the law applies to them.

Victoria's age of consent to sexual interactions is 16. The age of consent for same-sex relationships is the same as it is for heterosexual relationships.

There are some legal defences if the person having consensual sex is younger than 16 and their partner is less than two years older than them and does not have a caring or supervising role with them.

If an adult has a sexual relationship with someone in their care who is 16 or 17, it's also a crime, unless the adult reasonably believed the younger person was 18 or older.

People aged 18 and over can consent to sex with anyone aged 16 or over, unless they are supervising or caring for the younger person.

In Victoria, criminal laws apply to non-consensual sexual penetration, which includes anything that involves putting a penis into a vagina, anus or mouth (to any extent). It includes putting an object or a part of the body into a vagina or anus.

The law also applies to touching a person in a sexual way, like touching another person's vagina, penis, anus or breasts. Rape occurs when someone sexually penetrates another person who has not consented, including where the person cannot consent because they are asleep, unconscious or so affected by alcohol or drugs that they cannot consent. Sexual assault occurs when someone touches another person sexually without their consent.

Photo: iStock

SEXTING ††

In late 2014, Victoria introduced Australia's first "sexting" laws. These laws created offences targeting the distribution, or threats to distribute, intimate images of another person, and introduced exceptions to child pornography offences where young people engaging in non-exploitative "sexting" with their peers.

The Crimes Amendment (Sexual Offences and Other Matters) Act 2014 created two summary offences of "distribution of an intimate image" and "threat to distribute an intimate image" in circumstances contrary to community standards of acceptable conduct. These offences apply to young people and adults.

The distribution offence carries a penalty of up to two years in prison, and the new offence of threatening to distribute carries a penalty of up to one year in prison.

New exceptions to child pornography offences will ensure that those aged under 18 are not inappropriately prosecuted or added to the sex offenders' register for consensual, non-exploitative sexting with their peers. These exceptions do not apply in relation to images depicting a criminal offence such as a sexual assault.

MARRIAGE ††

Teenagers aged 16 or 17 can marry only if their parents or guardian agree, their partner is at least 18 and a court agrees the situation is special enough to allow the marriage – pregnancy may not be enough.

The court considers things like how long the couple has been together, their maturity, financial situation and how independent they are from their parents. If the court agrees, they must marry within three months.

CONTRACEPTION ††

Those under 18 may be able to get contraception, like the pill, from a doctor. The doctor must decide if the young person is mature enough to understand what they're doing and use the contraception properly. Anyone can buy condoms at any age; most chemists and supermarkets sell them.

PREGNANCY ††

Girls need to know they have options and people they can talk to, such as a counsellor, nurse or doctor. They can choose to keep the baby, adopt it out or have an abortion. There is no legal minimum age for keeping a baby or having an abortion. If the mother is under 16, a loved one concerned about their welfare or the baby can call the Department of Human Services. Abortion is legal in Victoria up to 24 weeks and after 24 weeks in some rare circumstances.

Family Planning Victoria provides advice and support // www.fpv.org.au

YOUNG FATHERS ††

A father is legally responsible for financially supporting their child. If they are at school and don't earn any money, they may have to pay later when they can afford to. If proven to be the father, they must pay child support until the child is 18.

CONTACTS

Useful websites with legal information for young people:
Go to // www.lawstuff.org.au
www.legalaid.vic.gov.au
www.youthcentral.vic.gov.au – follow link to "Know Your Rights"
www.youthlaw.asn.au
Get the free phone app // Below-the-belt sex, selfies, cyber-bullying at www.legalaid.vic.gov.au/below-the-belt

---

†† *Source Victoria Legal Aid. www.legalaid.vic.gov.au*

Profile // Justine Kiely-Scott

SEX & RELATIONSHIPS

Sex Education Australia's Justine Kiely-Scott says understanding the multifaceted nature of relationships is an important part of sex education.

"Relationships can be defined in many ways. When we commonly think of relationships we think of a monogamous commitment. But they can be many and varied.

"When it comes to sex and relationships, very important rules need to be applied regardless of the 'type' of relationship. A 'one-night stand' is a type of relationship, as is a short-term or long-term commitment.

"If we are to get the right information across to young people, it is essential that we are non-judgmental. The same rules apply for a casual sexual encounter as a longer-term relationship.

"We want young people to have respectful, consensual, pressure-free, guilt-free, STI-free pleasurable sex, no matter what the circumstance. Good communication and being able to clearly articulate consent and individual needs are vital.

"The hardest part of any sexual interaction is being able to communicate confidently what you want or don't want. If the rules about what is and isn't healthy and respectful are clear to all, then articulating individual needs shouldn't be so hard.

"Respect and choice should always be a part of a sexuality education program. Consent must never be assumed and … free agreement means just that – sexual activity without being pressured or forced, even subtly.

"Young people need to be able to recognise the warning signs of an unhealthy relationship and be confident they know who and where they can turn to for help. Some schools are doing a great job in this area, but we need to continue to build teachers' skills and confidence to teach this confidently and capably.

"A comprehensive sex education program will cover as many elements as possible in addition to the biological, for example the psychological aspects (emotions, attitudes, feelings, self-esteem, body image), the social aspects (friendships, dating, law, gender, stereotypes), and values (family, spirituality, religious, customs, culture, personal beliefs).

"Talking about what you would expect from a sexual/romantic experience is important. Discussing potential 'deal breakers' and the types of things that you would not tolerate or should not tolerate is important too.

"Gender stereotypes play a big part in how people communicate when it comes to sex. The messages are the same for boys and girls, but they may need to be delivered differently.

"We need to challenge the gendered assumptions that have become universal truths. Stereotypes suggest that in a heterosexual context for example, boys should 'make the first move' and girls need to be 'persuaded' to do sexual things.

"The importance of understanding what constitutes a respectful relationship and consent are the same no matter what your sexuality is. In this instance, the internet is the parents' friend – there is lots of comprehensive information available, along with communities that exist to reassure and inform young people.

"For parents, being as open and honest with your children is the key, but this ideally begins when they are little. It's a series of smaller conversations rather than one big 'talk'. Discussing relationships in general can be less confronting, and using examples from TV programs and movies can help.

"Parents need to let their children know they are there for them no matter what. They need to reassure them that they can come to them for advice and if they can't help, make sure young people know who can. This might be another adult or a support agency."

> "We want young people to have respectful, consensual, pressure-free, guilt-free, STI-free pleasurable sex, no matter what the circumstance."

Photo: Supplied

// Justine Kiely-Scott is co-founder and educator at **Sex Education Australia**, delivering sexuality and respectful relationships education in more than 60 government and independent primary and secondary schools, and universities, in Victoria. www.sexeducationaustralia.com.au

Profile // Dr Siobhan Bourke

OPEN COMMUNICATION & CONNECTEDNESS

Dr Siobhan Bourke is a sexual health physician. She believes it's important to talk frankly and to use correct terminology when talking to children about their bodies.

"When you talk in euphemisms, you create taboo subjects. This is true for a lot of topics, including sex. Kids are smart, and if you don't give things their correct name, they work out that you are trying to cover up something and they wonder why that is. They work out that sex is a taboo subject. Use the right language around sex and relationships so there is no mystique for kids.

"But for kids to be safe, they need to be able to approach their parents and have conversations about sex. In any realm, including sexual health, connectedness to parents is a safeguard for children. Being able to talk to mum, dad or a guardian is the biggest safety net that any child can have.

"But if you start making barriers because you can't say the words 'penis' and 'vagina', kids catch on to that. They realise conversations about sex and genitals are not to be had with parents – so they don't have them. Instead, they will look for information on the internet or they go to their friends, who may also be uninformed. I remember being a teenager and an older male friend telling me you can tell when a girl is not a virgin by the shape of her vulva! For the next few years I thought that was true!

"If you want to help your kids make big decisions in life, you need to have conversations and use truthful terms. Sometimes I think parents don't use the right terminology because they weren't taught to use the right terms themselves. Many women who see me in the clinic say they have an itch or pain on their vagina when they mean their vulva – the vagina is inside and the vulva is outside.

"I think a great resource for children is a guide called *Talk soon. Talk often.* **healthywa.wa.gov.au/Articles/S_T/Talk-soon-Talk-often**. It's a guide for parents talking to their kids about sex. It's written for the Department of Health in Western Australia.

"Some parents think that if they start talking about these things that kids will then want to have sex. The evidence has shown time and time again, the more knowledge kids have, the more likely they will make good decisions for themselves and they will delay sex until they are ready.

"You don't have to be a sex expert to help your kids. If you don't know the answer to a question, say so and find out the answer together. You'd help your kids work out how to open a bank account or get their driver's licence, and if you weren't sure about some aspect of that, you'd find out what you needed to know. Why does it have to be different with sex?

"Do the initial search for answers on the internet without your children. If you search sex terminology you may inadvertently come across some images that you don't want your children exposed to yet. Do the search yourself, particularly if your children are young, and then search with your child. Or go to the library and get some books so you know what you're looking at and are comfortable with it.

"Sexual relationships and relationships with other human beings are big decisions too and sometimes we are not equipping our children with the information they need because we are not having those conversations. If your child asks you a question about sex in the supermarket and you say that you'll discuss the topic later, it's important to do the 'later'. If you don't it signals to kids that they are not supposed to talk about it and they won't talk about it with you any more.

You want your child to be able to come to you with any of their problems. Open communication and connectedness are the greatest protective factors to keep children as safe as possible."

Photo: Supplied

// WHAT DO YOU CALL YOUR GENITALIA?

Here some parents share their personal names...

Hoo Hoo	Front Bottom	Tools
Tinkle	Fanny	Ball Bag
Pee Pee	Your Johnson	Trouser Snake
Vag	Charlie Carter	Below Stairs
V Jay Jay	Tackle	

// Siobhan Bourke is a sexual health physician with Centre for Excellence in Rural Sexual Health (CERSH), University of Melbourne; and Family Planning Victoria.

PARENT Q&A

Dr Siobhan Bourke answers a few of your questions.

Q. WHY IS IT IMPORTANT TO USE CORRECT SEX AND HUMAN BODY TERMINOLOGY FROM DAY ONE?

A "As soon as we use a euphemism, we're creating a taboo. We're saying to kids, it's not right to use the right language. They pick up on that – we won't talk about it, we'll hide it. And from not calling your penis your penis and not calling your vagina your vagina, it leads to other things that they're not supposed to talk about. And the whole subject of sex becomes taboo. When that occurs, we end up with kids not talking about some of the most important things in their life."

Q. SO HOW DO PARENTS APPROACH THOSE CONVERSATIONS?

A "It's not the conversation you have at the top of your voice in the middle of the supermarket, and there are appropriate levels of information. The key is to have little conversations and have them often. You don't have to give them a full-on manual, but you can discuss simply what goes on with sex and methods of protection against infection and pregnancy.

When girls are heading towards puberty and having their periods it is a great opportunity to have this conversation. For some girls they may know that mum or others are bleeding – they notice things in bathrooms or walk in on mum in the toilet, so the conversations may start even earlier than puberty. You can explain the function of periods and the menstrual cycle as your body preparing for pregnancy, and then, if not getting pregnant, a period comes; details will depend on the age of the girl."

Q. IS IT IMPORTANT FOR PARENTS TO REALISE THEY DON'T HAVE TO KNOW THE ANSWERS TO EVERY QUESTION?

A "Parents think they are supposed to know all about sex, but you don't have to know everything. It's about working stuff out together, like you would other topics. The most protective factor for kids for sex and drugs is that connectedness in families. If your child can ring you at 3am and say 'come and help me', you've maintained that connection. If they can say to you, 'I like so and so and want to talk to you about sex' or 'where do babies come from' and get an honest answer, that is the safest thing for kids going out into the world.

Sometimes conversations are awkward for both parents and children but they need to be had. If maintaining eye contact is making either party feel nervous, try having the conversation you have in the car or while doing the dishes. As the adults and guardians, we need to have these conversations."

Q. WHAT DO PARENTS NEED TO KNOW ABOUT PORNOGRAPHY?

A "Pornography is so much more accessible today. Porn also seems to be increasingly violent in nature, particularly against women. But it's also damaging for young people, especially men, because it takes away their understanding of what loving, caring and responsible relationships are. We need to be able to talk to our young people about pornography in conversations around their sexuality. That's why it's important to develop that ability for your young person to be able to talk to you about whatever."

Q. WHAT ARE THE MOST COMMON SEXUALLY TRANSMITTED INFECTIONS AFFECTING YOUNG PEOPLE?

A "Chlamydia is the most common bacterial infection – spread by unprotected sexual activity. It's simple to detect, with a urine test, and it's easily treated with antibiotics. The most commonly transmitted STI is the human papillomavirus or HPV. More than 80 per cent of people get it and it's very difficult to avoid but most people clear it without even knowing they had it. There are some types of HPV virus that cause changes to the cervix and can lead to cervical cancer down the track, but we now have a vaccine to prevent that.

The Australian government put this vaccine on the National Immunisations program for girls aged 12 or 13 (equivalent to year 7 at high school) in 2007 and then included boys aged 12 or 13 in 2013. This is showing to be a great protection against cervical cancer and other HPV-related cancers. There are other STIs around so simple advice is to use protection (condoms) and to get regular checks – sexually active people under 30 are recommended to have a urine chlamydia test once a year."

Q. WHAT ADVICE DO YOU HAVE WHEN PARENTS DISCUSS CONTRACEPTION WITH THEIR KIDS?

A "The first thing most people talk about is the pill but for young women, long-acting reversible contraceptions (LARC) that you don't have to remember and think about every day are more reliable and convenient. There are intrauterine devices and the Implanon implant, which are both available for young women – even those who have not been pregnant or given birth.

It is also good to remember when there has been a contraception failure the morning-after pill, or more appropriately called emergency contraception, can be taken up to 120 hours after unprotected sex, although it's most effective within the first three days."

> "Parents think they are supposed to know all about sex, but you don't have to know everything."

Profile // Dr Russell Pratt

THE EXPERT

Pornography is a minefield and parents are right to be concerned.

We cannot stop young people accessing porn, but experts say we can minimise the potential fallout. Forensic psychologist Dr Russell Pratt says children and young people can access pornography whenever and wherever they want on iPhones, iPads, laptops, tablets and gaming consoles.

"Pornography has also changed over the past two decades," he says. "'Porn with a story' from the mid-'70s through to the early '80s is now replaced by every permutation and combination of category and subcategory you can imagine, and some you most likely can't."

Writing for the Australian Psychological Society, Dr Pratt says there is more porn than ever and research shows that males aged 12-17 are the most frequent online consumers (Haggstrom-Nordin, Hanson & Tyden, 2005).

"Not only are we struggling to comprehend the extent and type of pornography our youth are being exposed to, but we also have to grapple with the impact this is having on their sexual practices and relational templates," Dr Pratt says. "The pornography industry appears to have brought about changes to both body image and sexual practices among young people.

"Here's some examples: the complete lack of pubic hair on virtually everyone under 30 – thank the porn industry; the research indicating that large cohorts of teenage girls do not regard oral sex as sex, but rather something that is provided to young men as a way of not having sex – thank the porn industry; the growing rates of reported anal sex amongst adult and teenaged heterosexual couples, to the point that for the first time ever, rates of practising anal sex were polled among Victorian school students in years 10-12 in a recent survey of sexual practices (the rates were recorded as nine per cent of the sample of just over 2000 youth in case you were interested; see Mitchell et al., 2014) – thank the porn industry."

Recent Australian research found that young men believe that what they are watching provides real templates for sexual activity (see Crabbe and Corlett, 2011). Dr Pratt says research also shows that children are engaging in sexual practices earlier and those who watch porn engage in oral sex and intercourse younger than those who don't.

"Over the past decade, we have seen a growing trend of younger children engaging in problem sexual and sexually abusive behaviours generally aimed at younger children – in other words, children sexually assaulting children," he says.

"Pornography is providing too many 10-year-olds with the mechanical knowledge to anally, orally and/or vaginally penetrate younger siblings, cousins and acquaintances."

Dr Pratt says to "porn-proof" kids we must have quality relation-based sex education and sexuality training for those who work with vulnerable youth. Parents must also help their children "decode" porn.

"Parents need to model respectful, loving relationships – with partners, friends and the children themselves," he says. "Nothing will assist young people more than a healthy familial relationship that allows them to measure what they see in 'porn world' up against what they see in the real world they are immersed in.

"If young people are exposed to gender inequality, family violence, taboos about discussing sexual and relationship matters, or a harsh and unyielding parenting regime, then the relationships portrayed in pornography may not look that comic, sad or alien to them.

"The other duty for parents is to get over the embarrassment and talk with children about sex and relationships. Nature abhors a vacuum, and if parents create one then pornography is just waiting to fill it."

Dr Pratt says no one can stop the pornography onslaught. "What we can do is assist youth to understand that pornography is fantasy, and relates to real life sex the way that *Die Hard* and McClane do to real life conflict management," he says.

Photo: Supplied

// **This is an edited extract of an article by Dr Russell Pratt, first published in April 2015 in *InPsych*, the bulletin of the Australian Psychological Society. To read more, go to www.psychology.org.au/inpsych/2015/april/pratt**

Profile // Hugh Martin

THE ADDICT

Hugh Martin was eight years old when he first saw pornography. It was the start of an addiction that nearly cost him his marriage and his family life.

"Some research shows that about 90 per cent of nine-year-old boys have seen porn. It's everywhere – and it isn't only touching the lives of 'bad' kids. Porn is now so accessible that you don't even have to look for it. Porn will find your child. Whenever your child is on the internet there's a high possibility that some link, somewhere, will lead them to something pornographic – regardless of what filters you have in place.

"Porn has moved from specialised porn sites into the mainstream social-media sites because porn producers, like drug dealers, are using every opportunity they can to expand their market. To create a future crop of porn users, they have to plant the seeds with younger people now. It's Marketing 101.

"I was first exposed to fairly tame stuff as a kid. A friend's father had an extensive collection of *Playboy* and *Penthouse* magazines. He knew we were looking at them but he never talked to my friend and I about what we saw. So I grew up assuming that what I saw in those magazines was 'normal'.

"When you take that idea to the internet and the incredibly graphic content available today, that's a real worry. Because children and young people don't have the emotional or cognitive intelligence to say 'hang on, that's not what things are really like'. They have no point of comparison.

"The new style of porn isn't about having a movie with a storyline – it's called 'gonzo porn', like gonzo journalism. Producers bring a woman into a room, interview her, she strips off and guys walk in and have sex with her. It fits nicely into the online format – you cut straight to the chase and kids enjoy hit after hit after hit.

"A lot of people say porn drove the development of the internet – paywalls, streaming and aggregation all come from the porn industry. Anecdotal evidence says the massive take-up of high-speed internet is due to the ability to access pornography, too. Because porn isn't produced by a geezer down a back lane – it's made by smart people who know exactly what they're doing.

"Porn has become so prolific it's the educator, and that's why parents need to have an open and frank conversation, just as they'd talk about alcohol or drugs to their son or daughter. Yes, it's uncomfortable, but if you don't have those conversations boys may assume it's normal for a woman to want to have sex with 10 guys, that girls are always available, and that they always want sex no matter what. They learn that women are to be used. That's what porn teaches them.

"And girls have expectations placed on them sexually. For example, they're expected to feel that anal sex is normal,

Photo: Supplied

> "Kids need a gravitational anchor by which they can make sexual decisions, moral decisions and respectful decisions around sex."

or that it's not really sex. For some young people now, oral sex is seen as akin to kissing – it's no longer seen as a serious thing. Porn has helped drive that perception.

"Kids need a gravitational anchor by which they can make sexual decisions, moral decisions and respectful decisions around sex. They need someone to talk to and to help them understand what they will see online.

"I don't think a lot of parents understand the nature of pornographic content today – much of it teaches young people that sex and violence can be the same thing.

"I run workshops with men who have developed an addiction to pornography. So much of their sexual education and what is 'appropriate' in a relationship came from pornography driven by violence and revenge against women to a certain extent.

"Parents need to have an ongoing conversation with their child. Be brave. Ask your kids if they've seen porn and what they thought of it. Don't judge. Just be curious. Keep the door open so eventually they can come to you when they see something that bothers them and say 'I saw something the other day ...'"

// Hugh Martin is a psychotherapist and founder of Man Enough, an organisation that runs presentations and workshops to help men make positive changes to their lives. www.manenough.com.au

ASSISTANCE

There are many places to get information and help.

Your doctor, community health centre, reproductive specialist or pharmacist.

Melbourne Sexual Health Centre
www.mshc.org.au
9341 6200 // 1800 032 017 (for outside Melbourne area)

The Women's Health Information Centre
1800 442 007 // 03 8345 3045

Dr Marie (Marie Stopes International)
www.mariestopes.org.au
1300 401 926

Domestic Violence Resource Centre
www.dvrcv.org.au
03 9486 9866

Centres Against Sexual Assault (CASA)
www.casa.org.au
Free call, after hours: **1800 806 292**

Transgender Victoria
www.transgendervictoria.com
03 9517 6613

QLife. Online chat 5.30-10.30pm
www.qlife.org.au
1800 184 527, 3pm-midnight, 7 days

Zoe Belle Gender Collective
www.zbgc.org.au

Rainbow Network for LGBTIQ+ youth
www.rainbownetwork.com.au

Emergency help: Kids Helpline on
1800 551 800 or Lifeline on **13 11 14**

Victorian Government Better Health Channel
www.betterhealth.vic.gov.au

The Royal Women's Hospital sex and sexuality
www.thewomens.org.au/health-information/sex-sexuality

ReachOut has relationships and sexuality information for young people at
www.reachout.com

Kotex site for girls
www.ubykotex.com.au/puberty

Women's and Children's Health Network
www.cyh.com

LEGAL WEBSITES
Victoria Legal Aid
www.legalaid.vic.gov.au
1300 792 387 Monday to Friday 8am-6pm
www.lawstuff.org.au
www.youthcentral.vic.gov.au
– follow link to 'Know Your Rights'
youthlaw.asn.au

TEEN SEX & RELATIONSHIPS WEBSITES
lovegoodbadugly.com
www.nellythomas.com/condom-dialogues
www.scarleteen.com

WHAT IF GENDER ROLES IN ADVERTISING WERE REVERSED?
www.good.is/articles/intermission-what-if-gender-roles-in-advertising-were-reversed

---

// RECOMMENDED READING

Getting Real: Challenging the Sexualisation of Girls by Melinda Tankard Reist (Editor) // www.booktopia.com.au/getting-real-melinda-tankard-reist/book/9781876756758.html
Raising boys & Raising girls by Steve Biddulph // www.stevebiddulph.com.
Speaking Out: A 21st-Century Handbook for Women and Girls by Tara Moss // www.harpercollins.com.au/9781460754535/speaking-out-a-21st-century-handbook-for-women-and-girls/
The Puberty Book by Kelsey Powell and Wendy Darvill (Hodder Headline Australia)
Sexpectations: Sex Stuff Straight Up by Craig Murray and Leissa Pitts (year 7 up) (Allen & Unwin)
Young adult literature // thestellaprize.com.au/2016/05/sex-in-ya/

OUT OF THE BOX // NORWEGIAN SEX ED

Newton is a science program from Norway for children and young people. The target group is from 8 to 12 years. The Newton series about puberty conveys openly and frankly what happens to the body in the transition from child to adult.

THE VIDEOS
Puberty: How does it start? Go to **goo.gl/8YBbyo**
Puberty: Breasts Go to **goo.gl/7UtkB1**
Puberty: Growth and voice change Go to **goo.gl/dXpAVf**
What's the deal with puberty? Go to **goo.gl/VFNa1L**

// FAMILY PLANNING VICTORIA

Family Planning Victoria (FPV) works in partnership with a range of local, regional and national organisations, including universities, community and women's health centres and other family planning organisations and is associated with International Planned Parenthood Federation (IPPF) and Family Planning Alliance Australia (FPAA).
Family Planning Victoria // www.fpv.org.au // 1800 013 952 // 03 9257 0100.

Family Planning Victoria publishes a range of online resources for young people, including our podcast 'Doing It'. www.fpv.org.au/resources // www.fpv.org.au/schools/podcasts

BOX HILL CLINIC
Ground floor, 901 Whitehorse Road, Box Hill (near Box Hill station)
03 9257 0100 or freecall 1800 013 952
Clinic hours: Mon-Fri 9am-5pm

ACTION CENTRE CLINIC
Level 1, 94 Elizabeth Street, Melbourne (near Flinders Street Station)
03 9660 4700 or freecall 1800 013 952
Clinic hours: Mon-Fri 8am-6pm

// LGBTIQ+ – IF YOU NEED TO TALK

LGBTIQ+ young people have never had so many support services. But they need to know how to access them and feel comfortable in doing so. If parents know or suspect their child needs this kind of support, they need to be supportive and help them access support groups.

Family Planning Victoria Action Centre visit // www.fpv.org.au/for-you/sexual-diversity/lesbian-gay-bisexual-transgender-intersex-lgbti or contact them on 03 9660 4700 or at action@fpv.org.au

Australian Human Rights Commission // call 1300 656 419 or visit www.humanrights.gov.au

Fair Work Ombudsman // call 131 394 or visit www.fairwork.gov.au

Victorian Equal Opportunity & Human Rights Commission // call 1300 292 153 or 1300 289 621 (TTY)
Visit www.humanrightscommission.vic.gov.au

// CHECK THESE OUT

Talk Soon, Talk Often. WA government resource // healthywa.wa.gov.au/Articles/S_T/Talk-soon-Talk-often
The Line. Victorian government respectful relationships program // www.theline.org.au
Note: Parents should check websites first, to make sure they are OK with them.

WATCH
Movies can provide a great base for discussing relationships and sex, but many are idealised, unrealistic and reinforce stereotypes. Some more realistic movies for teens include:
High Fidelity (2000)
Mean Girls (2004)
Superbad (2007)
Juno (2007)
500 Days of Summer (2009)
The First Time (2012)
The To Do List (2013)
Don Jon (2013)
Note: Some films are more explicit than others, so parents and carers should check the content first, depending on their child's age.

READ
The Wonder Down Under
by Dr Nina Brochmann
and Ellen Støkken Dahl //
published by Hachette Australia.
RRP $32.99.

// RESOURCES FOR TEACHERS

Thinking Ethically is a teaching resource that provides a framework for discussing challenging topics.
Topics include: Ecocide, Modern Slavery, Cyber Safety, Same-Sex Relations, Interfaith Tolerance, Animal Rights, Euthanasia, Legalising Cannabis, Cosmetic Surgery, Abortion, Role of Media, Mental Health, Refugees, Crime and Punishment, Just War, Surrogacy, Food Security, Aboriginal Reconciliation, Terrorism and Neurodevelopmental Disorders.
For more information, go to // cengage.com.au/secondary/teachers/thinking-ethically

Bullying. No Way! // www.bullyingnoway.gov.au

The Porn Factor DVD // www.itstimewetalked.com.au/resources-order-form/

www.ingramcontent.com/pod-product-compliance
Lightning Source LLC
Chambersburg PA
CBHW061539010526
44112CB00023B/2895